In Praise of
The Heart of Meditation

"A wise and wonderful book. *The Heart of Meditation* is surely one of the very best introductions to the art of meditation, which means an introduction to your real Self. I highly recommend that you dive into its warmth, and find the blissful, loving, radiant Self that you and all sentient beings truly are. This ever-present Self is the answer to your prayers, the object of all desires, the goal of all journeys—and it exists right here, right now, in the splendor of your own awareness. By following the simple and delightful instructions herein, you might very well discover for yourself this treasury of infinite freedom and fullness."

KEN WILBER

author of *A Theory of Everything—An Integral Vision for Business, Politics, Science, and Spirituality* and *One Taste*.

"A thoughtful, intuitive, and uncommonly well-written book, which can only be welcomed by all who follow the way of meditation (no matter the tradition) and especially those — the great majority of us, I suspect — who can always benefit from a good jolt of fresh energy and inspiration in our practice."

PETER MATTHIESSEN (MURYO ROSHI)

author of *The Snow Leopard* and *Nine-Headed Dragon River: Zen Journals 1969-1982*.

"*The Heart of Meditation* comes as a welcome gift. It answered a nagging question: once my meditation practice was established, how could I cultivate, deepen and expand it? After twenty-five years of meditation, my practice had become predictable and annoyingly routine. I had been searching for a way to revitalize and reinvigorate my commitment and enjoyment of meditation. This book literally opened door after door of inner possibilities."

ROBERT KUSHNER

artist whose paintings appear in the permanent collections of
The New York Metropolitan Museum, The National Gallery in Washington,
The Tate Gallery in London, and the Ufizzi Gallery in Florence.

"I have thoroughly enjoyed reading Swami Durgananda's new book, *The Heart of Meditation: Pathways for Deepening Your Practice*. The book is aptly named, since I have been able to put several of its enlightened insights and technique's to work in my own meditation practice.

"Durgananda writes with a clear and inviting style, drawing the reader into her message with warm and loving guidance.

She weaves a unique and beautiful tapestry through the masterful teachings of the Kashmir Shaivism tradition, and the enlightened masters, Swami Muktananda and Gurumayi Chidvilasananda.

"This is a practical book for the serious meditation student at any level, yet it is also an inspirational and educational book. I recommend it to anyone who is sincerely interested in pursuing the experience of the Divine Self through the art of meditation."

STEVE TWOMBLY

publisher and editor of *Natural Health* magazine, Weider Publications.

"Swami Durgananda powerfully reaffirms the core truth that it is ultimately love that binds the universe together. In *The Heart of Meditation*, she demonstrates step-by-step how the practice of meditation can lead us into direct relationship with that loving Ground Of All Being. While the practice she shares with us is based on the Siddha Yoga tradition, she makes it clear that all the great religious traditions have teachings and practices that lead us to that ground of being. The reader is encouraged to adapt what she is saying to their own spiritual journey."

ELISE BOULDING

author of *The Underside of History: A View of Women through Time* and
One Small Plot of Heaven: Reflections of a Quaker Sociologist on Family Life.

"I have enjoyed and understood *The Heart of Meditation* from the Introduction to the conclusion. Meditation and other similar interior spiritual practices have been surrounded in a cloud of mystery that seems to make the first step the most challenging, and therefore discouraging. Swami Durgananda has organized this work in a compelling and effective manner. Not only are we, the readers, presented with an understandable technique to practice meditation, more importantly, we are able to understand why we would want to practice meditation. I have been practicing some form of meditation for the past several years, and I have read scores of discussions about meditation practice. This work ranks on the top of the list for effectiveness and accuracy."

DONALD MASTERS

leader of meditation workshops based on the *Twelve Step Program*; program presenter for Contemplative Outreach International, Ltd.; and director of the National Partnership for Recovery & Prevention, a nonprofit organization in Colorado.

"*The Heart of Meditation*…a personal, inviting window into the world of meditation. This is a welcome, down-to-earth presentation of the process that could enrich our lives."

MARCIA LATTANZI LICHT

Hospice bereavement counselor and author of *The Hospice Choice.*

The Heart of Meditation

pathways to a deeper experience

The Heart of Meditation
pathways to a deeper experience

Swami Durgananda

A SIDDHA YOGA® PUBLICATION
PUBLISHED BY SYDA FOUNDATION
SOUTH FALLSBURG, NY

Published by SYDA Foundation
PO Box 600, 371 Brickman Rd, South Fallsburg, NY 12779-0600, USA

Art direction: Stephen Magner
Cover and book design: Cheryl Crawford, Christel Henning, Richard Laeton, Jodi Lether,
    Mary Orr, George Stefansky
Cover photograph: Timothy Sens
Print production: Ana Carolina Kapp, Patricia Stratton-Orloske
Production assistance: Juliana Carvalho
Production and editorial assistance: Lori J. Tomsic

Printed in the United States of America

First published 2002
08 07 06 05 04 03 02   5 4 3 2 1

Permissions acknowledgements begin on page 340.

Library of Congress Cataloging-in-Publication Data appears on page 344.

To Gurumayi

Whose wisdom reveals the pathways,

whose love opens the heart,

whose teachings form the essence of this book.

ACKNOWLEDGMENTS

This book came into being through the grace and the teachings of my Gurus, Gurumayi Chidvilasananda and Swami Muktananda. These great teachers have distilled from the vast ocean of the Indian scriptures that which is most helpful and nourishing for contemporary practitioners, infused it with their love and spiritual power, and offered it with unending generosity to their students. No words can express the depth of their guidance and love.

Many people helped in the preparation of this book. I would particularly like to thank Peggy Bendet for editorial support throughout the process, and Jonathan Shimkin, whose insightful comments gave me the courage to let go of inessentials and discover what really wanted to be said. Judith Levi provided many of the quotes that appear in the margins and prepared the index. Valerie Sensabaugh, Megan Bird, Karen Swezey, and Anne Malcolm lovingly supervised the editing and production process, while Polly Koch and Patti Hayes copyedited the text.

Thanks also to those who read the book at different stages and offered valuable feedback and suggestions: Paul Muller-Ortega, William Hayashi, Swamis Anantananda, Akhandananda, Apoorvananda, Ishwarananda, Kripananda, Madhavananda, Shantananda, Siddhananda, and Vasudevananda, Nada Clyne, Nancy Garrett, Marilyn Goldin, Margaret Simpson, Andi O'Conor, Kathryn Downing, Osnat Shurer, Anne Johnson, Robyn Jensen, Cynthia Franklin, Judith Levi, Rudy Wurlitzer, Barbara Yaffe, and John Friend. Special thanks to Robert Kemter, director of the Courses Department at SYDA Foundation, as well as Peter Walsh, Hector Campero, and the members of the 1998 Young People's Internship program in Shree Muktananda Ashram, whose Wednesday evening meditation classes gave me the opportunity to try out so many of the insights and exercises in these pages. I offer a global bow to the Siddha Yoga teaching swamis. Their insights into the practice of meditation helped form my own approach to practice, and many of them are reflected here.

Finally, now and forever, I offer deep and heartfelt salutations to Bhagawan Nityananda, the Parameshwara Guru of the Siddha Yoga lineage, whose grace supports this path of meditation. And I offer salutations to the original Guru of all the teachers of the lineage, Shiva Mahadeva, and to the ever-playful Chiti Kundalini, who has become all that is, and by whom we are all, in the end, set free.

CONTENTS

EXERCISES

FOREWORD

You are about to enter an exceptional book, one that is likely to deepen not only your meditation practice but your relationship with your own self, and your life. How will that happen? Let me offer you an analogy.

Running through the handsome city of Bern, Switzerland, is a wide and graceful green river, the Aare. A friend who grew up in a village a few kilometers upstream from the city told me of how he and others from his community used to swim to the middle of the Aare on summer days and ride the currents downstream, all the way into town. There, other friends who had come by car with provisions would meet them at the shore, and they'd have a picnic.

He said that if you got right into the flow of the current, the journey was easy and such fun. Those who held back from the center of the river, maybe out of fear, maybe out of ignorance of the gracious help the river offered, never got very far. They would end up bumping into overhanging trees and other things that jutted out from the shore, or getting caught in eddies or tangled in the reeds along the riverbank, or bruising themselves on the rocks in the shallows. Finally, worn out by their own effort, they'd climb out of the water.

So, whether you ended up exhausted on the shore or floating happily to a picnic was all a matter of knowing about and trusting the current, letting it take you where you wanted to go. This book is about how to let the current carry you.

SWAMI DURGANANDA HAS BEEN FOR MANY YEARS a teacher in the tradition of Siddha Yoga, and a disciple of Gurumayi Chidvilasananda, the spiritual head of our tradition. I often worked side by side with Durgananda under Swami Muktananda, the meditation master who introduced Siddha Yoga to the West, and later under Gurumayi. Already an accomplished writer when she met Swami Muktananda in 1974, Durgananda steeped herself in the teachings of the Siddha Yoga Gurus and, under their tutelage, became a highly skilled teacher. How can one convey the fullness of what a disciple receives while serving an enlightened master? To have been given direct and personal guidance for eight years by Swami Muktananda, and for twenty by Gurumayi, is a matter of the greatest good fortune. And now, with this book, Swami Durgananda continues to serve her Guru by sharing with others the fruit of her exploration, encouraging them to undergo their own personal transformation.

Durgananda has always been an avid reader and student, with formidable powers of retention. A natural scholar, she is one of the most knowledgeable people I know regarding the ancient spiritual traditions of India. She has formed an intimate friendship with the Upanishads, the Puranas, the *Bhagavad Gita*, Patanjali's *Yoga Sutras*, Vedanta, and the writings of Shankaracharya and many of the poet-saints. She also has extensive knowledge of Kashmir Shaivism. This is a philosophy that eloquently articulates how one supremely free Consciousness becomes everything in this universe, including our own limited individual awareness, and also maps the way our awareness returns to its original state of freedom. Durgananda is an excellent teacher of these subjects, adept at helping students translate philosophy into practical experience.

She is keenly interested in varied expressions of the mystical experience found in the accounts of spiritual masters and saints of many traditions. And she has included many quotes from their writings and songs in this book.

Because she has a journalist's curiosity about life and a writer's skill with words, she is able to express the classical teachings of yoga in a way that speaks to people engaged in active roles on the world stage, so that they may apply these truths to their work and to the way they move through this world.

All of Durgananda's strengths are expressed fully in her teaching of meditation. Having courageously explored her own inner world, she inspires others to do the same.

This book, like a good friend, can remind such seekers of their goal and untie them from their moorings, so they can get back into the current.

WHAT IS THAT CURRENT I've been speaking about? In order to explain it, let me tell you a little about the Siddha Yoga tradition.

Gurumayi Chidvilasananda, like her Guru before her, is a *shaktipat guru.* That means she has the ability to bring about an awakening in others that leads to the unfolding of their own innate spiritual power, the emergence of the inherent wisdom and strength of their own souls. In yoga, and in other spiritual traditions of India, this inner power is known by the name *kundalini shakti* and is said to exist within every human being, providing each of us with an innate capacity for spiritual growth.

As long as *kundalini* exists in us in a dormant or contracted form, our experience of who we are is limited. Except for rare glimpses or intimations of "something more," we identify ourselves with what our body feels, what our senses perceive, what our mind thinks, what happens to us—as if that were the sum total of our being. However, when our *kundalini* is awakened by a master whose own spiritual energy is fully unfolded, this inner power begins to expand to its original state of supreme freedom. And with this, our awareness expands beyond the apparent and surface reality to which we have been accustomed. What was once contracted, confined, or (you might say) dammed up, is released. The river begins to flow. Riding its currents, we are naturally drawn inside to the fullness of our own inner being.

Rather than trying to manipulate or influence the *kundalini* in any way, we learn to let it influence us, recognizing that it is a divine power that unfolds naturally. Being our own inner power, the *shakti* knows best what to do for us at any given moment. Gurumayi has said:

> The *kundalini shakti* is a supremely intelligent force. It will manifest only those things that are needed for your spiritual growth. Therefore, trust that the *kundalini* knows perfectly what is right for you.

As we learn to recognize and follow the natural inward pull of the awakened *kundalini shakti,* meditation, the entering into ourselves, begins to take place spontaneously, without a whole lot of strenuous effort.

Swami Durgananda's book presupposes that—no matter what words you might use to describe your path, your journey—there is an energy moving in you that is impelling you to establish a closer relationship with your own inner being.

Durgananda teaches us how to cooperate with that energy. Like an experienced river guide and trusty friend, she, having traveled the waters, presents us with guidance on how to navigate the currents and also how to keep ourselves in top form for the journey. She maps out numerous experiences we may encounter along the way, and gives us ways not only to understand them but also to make the most of them.

She writes, "...if we take our experiences as directional signals from the *shakti*, as doorways into deeper meditation, and follow them, any one of them can take us deeper."

She invites us to turn even the obstacles into great opportunities for self-discovery, perfect occasions for dialogue with ourselves. As many readers may have already discovered, we're likely to approach meditation in the same way we approach other parts of our lives. For example, if we are in the habit of pressuring ourselves, we'll pressure ourselves to meditate—or to have an experience, or to get it done with so we can move on to all the other things we have on our list. Meditation offers us the opportunity to become conscious of these constricted ways of being with ourselves and our lives and to release them, to be more and more completely here, and to discover for ourselves the fullness of every moment.

This book is replete with practical, helpful guidance, derived from Durgananda's own conscious engagement with the practice of meditation, done with a spirit of adventure and scientific curiosity, as well as with the longing to be united with the Self. It encourages you, the reader, to give yourself full permission to love your practice of meditation, to engage in it for the joy of it, in the way that suits your own temperament. Whatever your temperament, you will find exercises and guidance here particularly suited to your way of entering an experience. Durgananda writes, "The best reason to do any meditation practice is that you like it."

FOR THE PAST SEVERAL YEARS, my own main area of service has been the development of Siddha Yoga teachers. Moved by the ways in which Durgananda's book had affected my own practice of meditation, I enlisted her to engage with a group of twelve bright young adults in our Siddha Yoga teaching internship program.

Generously and enthusiastically offering her time and her wisdom, she worked intensely with them over a period of three months. I watched her guiding them through the study of the Siddha Gurus' teachings on the practice, sharing with them her own discoveries and understandings, leading them through many of the approaches to meditation that she had herself explored and found effective—approaches that she shares in this book. She encouraged them to approach their meditation practice as an experiment, a time of learning, and, as she has done, with a sense of lightness and permission to let themselves be playful. At the same time, she demanded a lot of them, assigning to them a daily conscious contemplation and detailed articulation of what they were discovering through their practice. Great learning, real discovery took place, as she knew it would, as it has for her.

I watched as these students changed and deepened. Every aspect of their studies was affected by their enriched practice of meditation, of touching into their own center. Their thinking became clearer, more creative, and their minds more readily grasped what they studied. As they became more self-aware, they also became better listeners, tuning in to what was being said behind a person's words. They became increasingly articulate, more clearly communicating subtle ideas and experiences. Their own loving natures became even more manifest as they consciously opened to the great support and guidance they received from within. They overcame the concept that taking the time to explore one's own being is a selfish act, discovering for themselves how much more strength and inspiration this inner work gives them for the selfless service they render to others.

There was one student in particular, exceptionally truthful and strong, who for some time had moved her colleagues and me with her deep and simple expressions of inner wisdom. Steady, kind, disciplined, and loving, she commanded great respect from her fellow students as well as each of her teachers. And yet the woman's view of herself, formed early in her life, was painfully self-deprecating. It seemed to me that she might never become a teacher, encased as she was in those chains of self-loathing.

It was during the exploration of her meditation that this young woman touched her own heart and connected with her worthiness so solidly and profoundly that the old self-image simply lost its power and came undone. Since then, every day she has grown stronger, clearer. Recently, she steered her whole family through a great crisis, holding them all steady with her unshakable conviction. Seeing with my own eyes what happened for her, I am reminded yet again that, ultimately, what changes us, what brings about genuine and lasting transformation, is the sustained contact with our own inner being, our own awakened power. As Swami Durgananda writes:

Meditation is the basis for all inner work. We might struggle conscientiously to change our limiting qualities; we might saturate ourselves with instructions and help, both concrete and subtle. Yet in the end, it is the direct, naked encounter with our own Awareness that shifts our understanding of who we are and gives us the power to stand firmly in the center of our being. No one else can do this for us. Only meditation unlocks those doors.

May this book encourage you to proceed joyfully on your inner journey with a courageous and adventurous spirit.

May you fearlessly ride the currents of grace all the way to your destination. May your life be a blessing to this world.

Swami Vasudevananda
Shree Muktananda Ashram
June 2002

PART ONE   Going Deeper

CHAPTER 1

Meditation for the Love of It

The book you are about to read is a report from a long, surprising, and still unfinished journey. In the early 1970s, Swami Muktananda initiated me into meditation by showing me that the field of my Awareness contained the whole universe. It happened quite unexpectedly, all in a rush. I was sitting with my eyes closed in a room with several hundred other people, very much aware of the sensations in my body and of the faint rustles, coughs, and other sounds around me. The next thing I knew, there was a kind of implosion. Instead of being around me, the room with all its sensations and sounds was now inside me. Then my awareness started to swell until I could feel the earth, the sky, and even the galaxy inside me.

In that moment, I understood, with a surety that was both terrifying and exhilarating, that there is only one thing in the universe: Awareness and that Awareness is me.

Joy is within.

Meditate.

SWAMI MUKTANANDA

The experience faded after an hour or so, but the understanding it gave me has never gone away. After that initiation, I was in a new relationship to myself and to my own inner world.

What had happened to me was an awakening of the *kundalini shakti*, the inner energy that nearly every esoteric tradition recognizes as the force behind spiritual transformation. *Kundalini* can be awakened in several ways; in the Siddha Yoga tradition, it is usually activated by the Guru. The Siddha Yoga masters, Swami Muktananda and my present Guru, Swami Chidvilasananda, or Gurumayi, specialize in transmitting their own spiritual power to disciples through a process called *shaktipat,* which literally means the descent of spiritual energy. *Shaktipat* and the awakening of *kundalini* bring the energy of the spirit dramatically into the foreground of our lives, shifting our priorities and stirring our hidden resources of love, understanding, and insight.

Kundalini's power becomes particularly evident when we meditate.* The awakened energy draws us into meditative states and begins showing us the tracks of our inner country even as it tunes the body and mind to a new level of subtlety and awareness. Over time, *kundalini* transforms our vision until we see the world as it really is: not hard and bumpy and irrevocably "other," but filled with a single loving energy that connects us with one another and with the world.

---

*A more detailed explanation of *kundalini* and its effects can be found in Appendix 1.

The effects of this awakening on my own life have been widespread and various. Mainly it has shifted my sense of being. Once I had seen that vastness, no matter how caught up I might get in my thoughts or emotions or agendas, a part of me would always know that I contain a reality beyond all that. That in truth, "I" am expansive Consciousness. Over the years, I have come to measure my spiritual progress by how much I am in alignment with that initial insight—by how firmly I am able to identify myself with Consciousness rather than with the person I sometimes think I am.

It has been a road with many sidetracks and hairpin turns. Yet, little by little, the alignment comes. Meditating with the inspiration of *kundalini* and under the guidance of two enlightened masters, I've come to count on entering the space of expanded Awareness for at least a few minutes every day. Over time, meditation has eaten away at the tight walls of my identification with the body, my feeling of being only this physical person, defined by my history and my looks, my intelligence, opinions, and emotions. Little by little, I have begun to identify—precariously at first, then more and more firmly—with that subtler part of myself, with that field of spaciousness behind thoughts, with the tender energy in my heart. With the pulsation of pure being that arises when thoughts die down. With love.

From the beginning, sitting meditation has been the most reliable way I know to touch the tenderness of pure being. I have treasured it. Of course, my love affair with meditation has been like any other unfolding relationship. It has had its ups and downs, its fertile seasons and its apparently barren ones. On the Siddha Yoga path, meditative states arrive spontaneously and naturally. They come in their own time and their own way, gifts of the unfolding *kundalini*.

I have fallen spontaneously into meditation while walking, writing, or sitting in a meeting. I have also had weeks when meditation didn't seem to want to come at all. *Kundalini*-inspired meditation is often surprising and certainly cannot be forced.

But neither can it be approached passively—which is the point of this book. The effort required of a meditator is quite subtle, a matter of attunement and awareness. We learn this attunement gradually, and we learn it by meditating. Fortunately, much of what we learn can be shared, and as I've talked to other meditators and taught classes in meditation, I've found that some of the attitudes and practices that have helped me have also been useful to other people. This book evolved as an offering to other committed meditators, as a way to share certain principles and attitudes that meditation has taught me, and that seem to work not just for me but for others as well.

The most important principle to understand about meditation is this: We meditate to know ourselves. We usually think of meditation as a practice or a process. Yet meditation is also a relationship. If it is a process, then it is the process of coming into relationship with our own Consciousness. In the *Bhagavad Gita,* Lord Krishna defines meditation for his disciple Arjuna by saying *dhyanen atmani pashyanti,* "In meditation, the Self [the pure Awareness that is our essential nature] is seen." This sounds like a simple enough statement, but as we meditate, we come to realize that knowing the Self is far from simple. Which "self" do we encounter when we meditate? The great Self, for sure, the *atman* as the Indian sages call it, the luminous Consciousness beyond the discursive mind. Yet on the way to the great Self, we also encounter a lot of other aspects of ourselves, including the parts of us that seem to hinder the experience of our essence. One of the boons of meditation, if we allow ourselves to engage in it fully, is that we not only come to see all this, we also learn how to move through it. In this daily act of plunging into our inner world, the separated parts of ourselves do come together. The loose ends of our personalities meld with our Awareness, and we become whole.

Of course, this level of transformation doesn't happen overnight. That is where we sometimes get confused. Most of us enter into meditation rather naively. We bring along expectations, ideas, assumptions. For instance, we sometimes imagine that successful meditation is a kind of prolonged honeymoon in which we rove through fields of bliss and float along deep lagoons of peace. If our relationship with the inner world becomes troublesome, boring, or more intimate than we bargained for, we feel frustrated. We might decide that we really aren't so good at meditation, and it is often at this point that we give it up.

We would be a lot less frustrated if we realized that meditation is like any other intimate relationship. It requires patience, commitment, and deep tolerance. Just as our encounters with others can be wondrous but also baffling, scary, and even irritating, our encounters with the self have their own moods and flavors. Like any other relationship, this one changes over time. And it is best undertaken with love.

WHAT IS NEEDED IS INTEREST

Meditation, as my Gurus often say, is not something that you need a special talent for, the way you need a talent for mathematics or art. The real key to going deep in meditation is *wanting* to go deep. The more you crave the taste of the inner world, the easier it is to meditate. In Sanskrit that desire is called

The spirit is so near
that you can't see it!
But reach for it...
Don't be the rider
who gallops all night
And never sees the horse
that is beneath him.

RUMI

mumukshutva, or the wish for the freedom that comes with Self-knowledge. Your desire doesn't have to be huge at first. Even a slight spark of interest is enough because the inner world is actually yearning to open up to you. Once *kundalini* has been awakened, it keeps pulsing inside, just under the skin. It is constantly sending you signals, whispering, "Here I am! Meet me! I'm your guide! I have so many things to show you about yourself!" That is why the moment you become truly interested in knowing your Self, in entering the field of your own Awareness, the inner world begins to reveal itself. It can't help it. That's what it exists to do.

The problem is that we aren't always interested in our meditation. Many of us, when we meditate at all, do it because we know it is good for us. Perhaps it is part of our ongoing self-improvement project or the fuel we use to keep going. Shortly after this book began taking shape, I spent some time with a friend who was complaining about her meditation practice. It had become flat, she said. It didn't deeply engage her. In fact, she didn't much enjoy meditating. I could tell from her tone that as a serious spiritual practitioner, she felt slightly ashamed about this. So I asked her, "What's the best thing about meditation for you?"

She thought for a minute, then said, "It's my therapy. When I sit down, I'm usually burning with inner upheaval, worried about something, or just stuffed with negativity. I repeat my mantra for fifteen or twenty minutes, and when I get up, my mind is calm. I feel quiet. I can go on with my day." Then she said, "I know I have to do it every day, or else my mind makes me crazy."

My friend is getting something important from her practice. In fact, she's experiencing one of meditation's major gifts: its power to clear the mind. Yet because that's all she wants, she gets up from meditation just at the moment when the real sweetness inside her could start to reveal itself. It's when the mind calms down that we begin to discern the wideness of our own being, the love inside. If, along with appreciating its therapeutic benefits, my friend could meditate for the sake of entering into herself, she might stay in meditation a little longer and go deeper than she is going now.

The people who seem to get the most out of their practice are the ones who simply enjoy the act of meditating. This doesn't necessarily mean that they have exotic experiences. Far from it. Some swear that they have never so much as glimpsed a light or seen even a fleeting vision or felt their consciousness expand beyond the body's boundaries. Yet if you listen to them talk about their practice, you realize that they are tasting the richness of their entire meditation experience in all its seasons.

When you approach your meditation with interest, that simple time of sitting becomes enjoyable in itself. You notice the breath, you savor the pulsation of the mantra as it sinks through the layers of your consciousness. You enjoy the rising stillness, the vagrant images flitting through the inner space, and the gradual shift into a quieter mind. Each moment, whether dramatic or seemingly boring, can be full of fascination. You are with yourself. You are with God. Your meditation is an entry into the cave of the heart, the cave of the spirit.

On the other hand, if you look at meditation as a duty, or if you approach it with impatience and rigid expectation, waiting for an *experience* and feeling bored or angry with yourself when your mind doesn't immediately get quiet, you fall out of relationship with your meditation. That is because meditation is anything but a mechanical act. Seeing your inner experience as boring, feeling discouraged when it doesn't unfold as you think it should, telling yourself "I'm not a good meditator anyway"—all this is actually a rejection of your own inner energy, your *shakti.* Just as a friend cools toward you when you hold back from her, the *shakti* that makes your meditation dynamic becomes elusive when you ignore it. But it will leap up to meet you once you begin attending to it with love.

So one of the secrets of deepening our meditation is to discover how to awaken our love for meditation and keep it alive—even when our experience is subtle or apparently dull.

At this point, you might want to take a few moments to look at your own relationship with meditation. What do you feel about meditation? Do you enjoy it? Do you approach it dutifully or methodically? Does it ever surprise you? What does meditation mean to you? You can also ask yourself how you feel about the Self you experience in meditation. What is your relationship with that Self?

THERE IS NO SUCH THING AS GOOD OR BAD MEDITATION

Here is how Swami Muktananda spoke of his own meditation practice:

> I did not meditate out of fear but with enthusiasm and faith
> and love. I did not meditate to please anyone or to get any bene-
> fits from anyone or to satisfy a desire, sensual or otherwise. I did
> not meditate to rid myself of any illness, physical or mental, nor
> to gain fame through the miraculous and supernatural powers
> I might acquire. No one forced me to meditate. I did not

In meditation, you find your own way of knowing and experiencing the truth of your own heart.

GURUMAYI
CHIDVILASANANDA

meditate because religion says that it is good to meditate.
I meditated solely for the love of God, because I was irresistibly
drawn toward the goddess [Kundalini], and to explore my
own true nature.

Most of us would like to feel this way about our meditation. We want it to be
a delight to us, a source of joy. For this to happen, it helps to stop worrying
about whether we have "good" meditation. The truth is that there is no such
thing as good or bad meditation. There is only the relationship to our Self, to
our unfolding *shakti*. We don't need to worry, "Suppose I blow this session?
Suppose I do something wrong? Suppose I waste my time?" Instead we can
look at meditation as an experiment or, better yet, as a game we are playing
with ourselves, as an exploration. We can give ourselves permission to be creative. For example, when we sit to meditate, we might ask, "What will happen
if I repeat my mantra as if I were calling the Beloved in my heart?" Then we
can try it and note the results. We might wonder, "How would it be if I spent
this meditation period just witnessing my thoughts?" and try that. We might
have an impulse to work with some classical form of self-inquiry, like "Who
am I?" and spend an hour noticing what happens to our feeling of identity. We
might think, "I'd like to have a more worshipful feeling in meditation," and
then spend a few minutes praying or invoking grace with some imaginative
form of inner worship like offering flowers on the altar of the heart. Or we
might decide, "Today I'm just going to ask for grace and see what the inner
energy does with me," and then surrender ourselves to whatever experience
comes.

PERMISSION TO PLAY

I had been meditating for many years before I fully realized that meditation yielded its greatest riches to me when I gave myself permission to play. For a time, I had let myself fall seriously out of relationship with my meditation practice. Though in earlier years I had meditated intensely—and experimentally—trying out different approaches and different techniques, constantly testing my Gurus' instructions against my experience, at some point my practice had become fixed in a certain routine. I had my accustomed ways of sitting, of focusing, and I rarely thought to go beyond them. It didn't occur to me to contemplate my meditation experience or to work with my practice. Instead I treated meditation as it came, enjoying the moments of contact with my deeper Self. When these moments didn't come, I sat my daily hour anyway, hoping that *kundalini* was somehow moving me along. In truth, meditation had become an almost unconscious act—something I did every day and took for granted, like eating and sleeping.

Then one day I found myself assessing my practice. What I found surprised me. I had been meditating for ten years. I had experienced many positive changes in my character. My mind had become calmer, sharper, and smarter. My emotions were less unruly. I felt an equanimity I had never had before. I was happier.

Yet it had been some time since I had moved deep into meditation. Usually my thoughts remained, like a substratum of static underneath everything. Usually my consciousness stayed on the surface of itself. In fact, I spent a lot of time drifting through realms of thought and reverie.

It was clearly time for a reevaluation. So I began asking myself some basic questions:

The true practice of [meditation] is to sit as if you were drinking water when you are thirsty.

SHUNRYU SUZUKI

Why do I meditate?

What is my real goal in meditation?

What do I like about my meditation practice?

What do I feel needs improvement or change?

Would I be willing to live with my current level of inner experience for the next ten years?

The answers I came up with were a little disconcerting. The first thing I realized was that the shallowness of my meditation was a symptom of lost clarity about my goal. If you had asked me what I wanted from meditation, I would have glibly answered, "to realize my true Self," but in reality I was not living as though Self-realization were a real goal. Instead I was using my spiritual practices as Band-Aids or perhaps as tonics—nourishing techniques that I employed to keep myself in good working order.

WHAT DO I REALLY WANT FROM MEDITATION?

At that point, I asked myself: "What do I really want from meditation?"

The answers came with a surprising power. I want freedom, I realized. I want an end to the anxiety and craving and fear that create so much unnecessary suffering in my life. I want meditation to take me beyond the neuroses, attachments, beliefs, and fears that still plague my inner world. And I want meditation to be what it was when I first discovered it—dynamic and engaging, a rendezvous I approach with love and excitement no matter what happens.

At that point, I stopped and reminded myself that meditation can't always be fun. Meditation is also a process of purification, I told myself, so there are bound to be days when sitting is somewhat boring and even painful—

Set fire to the Self within
by the practice of meditation. Be drunk with the
wine of divine love. Thus
shall you reach perfection.

SHVETASHVATARA
UPANISHAD

aching knees, long stretches of time when I just field my thoughts. If I insist that meditation be fun all the time, I won't last long as a meditator. I won't be able to sustain the simple daily effort it takes to sit every morning and keep my mind from wandering.

But wait a minute! I said to myself. Don't be so puritanical! Even if it's not always fun, surely meditation should engage me. Interest me. Create anticipation for the next meditation. Otherwise why would I do it? It's all very well to say that we meditate to become better people, or to give ourselves the inner wherewithal to live compassionately, or to be better parents or writers or bankers. Those are fine reasons to meditate, of course. Yet, I thought, the sages who first drew me to the spiritual path—Ramakrishna, Ramana Maharshi, Kabir, Muktananda—lured me with their joy in the quest, with their wonder at the experience of the inner world. There was a promise, in fact, that meditation would be dynamic, would open up something unseen and unheard, would surprise me, extending my senses to a new level of awareness. That it would be, in fact, joyful.

EXPERIMENTING

With this in mind, I decided to reenter my meditation practice as a beginner. I could still remember the excitement I had felt at certain moments over the years when a single instruction from my Guru had unlocked a doorway inside. I remembered how I would grasp at these instructions, sometimes almost trembling with impatience to put them into practice, to experiment, to make them real for myself. Because instructions from an enlightened teacher come empowered with the Guru's spiritual energy, they can sink into our consciousness like subtle depth charges and open up new pathways inside us. Following these instructions connected me almost instantly to the deeper layer of myself. In truth, I was still following the pathways that had opened up in those moments years ago.

What would happen, I wondered, if I reexamined those core instructions with a fresh eye? If I simply let myself go deeper into what I had been given? These teachings were, after all, the distilled wisdom of the Indian yogic tradition. Even though I had contemplated them many times, even though over the years I had often felt, "Now I understand this once and for all!" the fact was that there seemed to be no limit to understanding. Whenever I let myself ruminate about my practice, I always ended up rearriving with a sense of revelation at something that Gurumayi Chidvilasananda or Swami Muktananda had pointed out years ago or that I had read in one of the classical texts of meditation and thought I fully grasped. These simple principles were so subtle and true that they could be reentered and rediscovered over and over again.

So I began approaching my daily practice as an experiment. I decided that I would let myself work with the teachings in an open way, not looking for specific results. I wouldn't expect anything when I sat. I would simply regard the time I spent in meditation as a time of learning, as a time to be with my own consciousness and with the basic teachings of my tradition. I would see what was there. I also decided to meditate with a sense of fun. In other words, I would give myself permission to bring an element of lightness and spontaneity into my meditation. I would let myself play. In fact, each time I sat to meditate, I would consciously remind myself, "It's okay to be playful."

These two strategies—seeing meditation as an experiment and giving myself permission to play—turned out to be crucial to the process that followed.

The Infinite Goodness has such wide arms that it takes whatever turns to it.

DANTE ALIGHIERI

First of all, they helped shake loose the inner critic who usually hovered over my shoulder judging my practice. Second, they freed me from a tendency to make meditation into a routine. Fear of meditating in the "wrong" way had made me turn techniques that were supposed to be helpful guidelines into unbreakable rules, which became hedges around my imagination and intuition. The simple realization that it was fine to play with meditation uncoiled springs of tension so that I could begin to see what was actually there when I closed my eyes and followed the basic instructions of my tradition.

That was what I did that first day. Swami Muktananda had once defined meditation as "turning your mind and senses, which continually wander in the outer world, toward the inner Self." The focus on the Self—the underlying Awareness behind all experience—was the crucial part of the equation. Ramana Maharshi, one of my early heroes, had said the same thing in his own way: "Taking the Self as the target of your attention, you should keenly know it in the heart." I had often heard Gurumayi describe that same process as "entering the heart." Of course, I thought I "knew" the inner Self. I even had standard ways to turn toward the heart. But on this particular morning, I decided just to turn my focus inside. Not to work with any particular technique, just to sit with my attention trained on the field of my own mind, on the inner emptiness I saw when I closed my eyes.

Perhaps you would like to try this. It seems very obvious, but many of us completely ignore this most obvious thing, the field of our own consciousness. Close your eyes and notice what you see. Try to describe it to yourself. I'm not suggesting that you enter into some kind of altered state. Just be aware of what is there, the apparent emptiness behind your eyelids.

THE FIELD OF YOUR CONSCIOUSNESS

Here is what I saw: It was a field of grayish translucent energy, a kind of vibrational soup, that at first glance looked dull, opaque, and flat, except for some streaks of dim light undulating through it. For a while, I gazed at the streaky soup of my inner consciousness—though "gazed" is not quite the right word. More accurately, I let myself be with it, just be with it as it was.

As I sat with this emptiness, I noticed that I was observing it as something outside of me. I began to wonder what would happen if instead of keeping myself outside the screen of my consciousness, I were to actively enter into it. Would this bring me more deeply into the inner world?

At that point, I did something that is rather hard to describe: I entered the field. I did it by imagining a doorway in the inner soup and projecting myself through it. On the other side of the door, the field was no longer opaque. It had a quality of white light glimpsed through a curtain. I began to move through the field. The way to move through it, I found, was to *become it.* The experience was rather like being the little Pacman figure in an old computer game. Pacman moved by eating up other figures. I would "eat"—that is, take into myself— the field that I sensed before and around me. As I became that field, I could enter more deeply into it.

After a few minutes of traveling through this inner field, I found myself in a deep heart space. I call it a "heart space" because when I was in it, I felt rooted in myself: still, soothed, and full of loving tenderness—all feelings I associate with the heart. My mind was quite awake and from time to time would send up a thought or a query. But "I" was sunk deep into this heart space.

I began to explore it, to feel out its qualities and its subtle attributes.

I could feel a pulsation, a subtle ripple of movement, a resonance, and as I focused on that pulsation, it kept opening up further. Each time it did, it moved me deeper and deeper into the sensation of love. After a while, the murky quality of the energy gave way to a sensation of luminosity. It was like being inside a soft crystal—utterly transparent and shining.

From then on, my meditations became explorations of my inner energy field, that world of subtle sensation, love, and clarity. I felt as if I were penetrating the infinitely discerning substance that the Indian sage Kshemaraja called the *chidananda-ghana,* or "compact mass of Consciousness and bliss"—the felt experience of pure Consciousness. It got subtler the more I entered it, and the trick to deepening the experience (for me, at least) was to keep moving further and further into that field of energy. Sometimes I would do it by literally imagining doorways and moving through them. Sometimes I would feel myself swallowing up, "eating," or becoming each successive domain of Consciousness.

Sometimes the field of luminosity would take on colors or turn into a landscape—usually an emerald green meadow. More often it would remain a kinetic experience. Reading through my Gurus' books for clues to the experience, I found many references to the subtle touch of the *shakti,* which they described as thrilling, as the touch of bliss and the touch of love.

THE INNER BELOVED

At one point, I became aware of an elusive, loving presence, deeper even than the immediately accessible bliss. There was something intensely personal about the presence, as if I were being introduced to an inner lover, the Beloved that the Sufi saints speak of so enticingly. He (at the time, I related to it as "he," though obviously it has no gender) would seem to call me from inside at certain times of the day—around noon and in the late afternoon. The call took the form of an intense feeling of pressure in the heart. My attention would be pulled inside, so powerfully that it was painful to resist. If I found myself in a meeting or on a walk when the pull came, I would feel terribly irritable because resisting the inner pull to meditate was as uncomfortable as trying to resist hunger pangs or the need to sleep. It was that intense and that physical. If I was sitting at my desk, I would be almost forced to abandon what I was doing, close my eyes, and hurry down the corridors of consciousness toward the presence.

My afternoon and evening meditations became like successive rendezvouses with that inner presence. It was elusive, always slightly out of reach, yet each time it surrounded me with a blanket of love that, on different days, throbbed softly or strongly. On the days when I gave in completely to the call and sat until I came out of meditation spontaneously, the encounter with the Beloved was so entrancing, so ecstatic, and so subtly delicious that its afterglow would pervade my entire day.

For several months, my schedule allowed me to make time to sit in meditation for over an hour each morning and evening. I found, however, that I had to make meditation a major priority; otherwise a resistance—almost a resistance to the intimacy of the encounter—would tempt me to read or walk or in some way fill those hours with activities. But I discovered that if I kept my practice steady, the deepening process remained steady as well and that when I didn't honor the inner call, it created a kind of distance from myself, an energy barrier that made it more difficult to step into the heart space the next time.

There is a secret one
inside us;
The planets in all
the galaxies
pass through his hands
like beads.

KABIR

THE FRUITS OF DEEP PRACTICE

Not only has the process changed my relationship to meditation, but it has changed my relationship to myself. I have more confidence in myself, and I sense an inner solidity and decisiveness that are quite new. Instead of feeling unclear about my own truth and needing validation from others in order to accept my own insights as important and valid, I have begun to trust that my inner experiences, my gut feelings and reactions, are reliable guides to action. My friends tell me that I have become more spontaneous and more "real" in my relationships. More than that, deep layers of shame and unworthiness seem to be falling away. All this is the result of entering into direct relationship with my own *shakti,* with the Beloved inside me. One primary teaching of the Indian yogic traditions is that our fears, doubts, and suffering arise from ignorance of our real nature and are burned away through the knowledge of the Self. During this period, I often had the feeling that I was experiencing this directly—how an hour's immersion in my own wider mind or a few moments of recognizing the play of my own deeper energy in the movement of thoughts could shift my behavior and relationships.

Meditation is the basis for all inner work. We might struggle conscientiously to change our limiting qualities; we might saturate ourselves with instructions and help, both concrete and subtle. Yet in the end, it is the direct, naked encounter with our own Awareness that shifts our understanding of who we are and gives us the power to stand firmly in the center of our being. No one else can do this for us. Only meditation unlocks those doors.

To make use of the principles and practices in these pages, you don't need to commit yourself to meditating for hours at a time. What you do need is continuity of practice, even if it's only fifteen or twenty minutes a day. The act of sitting every day with a clear intention to explore your inner being will begin the process. Then, as you learn to pay attention to the signals from within, you'll know when it is time to begin meditating for longer periods. It is your intention, your sense of the goal, that makes even a brief meditation powerful and allows you to enter your own core.

I suggest that as you read, you try the exercises in the chapters. You can do this in several ways. First, you might like to read through each chapter and then go back and practice the exercises. Or else you could simply stop reading when you come to an exercise and try it for a moment or two. Many of these exercises, especially in the early chapters, are designed to make it easier to understand one of the principles being described. Grasping a concept intellectually and actually experiencing it are two entirely different phenomena. If you give yourself the opportunity to experience the concept, it will help you grasp it on a deeper level. If you also keep a journal or notebook beside you as you read, you can record your insights and experiences. In that way, reading this book can become an experiment in meditation and contemplation, an exploration of your own inner world. It is my hope that this exploration brings you revelation and delight, that it helps you open more deeply to yourself and to the greatness inside you.

Use your own light and return to the source of light. This is called practicing eternity.

LAO-TZU

CHAPTER 2

How Do We Experience the Inner Self?

For many people, the first great breakthrough in meditation practice comes when they begin to contemplate their goal. Until then, it is often a rather haphazard process. We close our eyes, follow the instructions that we've been given, then hope that something happens. We wonder if we're doing it right. Does correct meditation mean sticking like a limpet to the point that we are focusing on? Is it the focus that brings results? Or is the desired experience something that is just supposed to "happen," to arise on its own? Some of the most dedicated meditators I know have wasted months, even years, wondering what they should be doing or looking for to allow the meditative state to arise. When we have no real idea where we are going, we often end up in a kind of reverie instead.

Swami Muktananda liked to illustrate this problem with a story about a king who set out with a huge army in an easterly direction to meet his enemy. As the king was departing, the royal priest came running up and shouted, "Stop! Stop! Turn around! You're going in the wrong direction!"

"What are you saying?" the king asked impatiently. "I have thousands of men. I have war elephants. I have siege guns. I'm completely prepared and ready to go!"

"Yes, Your Majesty," said the priest, "but your army is marching east and the enemy is encamped in the west! You're moving in the wrong direction!"

Swami Muktananda said that in the same way, it doesn't matter how strong a meditator you are, how upright your posture, how skillful your ability to still the mind and to focus. If you don't know where you are going or what you are supposed to be meditating on, you will take yourself in the opposite direction to where you really want to go. Right at the beginning of meditation, you need to understand very clearly the nature of the Self that is your goal and how you can recognize it.

When I first heard this story, I was galvanized! It was the clue I'd been looking for. I began to ask the question, "What is the Self? How can I recognize it?" Over the years, I have found that this willingness to question our experience and to explore the nature of our own Self, looking for its footprints behind the thickets of thoughts and feelings, is the single most important effort we can make in meditation.

The ultimate goal of meditation is to experience the full unfoldment of our own pure Consciousness, the inner state of luminosity, love, and wisdom

The one you are looking for is the one who is looking.

FRANCIS OF ASSISI

that the Indian tradition calls the inner Self or the Heart. (A Buddhist might call it Buddha nature; a Christian might call it Spirit.) In fact, we want to do more than experience that state. We want to realize that we *are* that—not just a body or a personality, but pure Consciousness, pure Awareness. By this definition, a successful meditation is one in which we enter the Self—even if just for a moment. For this to happen, we need to approach each session of meditation with a conscious understanding that the Self is our goal and with an intention to experience it. Our intention gives directionality to our consciousness. It's like aiming an arrow. Yet even as we aim our attention toward the Self, we need to remember that we *are* the Self. As Ramana Maharshi said, "Knowing the Self means being the Self." When we forget this—that the Self is not only the goal of our meditation but also who we really are—we inevitably find ourselves stuck in one of the countless byways in the inner world.

The most common of these side roads is reverie—falling into the mazy realms of thought and image. We sit down to meditate and end up caught on some irrelevant thought train, letting it carry us from association to association ("Who was that blues singer? He was blind, from the Bahamas. I think his first name was John. No, Joseph. Jonathan would know. 'Gonna live that life I sing about in my song.' Jonathan's wife—Rachel? Roberta? How many children?").

Losing ourselves in thought is not the only way we can get distracted. I know people who have amazingly dynamic meditations: cascades of light, beautiful visions, and brilliant moments of insight. Yet their practice doesn't seem to change their relationship to themselves, nor does it help shift the platform on which they live their lives. This is because they treat their meditation like a light show, a play, or an entertainment. They are not looking for their ground, for the

The eye through which I see God is the same eye through which God sees me; my eye and God's eye are one eye, one seeing, one knowing, one love.

MEISTER ECKHART

Self, for their own essence in the midst of the movement within their meditation. For this reason, despite the gifts they receive in meditation, they don't feel they have gone deep. They don't feel peace. They don't experience satisfaction.

So the first key to deepening your meditation is to become clear about your goal. To begin to look for, to identify, and to identify *with* your essence.

IDENTIFYING THE SELF

The great secret about the Self, the inner God, is that it is us. As Ramana Maharshi said, "Be as you are. See who you are and remain as the Self." This is the knowledge that all the great spiritual teachers, from Shankaracharya to Meister Eckhart to Bodhidharma, have shared. We don't have to get into an altered state to experience it. All we need to do is to become aware of the part of us that sees and knows. When we touch that inner Knower, even for a second, we touch our essence.

The way I find this easiest to understand is to think of myself as composed of two different aspects: a part that changes, that grows and ages, and a part that doesn't. The changing part of me—the body-mind-personality part—looks very different now than she did when she was a twelve-year-old playing Fox and Geese with the neighborhood kids in Princeton, New Jersey. Her occupations and preoccupations have changed radically since then. Not only has this person played all kinds of different roles through the years—student, journalist, spiritual seeker, disciple, and monk—she also has taken on several dozen inner roles. So this changing part has various outer personalities and as many secret selves. There are aspects of us that seem ancient and wise and parts that seem impulsive, undeveloped, and foolish. They assume different attitudes as well. There is vast detachment along with a large capacity for emotional turmoil; there is frivolity and depth, compassion and selfishness. There are, in short, any number of inner characters inhabiting our consciousness, each with its own set of thought patterns and emotions and each with its own voice.

Yet amidst all these different and often conflicting outer roles and inner characters, one thing remains constant: the Awareness that holds them. Our awareness of our own existence is the same at this moment as it was when we were two years old. That awareness of being is utterly impersonal. It has no agenda. It doesn't favor one type of personality over another. It looks through them all as if through different windows, but it is never limited by them. Sometimes we experience that Awareness as a detached observer—the witness of our thoughts and actions. Sometimes we simply experience it as our felt sense of being: we exist and we feel we exist. The unknown author of *The Book of Privy Counseling*, a fourteenth-century Christian text, describes it as "the naked, stark, elemental Awareness that you are as you are." In Kashmir Shaivism, it is called *purno'ham vimarsha*, the "pure awareness of I-am"—the true "I" that is free of the body and continues to exist even after death.

When we focus in and get to know that Awareness, it becomes the doorway to our deeper Consciousness.

EXERCISE: BECOME AWARE OF YOUR AWARENESS

Sit comfortably, with your back upright yet relaxed, and your eyes closed. Spend a moment listening to the sounds in the room. Then, bring your

There is something beyond our mind, which abides in silence within our mind. It is the supreme mystery beyond thought. Let one's mind and spirit rest upon That, and not anything else.

KENA UPANISHAD

awareness into your own body. Notice how your body feels sitting in your posture. Become aware of the sensation of your thighs meeting the seat you're sitting on, of how the air feels against your skin, how the clothes feel against your body. Notice whether your body is warm, or cool. Now feel the sensations in your inner body. Perhaps you are aware of your stomach rumbling. Perhaps you notice sensations of contraction or relaxation in your muscles.

Become aware of your breath—the sensation of the breath entering the nostrils, the slight coolness as it comes in, the slight warmth as it goes out.

Become aware of what is going on in your mind. Observe the thoughts and images that move across your inner screen. Notice the deeper feelings, the emotions, any mental static that arises. You are not trying to change any of this. Simply hold it in your awareness.

Now turn your attention to Awareness itself. Become aware of your own Awareness, the knowingness that lets you perceive all this, the inner spaciousness that holds together all the sensations, feelings, and thoughts that make up your experience in this moment. Focus your attention on your own Awareness, as if you were paying attention to attention itself. Let yourself be that Awareness.

If you keep exploring Awareness in meditation, it begins to emerge more and more distinctly. Thoughts and other sensations gradually recede, and you begin to experience the still yet fluid field of bare Consciousness that is the underlying ground of you. Eventually, the Awareness that was at first only perceptible in snatches will reveal itself to be a huge expanse of being. "No words are necessary to see into reality," Rumi wrote. "Just *be* and It is."

According to most of the great Eastern spiritual traditions, our inner awareness/energy, or consciousness, is actually a limited, contracted form of the great Awareness/energy that underlies, creates, and sustains all things.* The Upanishads call it Brahman, the Vastness. The sages of Kashmir Shaivism called it Chiti (universal Consciousness), Paramashiva (supreme Auspiciousness), Parama Chaitanya (supreme Consciousness), or Paramatma (supreme Self). The great Shaivite philosopher Abhinavagupta called it Hridaya, the Heart. Physicists today call it the quantum field. In Buddhism it is called the Dharmakaya, the "body" of Truth. And, of course, we also call it God.

In its original, expanded form, that vast creative intelligence encompasses and underlies everything. In one of its limited forms, it is the mind-stuff (in Sanskrit, *chitta*) that forms the background of our thoughts, perceptions, and feelings. Kashmir Shaivism, which elaborately describes the different stages that this creative intelligence passes through in the process of becoming the material world, in the end has a simple formula for it: "Supreme Consciousness *(chiti),* descending from its state of complete freedom and power, becomes the mind-stuff of a human being *(chitta)* when it begins contracting into the form of objects of perception." In other words, the moment we begin to focus on

---

*In order to avoid confusion, the initial "c" in "consciousness" is capitalized when the word refers to pure or absolute Awareness. It is written in lower case when it refers to consciousness in one of its ordinary psychological usages, as the state of being aware of something or as a synonym for the human psyche with its faculties of perception, cognition, sensation, and volition. The word "awareness" also receives this treatment.

The Supreme Self, the still center of your own being, holds you together when everything else is falling apart. Good and bad swirl around it like children swinging around a maypole, but the center holds fast.

GURUMAYI
CHIDVILASANANDA

objects—including thoughts, perceptions, and ideas—we lose touch with the underlying vastness within us. And because thoughts, feelings, sensations, and perceptions fill our awareness almost every moment of our existence, it is no wonder that we rarely see the ocean of Consciousness inside us.

Some years ago, a friend of mine had an automobile accident. She was thrown clear of the car. As she lay on the ground, she found herself in a subtle state of awareness that was new to her, yet strangely familiar. She felt bodiless, yet very secure, joyful, and free. For what seemed like a long time, she simply rested in a vast expanded space of love. Then, as slowly as an ant crawling across a windowpane, words began to trickle into her mind: "I . . . wonder . . . if . . . they'll . . . think . . . this . . . was . . . my . . . fault."

The moment she perceived that thought clearly, she was back in her body, in her so-called normal state, feeling her bruises. She saw that she had actually experienced how the contents of the mind limit Awareness. It is not only thoughts that are limiting. The very act of perceiving something as a separate object contracts Awareness, as do the energy patterns created inside us by desires and their attendant emotions or the waves set up by dreams and fantasies. Everything, in short, that coagulates the subtle energy of the mind, or makes it undulate into waves and ripples instead of remaining steady and calm, helps to disguise the luminosity and openness of our inner Consciousness.

The work of yoga is to coax the mind into letting go of the perceptions and ideas that keep it stuck, so it can expand and reveal itself as it really is. As vast creative Awareness. Pure light and ecstasy. An ocean of peace and power. The Self.

WHAT IS THE SELF? OR DESCRIBING THE INDESCRIBABLE

The word "Self" as it is used in most English translations of Indian philosophy refers to the Sanskrit word *atman,* which is sometimes also translated as "itself." This is actually a good word for something that is wordless, formless, and essentially ungraspable, something that doesn't look or feel like anything in the sensory universe and can only be known by direct experience. Lacking form, it also is without name. So the sages called it *atma* (Itself) or *tat* (That). The forest-dwelling sages of Vedic India, whose teachings, collected in the Upanishads, are the basis of the vast body of Indian spiritual philosophy, tried to describe the indescribable using the language of simile, analogy, and metaphor. Images like these suggested the experience of pure beingness:

Like oil in sesame seeds, like ghee in butter, the Self lies within the mind.

The Self is that which makes the mind think,
but cannot be thought by the mind.

That which shines through all the senses, yet is without senses.

Any one of these statements, if you were to ruminate over it, would give you a feeling for the Self, for pure Awareness. Oil and ghee are subtle elements that are extracted from the grosser seed and the thicker butter, just as the pure Awareness that is the Self is a subtle essence that needs to be extracted from the cloudy substance of the mind. The Self gives power to the mind and the senses so that they can think or perceive. Yet because the Self empowers thinking, our ordinary mind can't find a way into it any more than a puppet can perceive the person pulling its strings. When we look for the Self, what we are looking for is actually what is doing the looking. Zen teachers delight in describing how impossible it is to see the Self with our ordinary perception. "It is like an eye looking at an eye," one Japanese master wrote.

EXISTENCE-CONSCIOUSNESS-BLISS: THE NATURE OF OUR INNER REALITY

Even though the Self is indescribable, the sages did find ways of describing its characteristics so that we could begin to recognize them. One of the most important things they have told us is that the Self, *atman*, is not the same as the empirical, personal ego. It is not the "me" that identifies with the body and personality, that creates boundaries and sets limits, and that is always telling us where "I" ends and the "outside" begins.

One of the ways we know we are experiencing the ego and not the Self is that the ego (*ahamkara* in Sanskrit) always experiences itself in comparison to others. The ego never feels fully equal to others: it sees others as higher or lower, as better or worse, as friendly or potentially hostile. The Self, on the other hand, just is. The Self sees everything and everyone as equal to itself.

The ego bears the same relationship to the Self as a lightbulb does to the electrical current that runs through it. The bulb looks as if it gives light independently, but in fact it doesn't. It is just a container. The true source of illumination is the electrical current that runs through the bulb.

In the same way, it is the Self that gives energy to the ego and enables the ego to perform its function of making you think that the boundaries it sets are the real you. The ego is a useful instrument. For one thing, if it weren't for the ego, we would have no feeling of being a personal self at all. The ego tells us who we are in the limited, worldly sense: where the body comes from, how old it is, what we "like" and "don't like." So the ego is not always a bad thing, an

No, my soul is not asleep.
It is awake, wide awake.
It neither sleeps nor dreams,
    but watches,
its eyes wide open
far-off things, and listens
at the shores of the
    great silence.

ANTONIO MACHADO

enemy that we need to pound out of existence. It is simply limited—and limiting. To become fully immersed in the Self, to experience the Self as it is—pervasive, totally impersonal Consciousness that is both connected to everything and boundless—we need to penetrate beyond the ego's confining messages. Once we let go of the tendency to identify with our particularity, then we naturally experience ourselves as vastness, as pure being, as joy, as Awareness, as light. As any and all of the many ways that the Self can manifest itself. "The whole purpose of yoga," Gurumayi Chidvilasananda writes, "is to erase the small 'I' and expand one's awareness until it is capable of attaining *purno'ham,* the pure 'I,' the perfect 'I.' This purified sense of self is . . . perfect oneness with all things, and its nature, its *svarupa,* is *prema,* pure love."

The sages of Vedanta tell us that the Self has three basic qualities. It is *sat,* or ever existent and permanently real. It is *chit,* or aware of itself and everything else. And it is *ananda,* or joyful.

THE SELF IS EVER EXISTENT

Unlike the ego, which comes and goes, inflating or deflating according to its position in relationship to other egos, the Self never moves. It is the part of us that never changes. Everything else in our life changes and shifts. Our bodies grow and age. We put on weight and lose it. Our circumstances change. And, of course, our personalities are subject to strange shifts and discontinuities. But through it all, the thread of the Self remains constant. It is present when we are asleep and dreaming as the Awareness that remembers our dreams. It is also present during deep sleep, though this is something we aren't conscious of until we advance considerably in meditation. When we are awake, of course, the Self is present as the awareness that allows us to experience our lives. In fact, this is the great liberating secret about the Self: it provides the context for our entire life experience, the thread on which the beads of our thoughts, experiences, and perceptions are strung.

Even though it is easier to experience the purity of Consciousness when the mind is quiet, the Self doesn't go away when the mind is full of thoughts. In fact, the Self is the source of those thoughts: all our thoughts and emotions arise from and subside into the same Consciousness-stuff. Whether we are happy or sad, agitated or calm, the Self as our inner field of Consciousness, our inner Awareness, underlies and contains all these feelings.

This means that at any moment, even in the midst of our thoughts, we can drop into the Self. As the Siddha poet Kabir said, "Wherever you are is the entry point." This is one of the secrets that every true spiritual tradition reveals. Though many techniques can help us enter meditation, the final truth is that the Self is so present in our ordinary experience that we can contact it merely by focusing on the gap between one breath and another or one thought and another. The fractional pause in the flow of the breath or in the flow of thoughts then opens out into the vastness of Consciousness, into what in Sanskrit is called the *madhya* (midpoint), the center, the inner space where we experience our connection to the whole.

Traditionally, the way to enter the *madhya*, the space of the heart, is through the instructions and grace of a Self-realized Guru. Because such a teacher lives in constant contact with that inner space, she not only can point it out to us, but can also open the inner door that reveals it. That is why following the instructions of such a teacher can be so revolutionary: the instructions contain a subtle power that can bring them to fruition.

Who is it who knows when the mind is filled with anger or with love? Who is it that is awake when we are sleeping? Who knows that we slept and reports to us on our dream? We have to meditate on that One who is the witness of everything.

SWAMI MUKTANANDA

Once I was meditating with Swami Muktananda when he gave us an instruction: "Meditate on the space from which the mantra arises and into which it subsides." Intrigued, I began to look for the little gap in the flow of the words I was repeating, the space at the end of the last syllable of the mantra and before the first. Did the mantra really arise out of that space in the mind? As I "looked," focused, and tried to feel that space between repetitions of the mantra, I felt myself dropping, like Alice down the rabbit hole, into a huge space. I could still feel my body, but I didn't feel confined inside it. Instead, "I" surrounded the body and somehow contained it. My thoughts and emotions were also inside my Awareness. It was impossible in that state to take my small, anxious mind seriously. There was no doubt at all that this calm wideness was the real me.

This state lasted for several days. While I was in it, everything felt different, especially being with other people. Normally in social situations, I felt a slight alienation and insecurity, a sort of low-grade discomfort. In this state, that feeling was gone. Without that discomfort, it was easy to feel affectionate toward people — even people I didn't usually "like." I felt easy, flexible, tender, and secure in myself in a new way. I literally felt that I rested in my own center.

What had happened? I had entered into the space of pure Consciousness, the baseline experience of the Self. The Guru's instruction had opened the doorway, and following his instruction had allowed me to slip through it.

This experience showed me two things: how close the Self really is, and how easily the blessing, the grace, and the energy we receive from the Guru can reveal its presence.

THE SELF IS AWARE

The Self permeates our experience in much the same way light permeates the room you are sitting in. If you were asked to describe that room, what would you say? You might mention the furniture, the color of the walls, the paintings, the objects on the table or desk, even the lamps. But would you mention the light in the room? Would you even notice it? Yet only because the light is present can you see what else is in the room. In the same way, just as the ever-present Self gives us our sense of being, it is the Self that allows us to experience everything. The Self is the screen on which we experience our inner and outer life. It is what makes it possible for us to see, to know, and to experience. The *Kena Upanishad* says that the Self "shines through the mind and senses," which is a poetic way of saying that it is the power of the Self that allows the mind and senses to function. So the eternally conscious Self is what makes us conscious. Essentially, it is light.

At times when our inner vision becomes pure enough to let us see through the layers of psychic debris that thicken our consciousness and make it opaque, we realize that everything is actually made of light. We understand that we are light, that the world is light, and that light is the essence of everything. This is why so many people's experiences of touching the Self are experiences of light—visions, inner luminosity, or profound and crystalline clarity.

However, there are other ways to experience the luminosity of the Self. It also reveals itself as our capacity to know, to be aware, and to experience. We don't have to see the inner light to feel how the Self illuminates experience; we only have to notice what it is that allows us to know things. It's not the mind that lets us know what we are experiencing—the mind is part of what is known.

That which cannot be expressed in words, but by whom the tongue speaks— know that to be the Absolute. That which is not known by the mind, but by which the mind knows—know that to be the Absolute.

KENA UPANISHAD

In the same way that we can be the "witness" of our hand or arm, we can be the witness of our mind. Shankaracharya, the great exponent of Vedanta, famously defined the Self in this way, as the witness of the mind. Swami Muktananda would say, "Meditate on that one who is always meditating on you, on the one who is constantly aware of what is passing through the mind."

So one way to locate the Self is to try to become aware of the part of you that is watching your experience, the part of you that is aware of your thoughts. Try to identify that witness, that knower. Perhaps you could ask yourself, "Who knows that I am thinking?" and wait to see what arises. Eventually you will become aware of a sort of knowing spaciousness, a feeling of watchfulness that sometimes seems to be located just behind and slightly above the head.

If you focus on that knower for a while, you will probably become aware of another knower just beyond it. You might go on focusing on the knower of the knower of the knower almost indefinitely, without ever completely grasping it. So now, instead of trying to *find* the knower, have the feeling that you *are* the knower. As you keep this up, sooner or later you may notice a shift in your state. Thoughts move to the background. The knowing Awareness moves to the foreground. You might experience a sense of huge clarity and freedom, as if the boxy walls that normally contract your consciousness have dropped away, setting you loose into a skylike state that is potentially infinite and infinitely relaxed, infinitely peaceful, silent, and aware. You will have moved into the experience of what we could call the "absolute knower," the pure Awareness that doesn't change or slip away. The Awareness that not only knows everything else, but also knows itself. You will be meditating on the one who is always meditating on you: consciousness facing Consciousness, awareness reflecting on Awareness, the *aham vimarsha*, or "I experiencing itself," of which Kashmir Shaivism speaks.

THE SELF IS JOYFUL

The third aspect of the Self is *ananda*, or joy. The *ananda* aspect of the Self encompasses many different kinds of experience, including love, bliss, and ecstasy. *Ananda* is also the source of all true creativity: the impulse to make something—to do anything—actually comes out of our inborn joy, excitement, and delight. The Siddha philosopher Abhinavagupta explained how the whole world arises out of divine delight, which he called the *ananda chalita shakti*, or the divine energy leaping forth in bliss. The *Taittiriya Upanishad* says, "All things are born out of bliss. They live in bliss and dissolve into bliss."

Of course, this is one of the most basic teachings of yoga. One of the first things that we read or hear when we start becoming aware of the yogic view of life is that our experiences of happiness are possible only because happiness is already inside us. In short, it is not the other person, the beautiful scene, the film, or the chocolate soufflé that creates joy. These things may trigger it, but the joy is intrinsic to us. In fact, the pleasure we experience through the senses is literally a shadow of the joy we have inside.

The deep joy we call "the bliss of the Self" bears the same resemblance to our ordinary states of pleasure as a panther does to a Siamese kitten. It is the same happiness, true, but it is infinitely fuller, more expanded, and more thrilling. Moreover, it gives us a sense of fulfillment. Instead of exciting the mind and creating a craving for more, the experience of *ananda* feels complete. That's because the *ananda* of the Self is self-sustaining: it doesn't come and go according to the

Who could live, who could breathe, if that blissful Self dwelt not within the heart? It is That which gives joy!

TAITTIRIYA UPANISHAD

38

conditions of our lives. Once we learn how to call forth the pure bliss within us, it often rushes up from inside all by itself, with no sensory trigger at all. *Ananda* is there when things are going well for us. *Ananda* is also there when things are falling apart.

His experience of *ananda* allowed Saint John of the Cross to write sublime poetry while living in a prison cell too small for him to lie down or stand up. It gave the Sufi Mansur al'Hallaj the ability to laugh while he was being executed. It allowed Bhagawan Nityananda to remain ecstatic even when village boys pelted him with stones. Many people discover that pure *ananda* when *kundalini* awakens. "Oh, now I understand what they mean when they talk about bliss," people often say to me, describing how, in the moments after receiving *shaktipat,* they caught their first steady glimpse of that underlying happiness.

The experience of that deep joy, which we often begin to feel as soon as *kundalini* comes awake and which deepens through our meditation practice, is one of the ultimate gifts of the spiritual journey. Even though in the West we have an odd tendency to distrust joy as somehow frivolous, the fact remains that for Christian mystics as well as for Islamic seers, and certainly for the sages of the mystical traditions of India, the pinnacle of inner experience is the joy of divine love. Love is itself the highest goal of meditation because the very fabric of the Absolute is love. As Gurumayi once said, "You feel love for God, and that feeling itself is God."

It seems that everyone who pursues the path to the ultimate reality discovers this eventually. Though different traditions give different names and attributes to it, they all agree that the nature of the ultimate reality is love.

THE MOMENT OF LOVE

Because joy and love are intrinsic to the Self, the sages tell us that we can enter the experience of its expansive happiness through the doorway of our ordinary feelings of happiness or affection. All of us have moments of spontaneous joy in our lives, and, whether we are aware of it or not, those moments give us profound and significant glimpses of our deeper truth. The key is to separate the experience of happiness from its external trigger. If you think that being with Joan is what makes you happy, then you will tend to seek out Joan in the expectation of feeling good—even though you may be aware that being with Joan doesn't always do that! However, if you can enter the moment of immediate enjoyment or happiness, the moment when you feel love, and *hold on to the feeling without attaching it to the person or sensation that may have triggered it,* the feeling itself can expand and allow you to enter the Self.

The *Vijnana Bhairava,* considered one of the key texts on meditation in the Hindu Tantras, is a compendium of techniques for entering into the pure Self through the avenue of our so-called ordinary experience. The following exercise is based on a verse from this text.

*It is my nature that
  makes me love
    you often,
For I am love itself.
It is my longing that
  makes me love
    you intensely,
For I yearn to be loved
    from the heart.
It is my eternity that
  makes me love
    you long,
For I have no end.*

MECHTILD
OF MAGDEBURG

EXERCISE: FOCUS ON AN EXPERIENCE OF LOVE

Close your eyes. Focus on your breathing, following the breath for a few moments to let your mind calm down. Then think of someone for whom you feel love or whom you have loved in the past. Imagine that you are with this person. Visualize him or her before you or beside you. To anchor yourself in the memory, you might notice what this person is wearing or become aware of the setting. Let yourself feel love for this person. Open yourself to the feeling. Once you are fully present with that feeling of love, let go of the thought of the person. Focus entirely on the feeling of love. Allow yourself to rest in it. Feel the energy of love within your body and within your heart.

You may need to repeat this exercise a few times before you get the hang of it. Once you have experienced how the felt sensation of love and happiness remains even after you let go of the idea of the person inspiring it, you will begin to realize that your love is actually independent of anything outside yourself. This is one of those insights that can change your relationship to other people, and certainly to yourself.

So, the experience of the Self—any experience of the Self—has the following qualities. It is an experience of pure being. It is an experience of awareness: the Self knows itself. It is witness to its own existence as well as to everything else. And it is an experience of bliss, for the Self is joyful, loving. Sometimes one of these qualities is so dominant that we may not be aware of the others. But when we enter into any experience of our deeper reality and allow its facets to reveal themselves, we will eventually find that all these qualities are there.

The question is, how do we know that we are experiencing the Self? Is it as simple as it sounds when we say that the Self is our own thought-free Awareness? Or is it only really accurate to call the Self a condition of expanded Consciousness, the spaciousness we enter when we shift out of ordinary awareness into a larger, wider, and deeper state? Are we in the Self when we experience pure joy? Or is the joy of the Self that huge, all-encompassing love that can sometimes seem too big for our body to bear? Is the tiny light we see at times in meditation the Self? Is the Self the rush of exaltation we feel when we watch the moon come up over the ocean, or the first snowfall? Or are these moments just glimpses of something much bigger and more extraordinary, something that we can only fully experience in a state of expanded or transpersonal Consciousness?

Here is one way of looking at it. Our experience of the Self is a continuum. Since the Self is always present, we can experience it in different degrees and in many different ways. The Self is both an extraordinary experience and something very close, simple, and familiar. It is light, bliss, and an Awareness so global that we feel everything is a part of us. It is also the calm that arises when you identify with the watcher of thoughts. You are experiencing the Self when you look into the eyes of someone who annoys you and realize that the same Consciousness is peeking out of his or her eyes that you experience in yourself. Or when you look at a flower and sense the creative force manifesting as color, fragrance, and curving petal and leaf. Or when you enter the state of "flow," of perfectly skillful action with no sense that you are acting. Or when you have a moment of utter trust in the processes of life. One of the major boons of awakened *kundalini* coupled with an ongoing daily meditation practice is that such experiences come regularly and often—and not always in meditation. The experience can arise at any time.

A friend wrote "Yesterday I was walking in the woods, watching the leaves fall. I looked up and found myself following a single leaf as it descended. There was a kind of hush. My awareness shifted. There was nothing in existence but the leaf and me. I saw the leaf falling, and it seemed to be falling through a vast space, and my own awareness became the space."

For many of us, the "big" experiences of expansion happen outside of

He who goes to the bottom of his own heart Knows his own nature; And knowing his own nature, he knows heaven.

MENCIUS

42

meditation, with our eyes open, as in this account from an American woman waiting for a flight:

> I was at the airport in the passengers' lounge. My plane was delayed, and I faced a long night of waiting. For some reason, though, I didn't feel bad about it. I was looking around the lounge, repeating my mantra and noticing the expressions on people's faces. Then I glanced down at the rug. It was an ordinary utility rug, the kind they have in airports. Grayish brown. Stained. Then, quite matter-of-factly, as though it was the most natural thing in the world, I became aware that this rug was pulsating with light. It was divine. It was God. I just sat there, staring at the rug. I was feeling so much love. I could actually see, with some subtle sense that I don't ordinarily use, this shivery presence in the rug. I knew it was in everything else, too. Tears were standing in my eyes. I realized how humble God is. He is perfectly willing to become this rug, this dirty, stained rug that we were all walking on. It doesn't matter to Him at all.

Such full-blown, dramatic experiences of expanded Awareness, such powerful shifts of vision, are gifts. We can't make them happen. They come to us through grace, in their own time according to their own will. No technique, no practice, and no amount of longing can force the Self to reveal its vastness.

And yet, here is the paradox. Even though we can't make that experience happen, we can invoke the power that brings revelation. This is one reason why the relationship we form with the Self, with our meditation practice, and with the inner *shakti* makes such a difference. The more we learn how to honor the loving power that inspires our meditation practice, the more we remember it and invoke it, and the more we learn to love it, then the more we experience its presence and its blessings.

CHAPTER 3

In the Beginning

Several years ago, a man told me an interesting story. In the early seventies, he had set out on a spiritual quest, going from India to Japan, from teacher to teacher. Like so many others during those years, he wanted to have a palpable experience of the Truth. He wanted to know unity; he wanted to know God. Finally, after years of unsuccessful practice, he decided to give his inner Self an ultimatum. He sat down one evening on his meditation mat and announced, "I'm going to sit here until dawn. If I don't have an experience by then, I'll get up and never practice meditation again."

Nothing happened. Nothing at all. So he got up and went about his life, determined that he wouldn't turn inside again.

There is an unseen presence we honor, that gives the gifts.

RUMI

Ten years later, a friend brought him to a Siddha Yoga meditation center in Los Angeles. He went into the meditation hall and sat down in the dark. As he sat there, he felt a sensation of great sacredness. He realized that he was in a place where many, many people had performed spiritual practices. He felt strangely humbled, imagining their sincerity and their effort. His heart turned over with an unaccustomed feeling of reverence.

Suddenly, without warning, a vast feeling of love rose up inside him. Then, as if an inner window had opened up, he was ejected out of his ordinary self and into a huge inner sky. All around him was deep, shimmering light, light in rainbow colors, vibrating with this same awesome love.

Challenging the universe to give him an experience of his inner world hadn't helped at all. Love, gratitude, and reverence opened the door. The *Katha Upanishad* says, "The Self reveals itself by its own will." The inner world can't be forced open. Try as we might, we can't make meditation happen. But our inner attitude can coax it forth. With love you can, as Rumi wrote, "make a way for yourself inside yourself."

It comes back to relationship. The Self, the inner Consciousness, is not some dry, mechanical energy, but a living, dynamic, love-filled intelligence. Some mystical poets call the hidden divine part of us "the Friend." Like any friend, it reveals its secrets where there is trust and respect. The Self is love, so it responds to love. The Self is subtle, so it is attracted to subtlety. The Self is tender, so of course tenderness calls it forth. We draw close to the Self when we make ourselves like the Self—loving, subtle, tender, and generous. We draw the Self close to us when we invoke it with honor and when we ask for its grace by being gentle both with ourselves and with the energy inside us.

In this chapter, we will look at different ways to create this open, loving state, the state that can draw forth the grace of the inner Friend.

HONOR YOUR PRACTICE

The most basic way to invoke meditation is simply to honor our practice, to treat the time we have set aside for meditation as sacred, and to enter into it with respect. It helps to create some simple rituals around our practice—things that we do with the body to induce a feeling of respect.

Cleansing ourselves is the first step. When we shower or even just wash the face, hands, and feet before meditating, we are performing a basic and time-honored act of physical and mental purification. The sages recited mantras while they bathed. Even if we don't do that, we can have the feeling that the water running over our bodies is also washing impurities from the mind. We can also wear clothes that we keep for meditation; in time they will become saturated with our meditation energy so that wearing them will make it easier for us to go inside. Before we sit, we can light a candle and incense. And we can bow.

Bowing is important. In the Indian tradition, yogis bow to each of the four directions before meditating, acknowledging that the divine source is everywhere. Then they bow to their own meditation seat. When we try this practice, we soon discover all kinds of nuances in it. Honoring the seat of meditation is not only a way of honoring the power of meditation that gathers in the cushion we sit on, but also a way of signaling to our inner being that we honor ourselves. The great Sufi poet Hafiz wrote:

> The Friend has such exquisite taste
> That every time you bow to Him

Your mind will become lighter and more
Refined;
Your spirit will prepare its voice to laugh
In an outrageous freedom.

Whether we bow at an altar or simply to the universe itself, we can have one of the following thoughts: "Let the shell that separates me from love melt," or "I offer myself just as I am, with humility and love," or "I take refuge in the Self." The idea is to soften the stiffness that clings to our heart and to allow a feeling of inner surrender and tenderness to emerge.

Gurumayi once remarked that it is important to do all this slowly and consciously; if you enter meditation in a hurry, it actually brings an attitude of restlessness to your entire meditation. In fact, she suggested that if you notice a feeling of agitation in meditation, you go back and mentally redo the preliminary ritual—the bow, the waving of the incense—taking it very slowly and noticing how when you do this, it brings your mind into a more balanced state.

Another very basic way to draw close to the Self at the beginning of meditation is to relax. It sounds simple. Just relax. Yet sometimes it is the last thing we think to do. So many times I have sat rigidly upright for an hour, doing hard practice and keeping myself one-pointed by a mighty effort. Then, once the hour was over, I would draw my legs up to my chest, and with the feeling of taking off a tight belt, I'd relax. At that very moment, the contraction that had been keeping my consciousness limited and my heart small would release, and I would be in deep meditation.

Rather than waiting until after meditation to relax, it makes sense to relax in the beginning. We relax the body with the breath. We relax the mind by accepting ourselves as we are in that moment, in whatever state we happen to be, and by entering into meditation without demands or expectations. An expectation is different from the intention described earlier. Having a strong intention, an awareness of the goal, helps focus us in the right direction. But having an expectation actually blocks our experience of the goal because it superimposes an idea of what is meant to happen over the spontaneous actuality of the unfolding moment.

It is a good idea to give yourself time at the beginning of meditation to scan the body, noticing where your muscles are holding tension. Then you can breathe into each place of holding—into your tight shoulders and belly and forehead—and breathe out any tension found there. In the same way, you can breathe into the energy held in the mind, into the tightness of your coagulated thoughts, and let the thoughts flow out with the exhalation. As you focus on your practice, keep that sense of relaxation, remembering to keep your attention soft and to release any sense of strain. This form of relaxed attentiveness is sometimes called "effortless effort."

INVOKING THE GURU

What allows us to relax into meditation, to make our effort without straining? Essentially, it is trust. First, we trust that the Self, the goal of meditation, is real and can be experienced. Second, we trust that we are connected to a greater power, a power that supports our meditation and brings it to fruition. We can invoke that supportive power by invoking the Guru. When we begin meditation by remembering the Guru, the enlightened teacher, we link ourselves to the secret source that brings meditation alive. Tukaram Maharaj, one of the poet-saints of the Maharashtrian tradition, wrote in the seventeenth century: "Place your faith and love at the Guru's feet. God lives with the Guru. So remember the Guru. Bring him into your meditation. When you remember the Guru, you find God both in the forest and in the mind."

I often contemplate what Tukaram meant by saying that God lives with the Guru. It is one of the great mysteries in this universe: how the universal power of grace, the principle of divine help, roots itself in the person of an enlightened teacher, then flows into anyone who connects to that teacher.

Grace is everywhere, of course, and flows to us from every corner of the universe. Nonetheless, a meditator usually needs to link himself to a living spiritual lineage in order to experience the form of grace that ignites an experience of the Truth. "The established method for knowing the Self is through the relationship between Guru and disciple," says Lord Krishna in Jnaneshwar Maharaj's thirteenth-century commentary on the *Bhagavad Gita*. In a mystical poem called *Amrit Anubhava (The Nectarian Experience)*, Jnaneshwar wrote, "If one could see his own eye without a mirror, there would be no need of this sport of the Guru." At every stage of the journey, from the moment of initiation until long after final realization, the Guru's grace gives power to our practice and opens the inner world. "My Guru gave me the grace to see that inside and outside are one," wrote the Sikh Guru Nanak. The *Katha Upanishad* says:

> Unless taught by a teacher, there is no access there,
> For—being more subtle than the subtle—
> That is inconceivable.
> Dearest one! This knowledge is not attained through reasoning.
> Truly, for ease of understanding, it must be taught by another.

O grace of the Guru, one who is supported by your favor becomes like the creator of the whole world of knowledge.

JNANESHWAR MAHARAJ

And the poet-saint Kabir sang:

> Think this over and understand it.
> The path is very narrow and precarious;
> it is so subtle that you need the Guru's help to discern it.

The Guru's instructions aren't simply verbal. The real help a Guru gives us is a kind of quickening, a subtle and constant transmission of her own state to us. This goes on not only when we are in her physical presence but in all states of consciousness, including dreams, meditation, and the states after death. When there is a real connection with the Guru, her guidance is with us no matter where the Guru happens to be or what inner state we happen to be in. That's one reason why, in the tradition of Siddha Yoga meditation, the inner connection with a living Guru is considered indispensable for dynamic meditation. Like the enlivening sap that brings buds and blossoms to a winter-barren tree, the spiritual force that flows from the living Guru and the Guru lineage gives life, juice, and potency to practice. It can kindle our desire to meditate, make the hidden Self discernible, enliven a technique so that the secret landscapes of our inner consciousness open to us. Just remembering the Guru can open the door to that transmission, and lift a routine meditation to an entirely different plane.

Here's an example: In 1994 I was meditating in Shree Muktananda Ashram in upstate New York. Gurumayi was in India. It was a holy day, the death-anniversary of one of the sages of our tradition. Such days are supposed to be especially propitious for asking blessings of the universe. As I was contemplating what blessing I could ask for, I turned inside and asked for the Guru's grace to guide me in making the perfect prayer. Suddenly Gurumayi's face appeared before me. She was laughing. "Ask for me!" she said.

I don't normally have visions, so I took this seriously. Actually, I was unnerved. I knew that "asking" for her did not mean asking for her to walk into the room. It meant asking for her enlightened energy, her inner state, to enter my being. An ancient fear of the higher forces of the universe swept over me. What would happen if I totally opened myself to that state? Would I lose myself? Would I get swept away, subsumed, taken over? Then I realized that my fear was just the static thrown up by the part of me that prefers to remain small and separate. It was that old self-limiting voice that always arises just as a great expansion is about to happen in meditation and that we just have to ignore if we want to go deep. So I inwardly set the fear aside and said to the laughing face in the field of my mind, "Yes! I ask for you!" At that moment, Gurumayi's face dissolved into light, and so did my mind. It was like becoming an ocean of light, rippling with tides of love. Even now, remembering that moment, I can feel the freedom of it.

When we ask the Guru to be present in our meditation, what we are asking is that the Guru's inner state of clarity, love, and subtle Awareness come alive in us. In fact, we are opening ourselves to the light inside us, to the meditation-bestowing presence of our inner teacher, the unseen guide whom each of us carries inside.

For lifetimes this inner teacher has lived within us, unseen and unknown yet constantly drawing us along, guiding us through different experiences, and bringing us to the point where we are ready to turn inside and know ourselves. When that moment comes, the inner teacher brings us to the physical human being destined to be our Guru. The inner teacher draws us to the outer teacher so that the outer teacher can make us conscious of the presence of the teacher inside. Meeting our Guru is often signaled by a profound sense of recognition, a feeling of homecoming. We may feel that we have never been seen as the Guru sees us or loved as the Guru loves us. Yet what we are recognizing, in truth, is the vision and love of our own Self. The physical teacher holds that vision—indeed, she triggers it in us. Most of us need the connection, the teaching, and the grace of the human teacher if we are to activate that highest vision inside ourselves. But the more we experience our own heart, our own inner love, the more we recognize that the guiding, loving, enlightening presence inside us is no different from the presence we feel in our human teacher. Ultimately we come to see the human teacher as a kind of embodied form of the wisdom and love of our own soul. This is one of the basic axioms of the Guru-disciple relationship; as the *Guru Gita*, a Sanskrit poem on the Guru, tells us, "The Guru is not different from the conscious Self."

So when we invoke the Guru at the beginning of meditation, we are not doing it to flatter the Guru or because we are psychologically dependent on the Guru or to create a cult of personality around the Guru. We invoke the Guru so that the Guru's enlightened state can touch our own concealed enlightenment, activate the enlightened teacher inside us, and enliven, give life to, our meditation.

Sometimes we hold back from invoking the Guru because we don't feel particularly loving or devotional. Yet, this is precisely when we most need to invoke the teacher. One friend of mine, a scientist, has an efficient, cut-to-the-chase attitude about her practice and a preference for meditating on pure Consciousness rather than on forms of any kind. At one point, her meditation became so dry that she could hardly find the interest to sit. Then she signed up for a meditation retreat in which every session began with a series of elaborate devotional practices: bowing to each of the four directions, saying prayers to the

Affix to the bow the sharp arrow of devotional worship; then, with mind absorbed and heart melted in love, draw the arrow and hit the mark—the imperishable Absolute.

MUNDAKA UPANISHAD

Gurus of the lineage, and chanting. Back home she added this ritual to the beginning of each meditation session.

"I did it very mechanically," she said. "I really didn't have much feeling about it. I just did it—doing my bows, remembering my teacher, praying. After a few weeks, my heart started to feel tenderized. Literally tenderized. Now I just start the invocation, and this tender feeling rises up, and my whole meditation practice is full of love."

Her story reminded me of something an acting coach told me years ago. He said that when you have to act the role of being in love with someone, the way to do it is to pay very close attention to the actor you are supposed to love. The audience, he said, will feel your attentiveness as love. In spirituality, paying close attention doesn't just simulate love, it actually evokes it. Practicing prayer, invocation, and surrender will always eventually create feelings of devotion, even if we start out mechanically. That's why we do the practices: because they give rise to love inside us. The Sanskrit word for devotion is *bhakti,* which comes from a root that means "to relish." Prayer, invocation, praise, remembrance, worship, and ritual—the practices that come from the tradition of *bhakti*—are actually means to relish the different flavors of sweetness inside us. They give rise to very high and subtle feelings of enjoyment, and that enjoyment enlivens our whole practice.

Invoking the teacher can be as simple as taking a moment to invite her to be present or as elaborate as the practice Swami Muktananda describes in his spiritual autobiography, *Play of Consciousness.* He would install his Guru's form in his own, imagining that his Guru's head was his head; his Guru's torso, his torso; the Guru's legs, his legs. When Swami Muktananda did this, he always began by reminding himself that by invoking the Guru he was calling upon a universal power, the force of grace itself. He would feel that his Guru's essence pervaded every direction, that the sky was the Guru's head and the earth, his body. So when he identified himself with his Guru, he was actually identifying himself with something vast and sacred as well as with his beloved teacher. Practicing in this way, he said later, he would begin to feel that he, too, contained the universe.

In fact, Swami Muktananda always said that our attitude toward the Guru and ourselves determines how much we imbibe from the Guru. If we see the Guru simply as a teacher or as an evolved human being, then we will receive what the Guru has to teach. If we see the Guru as a human being who embodies the divine and realize that this same divinity is inside ourselves, then our devotion to the teacher will draw forth our own hidden divinity. "I saw my Guru as the Self," Swami Muktananda wrote. "I thought he was the image of happiness, and I had great faith that he would show me how to attain that happiness. . . . So that is what I attained from the Guru."

An invocation like the one below, where we imagine the Guru as a distinct being outside ourselves, affects us most powerfully when we do it with the feeling that the Guru is a form of our own inner teacher, that the Guru is a part of ourselves.

You can practice this invocation with the spiritual teacher with whom you feel the closest connection, whether or not that teacher is physically in this world. If you don't feel connected to a particular teacher, you might like to invoke the presence of Bhagawan Nityananda, Swami Muktananda's Guru, the founder of the contemporary Siddha Yoga lineage. Nityananda, whose name

I am the same Self in all beings; there is none hateful or dear to me. But those who worship me with devotion, they are in me and I am also in them.

BHAGAVAD GITA

means "eternal bliss," was a being who existed in a skylike state of oneness with the universe. From his youngest days, he lived without personal agendas, acting purely to offer blessings and to help others turn toward the truth of their own nature. He continues to do that even after having left his body. His help and grace are available to anyone who calls on him, whether or not they consider themselves students of Siddha Yoga meditation. You don't need to know much about Nityananda to call forth his presence. His name is enough.

*From the blossoming
    lotus of devotion, at the
    center of my heart,
Rise up, O compassionate
    master, my only refuge!*

JIKME LINGPA

EXERCISE: INVOKING THE TEACHER

Sit in a comfortable, upright meditation posture and close your eyes. Let your attention merge with the breath, following the breath as it comes in and goes out.

Imagine that you are sitting before your Guru, or before the great saint or enlightened master with whom you feel most connected. Have the awareness that your Guru is not simply an individual being. Understand him or her to be the embodiment of the entire power of grace that runs through countless lineages of enlightened masters.

It is not necessary to "see" your Guru. The most important thing is to feel his or her presence, to allow that presence to be fully real for you. Feel this presence as a divine awakening force, a power of grace with which you are deeply familiar and deeply connected. Recognize that this is the particular embodiment of the grace-bestowing power that has chosen to draw you close to the state of enlightenment, the state of Truth. Your Guru is showering blessings on you. And it is happening through the breath.

As the Guru breathes out, s/he breathes into you the entire power of love and all the blessings of a vast lineage of enlightened beings. As you inhale, you breathe the love and blessings into yourself. As you exhale, you breathe these blessings through your whole body, feeling the Guru's love filling you from head to toe.

Now sit with the feeling that the love of your Guru and your Guru's entire lineage fills your body. Feel the energy of those blessings within yourself. Rest in the blessings you have taken in. Offer your thanks.

Give up to grace.
The ocean takes care
of each wave
Till it gets to shore.
You need more help
than you know.

RUMI

If you don't want to do such an elaborate practice of invocation, simply remember your Guru and then ask for his or her grace. Your invocation can be simple and short or elaborate and poetic. If you are full of longing, fill the invocation with your longing. If you feel dry and uninterested, confess your dryness and ask for help. If your mind is disturbed by anger, fear, or worry, offer the mind up to be transformed. Your invocation is your dialogue with the power of grace, and the more personal, direct, and heartfelt it is, the more effective it will be. Just as it is important to feel the largeness of the teacher's grace-bestowing power, it is equally crucial to understand how close the Guru is to you. Instead of thinking that the Guru is far away and superior, you can remind yourself that the Guru is actually present within you, part of the inner fabric of your being. The power of grace you are invoking is not coming from somewhere else. It is manifesting from within you.

Once you have opened yourself like this, once you have touched the power of grace, you are standing at the threshold of meditation. It is time to choose your gateway, the portal you will step through.

CHAPTER 4

Choosing the Right Doorway

In my early years of meditation, I wasted countless hours wondering which technique to use. Some early mentor had told me to decide on one technique and stick with it, and I reasoned that if I had to choose one practice, it had better be the right one. So I worried. I worried about which mantra to use, about whether to meditate on the witness or on the breath, about when it was permissible to leave the technique behind and just relax into myself. It wasn't until I stopped making techniques into icons that I began to discover how liberating it can be to work with different practices—and how important it is ultimately to move beyond them.

We use techniques in meditation for a very simple reason: most of us, at least when we

*This alone is obligatory,...
that the mind be firmly
applied to the true reality.
It matters little how this
is achieved.*

MALINI VIJAYA TANTRA

begin meditation, need support for our mind. A technique provides a place for the mind to rest while it settles back down into its essential nature. That's all a technique is really, a kind of cushion for the mind. No meditation technique is an end in itself, and no matter which meditation technique you use, it will eventually dissolve when your meditation deepens.

I like to think of meditation techniques as portals, entry points into the spaciousness that underlies the mind. The inner spaciousness is always there, with its clarity, its love, and its innate goodness. It is like the sky that suddenly "appears" over our heads when we step out of the kitchen door after a harried morning and glance upward. The Self, like the sky, is ever present yet hidden by the ceiling and walls of our minds. In approaching the Self, it helps to have a doorway we can comfortably walk through, rather than having to break through the wall of thoughts separating us from our inner space. When the practice comes from a recognized Guru lineage, it also carries an empowerment that can impel us through the doorway and straight into the experience. In Siddha Yoga meditation, once *kundalini shakti* has been awakened, the technique becomes a vehicle that connects us to that subtle inner power. Then the *shakti* itself carries the outgoing awareness inside, into a state of meditation. (It's also been my experience, as we'll see in a later chapter, that techniques can arise spontaneously from the awakened *shakti.*) Different techniques often seem to lead us into different corners of the inner kingdom. The Self is one, yet it has endless facets. So working with a technique that's new to us can land us in a part of the inner country we may not have known before.

There's another reason why it is good to experiment with techniques: the technique we are currently using may be keeping us stuck. That happens to a lot of people. They learn one practice, then they stick with it, even if it doesn't help them go deeper. After a while, they feel that they aren't good meditators, or that meditation is just too hard or too boring, or even that it comes so easily they miss a feeling of growth. Often their only problem is that they are trying to enter meditation through the wrong doorway or through a door that once opened easily but is now stiff on its hinges.

The best reason to do any meditation practice is that you like it. This piece of advice comes from no less an authority than Patanjali's *Yoga Sutras*, a text of meditation so fundamental that every yogic tradition in India makes it the basis for meditation practice. After listing a string of practices for focusing the mind, Patanjali ends his chapter on concentration by saying, "Concentrate wherever the mind finds satisfaction." How do you know that the mind is finding satisfaction in a technique? First, you should enjoy it. You should be able to relax within it. It should give you a feeling of peace. Once you've become familiar with it, the practice should feel natural. If you have to work too hard at it, that may be a sign that it is the wrong practice for you.

Most people who've meditated for a while have a sense of which modes of meditation feel most natural. Some people have a visual bent and respond well to practices that work with "sights"—visualizations and the like. Others are more kinesthetic, attuned to sensations of energy. There are auditory people, whose inner world opens in response to sound, and people whose practice is kindled by an insight or a feeling.

Once we become aware of how we respond to different perceptual modes, we can often adjust a practice so that it works for us. Someone who has a hard time visualizing can bring a visual form to life inside her if she imagines its presence as energy or an inner sensation, rather than trying to see it as a visual image. A highly visual person might get bored with mantra repetition when he focuses on sounding the syllables, but feel the mantra's impact if he visualizes the letters on his inner screen. One person might experience great love when he repeats a mantra with a devotional feeling, while his friend's meditation only takes off once she lets go of all props and meditates on pure Awareness.

We each have to find our own way. To do this, we need to give ourselves full permission to play with the different practices we are given.

THE POSTURE

The core, the foundation, the basis of all practice is posture. A correct meditation posture is comfortable enough so that you can sit in it for a while, steady enough so that you feel free to forget the body, yet strong enough so that it helps you stay alert. Here is a set of simple posture instructions that you can use when you practice the meditation exercises on the pages that follow. At this moment, as you are reading, you might want to align your body in this posture.

POSTURE INSTRUCTIONS

■ The most important aspect of a meditative posture is that the spine be held naturally erect, so that the energy of meditation can flow freely. If you can sit on the floor, sit in a comfortable cross-legged posture with a firm pillow, yoga wedge, or folded blanket under your hips. Raising the hips helps to keep your back from rounding or slumping and maintains

A yogi in a steady posture easily becomes immersed in the heart.

SHIVA SUTRAS

the natural curve of the lower back. Your knees should be parallel to your hips or slightly lower.

- If you would rather sit in a chair, place your feet flat on the floor, hip-width apart. Sit forward on your chair or cushion, so that your upper back doesn't round and slump. You may also support your lower back by placing a small cushion between the small of your back and the back of the chair.

- Place your hands palms down on the thighs with thumb and forefinger touching, or fold them palms up in your lap with the back of one hand resting in the palm of the other.

- Feel that your hips and thighs are heavy and grounded, as if they were sinking into the chair or the floor. Feel that your spinal column rises out of this grounded base, straight up through the crown of the head. Let your neck be soft.

- Let your head float freely, rising upward in line with the spine. Soften your face. Let your eyelids and cheeks relax. Let your tongue rest on the floor of the mouth.

- Inhale gently, and on the exhalation, allow your chest to open and lift, as if you were lifting it from the heart. Inhale, and on the exhalation allow the shoulder blades to melt down the back.

- It is important to be at ease in the posture, so if your body feels uncomfortable during meditation, feel free to adjust it. However, let your movements be mindful and slow, so you don't bring yourself out of meditation.

- Once your body is aligned, let the breath help relax you in the posture. On the inhalation, let the breath flow into any places in the body that feel tired or tense. On the exhalation, allow any tightness or constriction to flow out with the breath. This opens the body, softens it, and prepares it to hold the energy released in meditation.

- Sit for a moment in the posture. Close your eyes, and let the breath come in and out naturally. Listen to the sounds in the room. Feel the sensations in your body. Let yourself fully experience the sensation of being inside your body, in this posture, in this moment. Let yourself be where you are.

BASIC PRACTICES

Siddha Yoga uses several basic types of meditation techniques: a sound form (repeating a mantra), a kinesthetic or energy form (following the breath or focusing on the space between the breaths), and various visual forms. We also practice meditation by focusing on different inner centers, like the *sushumna nadi* (the subtle channel that runs up the spinal column) or the heart center. Another basic practice, meditating on the Witness or on bare Awareness as described in chapter 2, works directly with the formless, with Consciousness itself. These techniques can often be combined. For example, you might combine the mantra with the breath, or you might observe the breath and allow yourself to gradually become aware of the Awareness that is "doing" this observation. I often begin meditation by focusing on the space between the breaths until my attention becomes centered, and then rests in the space of the heart.

Before we examine these practices in depth, we will look at some principles that can help bring a practice to life for us.

THE SUBTLE ESSENCE OF A PRACTICE

The most important thing to remember about any practice we do (aside from the fact that it should be one recommended by the teachers of a recognized Guru lineage) is to keep looking for its subtle essence. Every technique we work with has its own unique feeling tone. It creates an energy space inside us. For example, when repeating a mantra with the breath, you might feel a specific sensation of air moving between the throat and the heart, as well as a subtle feeling of expansion or pulsation in the heart space when the mantra syllables "strike" it. Focusing on the space between the breaths, you might begin to feel the breath moving in and out of your heart and notice a subtle expansion of the heart space until it seems to include everything outside. You might notice that certain parts of the inner body are activated by a particular practice: the space between the eyebrows, for example, might begin to pulsate when you turn your attention to your own Awareness. Taking a deep breath might make you especially aware of the currents of energy flowing through your body.

That energy sensation, or feeling sense, is the subtle effect of the technique and its real essence. It is the feeling sense that a technique creates, rather than the technique itself, that opens the door into the Self. For this reason, we want to keep moving into the space created by the practice: into the *feeling* of the mantra as it drops into our consciousness, into the *sensation* of the breath as it pauses between the inhalation and the exhalation, or into the *vividness* of the object we are visualizing. As we do this, we automatically release ourselves into a subtler level of our being.

To know the Self as it is and become one with it: that is true meditation.

SWAMI MUKTANANDA

65

GOD IS IN YOUR FEELING

Another way to discover the inner essence of a technique is to work with *bhava*. *Bhava* is a Sanskrit word that means "feeling" or "attitude" or "conviction" about oneself. According to Indian tradition, *bhava* is so powerful that it can transform our experience of reality.

We are always holding onto one *bhava* or another. It is just that we don't think of our identification with being a woman or an accountant, our feeling of discomfort, or our sense of being responsible for the universe as attitudes or convictions. Instead we think they are the truth, that they are who we are. We look at the world through the glasses of our particular set of *bhavas* and imagine that what we see is the way things really are when actually we are seeing only the reflection of our *bhavas*. That is why a shift in our attitude makes such a change in our daily experience of the world. Any time we decide to focus on forgiveness instead of anger, or to look at a situation from someone else's perspective, or to dwell on our own good qualities instead of brooding about our failings, we discover the power of *bhava* to transform our experience.

The practice of consciously creating an internal *bhava*, or articulating a specific spiritual feeling, is called *bhavana*, sometimes translated as "creative contemplation." Each *bhavana* has its own effect on us. For example, if you practice the *bhavana* of offering your practice to God or to humanity, it creates a feeling of selflessness in your practice and helps take you beyond grasping for a particular experience or inner state. Remembering love or grace — as in the practice of breathing in with the feeling that you are breathing in love — expands the heart and gives a sense of contentment and protection. Feeling that everything is a part of your own Consciousness loosens the grip of limitation.

When a man meditates on the thought that he is rooted in the divine, and he prays to God, then he performs an act of true unification.

BA'AL SHEM TOV

66

If you practice a particular *bhava* long enough, it will become natural—
it will actually become real for you. That's because your consciousness is so creative that it can shape itself completely around any feeling you hold and recreate
itself in that image. Once the feeling that you have been practicing begins to arise
spontaneously as experience, you will discover the truth of what Tukaram
Maharaj meant when he wrote, "God is in your *bhava*."

Tukaram was an impoverished grocer from a tiny village called Dehu in
western India. He had nine children and a fiercely disappointed wife, but despite
everything, he spent his days chanting and singing to God until he eventually
attained a state of God-realization. A master of *bhava*, he used to talk to God in
a different mood every day. Sometimes he called out to God with love, sometimes he railed in angry frustration, and sometimes he declared that he belonged
to God and God belonged to him. It was Tukaram who articulated the secret of
bhava. He understood that our spontaneous feelings are what connect us to the
higher power. In short, when we love God, we actually experience divine reality
in our love. If we are afraid of God or angry at God, we experience God as fear
or anger. When we feel one with God, God's presence reveals itself as our inmost
being. When we long for God, we discover that God is in our very desire. By
practicing these *bhavas,* we bring them alive inside us.

As we look further at the basic Siddha Yoga meditation techniques, we
will also look at how we can merge them with different *bhavas*.

MANTRA REPETITION

The word "mantra" means "a tool for the mind." Specifically, mantras are physical sounds that approximate the "unsounded sound," the vibration of the Infinite

The Word without a word,
the Word within
The world and for
the world;
And the light shone
in darkness and
Against the Word the
unstilled world
still whirled
About the centre of the
silent Word

T. S. ELIOT

that throbs in the silence of pure Consciousness. These inner vibrations are far too subtle to be heard by the physical ears or articulated by the tongue. However, the traditional mantras of a Guru lineage—heard by sages in deep meditation and then transmitted to their disciples—carry that high, subtle vibration embedded in their syllables. Such mantras are called *chaitanya* in Sanskrit because the full power of pure, universal Consciousness *(chaitanya)* is within them. Repeating such a *chaitanya* mantra gradually draws the mind inward, back to the source of the mantra. That is the basic principle of mantra practice. However, the way the mantra works and the secrets of how it works are quite subtle. To understand the inner practice of mantra, we must turn to the texts of the Indian Tantric tradition, where the science of mantra is explained in all its complexity.

One thing all these texts agree on is that a mantra is effective only when it is empowered by a recognized lineage of teachers. That's because the words of a mantra are only its shell. The real mantra is the energy embedded in the syllables, which needs to be activated in order to work for us. When the mantra comes from a lineage, it is imbued with the realization, the enlightened experience, of the lineage-Gurus and also with their *shakti*, their spiritual power. Most of the exercises in these pages work with the empowered mantra of the Siddha Yoga lineage, *Om Namah Shivaya* (pronounced *Ohm nuhmmuh shivAHya*). However, if you have been initiated into another mantra, please feel free to use that.

The simplest, most basic way of working with the mantra is to combine it with the breath. You breathe in softly, thinking the mantra with the inhalation. You exhale gently, thinking the mantra with the exhalation. Because *Om Namah Shivaya* is a long mantra, some people find it hard to coordinate it with their breathing. One solution is to adjust the speed of your mantra repetition to the speed of your breathing. If you begin by mentally repeating the mantra rather quickly, you will probably find that your repetition slows down automatically as you get deeper into meditation and your breath slows. Another solution is not to try to coordinate it with the breathing, but simply to think the mantra to yourself over and over again.

Many people find there is a lot of power in enunciating the syllables of the mantra precisely and distinctly. I've found, however, that the mantra opens up for me more easily if I don't try so hard to enunciate. Instead I allow a slight slurring, a blurring together, of the syllables. I've noticed that when I repeat a mantra with "hard" focus, trying to keep each syllable separate, I tend to create a sense of difference between myself and the mantra, and this can become a barrier that keeps me from releasing into meditation. In mantra practice, as in any technique, the effort we make needs to be soft and subtle—the effortless effort that we spoke about in chapter 3. We focus, yes, but our focus is not a grasping concentration, not a mental fist gripped around the technique. To use one of Gurumayi's images, we hold the mantra in our awareness as if we were holding a butterfly in the palm of the hand.

THE LEVELS OF MANTRA

As we become more intimate with a mantra, we begin to experience it on progressively deeper levels. A mantra has three basic aspects. On the simplest level, of course, the mantra is an object of focus. It is a thought we can cling to in order to keep other thoughts at bay. On a deeper level, the mantra is an energy that

The one truth, formless ...eternal,...infinite, imperishable, inaccessible to mind and speech, shines forth in the conjunction of the great mantra and its profound meaning.

KULARNAVA TANTRA

comes from, and connects us to, the Guru lineage; it functions within us as a subtle force of transformation. On the deepest level of all, the mantra is pure radiance, pure silence, and pure love. According to the *Shiva Sutras,* this is the *rahasya,* or secret, within the mantra. At its core, a mantra is the light of supreme Awareness itself. The *Parasurama Kalpa Sutra,* one of the esoteric texts of the North Indian yogic tradition, says *Mantra maheshvara,* or "Mantra is [a form of] the supreme Reality."

HOW THE MANTRA WORKS

Of course, all this is not necessarily apparent to us at first. When we initially begin to work with a mantra, we are usually working purely with the syllables, and we seem to spend much of our time in meditation losing track of them. We try to stay with the mantra, but without even knowing how it happens, we keep finding ourselves somewhere else—thinking about the laundry, worrying about what our brother-in-law said yesterday, or wondering whether to drive to the city or to take the train. This moment when we catch ourselves thinking, however, is a powerful point of practice. At such a moment, we can choose to follow the original thought or to let ourselves get caught up in an inner commentary on the process—such as berating ourselves for thinking—or we can choose to bring ourselves back to the mantra. Without surrendering to the reverie or getting upset with ourselves for thinking, we just come back to the mantra. After a while, the mantra begins to act as a sort of magnet that aligns the iron filings of our scattered attention. This practice of gathering up the rays of our mental energy and bringing them into alignment is referred to in Patanjali's *Yoga Sutras* as *dharana,* which literally means "concentration."

At any point in this process, the *shakti* embedded in the mantra can plunge us into meditation—sometimes right in the middle of a particularly nagging thought! Here is where the right *bhavana* can often help, quickening the mantra energy by adding feeling to our practice.

Someone once told me that the mantra *Om Namah Shivaya* seemed impenetrable to her—"just Sanskrit words with no meaning"—until she was asked to repeat the mantra with the feeling that she was gently dropping the syllables into her heart. That *bhavana* made the mantra more personal for her. She began to notice that when she dropped the mantra into her heart region, she experienced a soft expansion of tenderness there, as if she were receiving an inner caress. Love began to arise in her. The mantra syllables seemed to merge into her heart.

For this woman, a devotional *bhavana* had helped open up the mantra. For someone else, repeating the mantra with the feeling that the syllables pulsate with enlightening energy, or offering the mantra to the inner Beloved, might provide the opening. You could think of the mantra as light or even visualize the syllables in letters of light inside your awareness. If you are a visual person, in fact, you may need to do a visualization as you repeat the mantra before you succeed in opening the mantra for yourself. If you are more auditory in style, try having the feeling that the mantra is being sung to you, try to hear it being chanted inside, or try repeating it while remaining aware of its meaning: "I honor the God within myself and all things." If you tend to be kinesthetic, feel for the pulsation in the mantra, the energy experience of it. I'm a kinesthetic person myself, and the mantra only began to work strongly for me after I learned to think of the syllables as energies and to feel each syllable pulsating inside me as

During worship,
all the actions performed
merge into the mantra.
The mantra, which
is the name,
merges into the mind.
When the mind merges,
everything dissolves.
Then the world of the seen,
along with the seer,
assumes the form
of Consciousness.

LALLA DED

71

I repeated it. Then the energy of the mantra began to open up for me into a pulsing sweetness, a feeling of gathering love.

Eventually, as we become sensitized to the feel of the mantra, we learn how to hold the syllables within our awareness in such a way that we can actually sense the vibration, the throb of *shakti,* in the syllables. At this point, we begin to discover why the sages have told us that the syllables of the mantra are just a kind of jacket, like the skin of a fruit. We start to experience the subtle vibration inside the syllables, which is the real source of the mantra's sweetness. We begin to learn how to merge our attention into the mantra energy, and, as we do, we feel the mantra beginning to sink through the layers of our subtle being and to affect us at deeper and deeper levels. It moves from the conscious level, where we have to repeat it distinctly with every breath, to a more subconscious space, where we feel the mantra pulsing often quite indistinctly beneath our conscious awareness. Eventually the syllables seem to pulsate with love, with Awareness, with an expansive feeling, or with light. In other words, we begin to experience a palpable sense of presence in the mantra as we repeat it. One of the important Shaivite texts, the *Spanda Karikas,* refers to that presence as the *spanda,* or the original pulsation of divine energy that creates the universe and remains embedded within every particle of it. The mantra is actually one of the main vehicles we can use to become aware of that ground energy.

Once you start to feel that energy, you begin to love repeating the mantra. Like the poet-saints Tukaram and Namdev and Jnaneshwar, whose essential practice was to repeat the names of God, you experience deep joy in simply turning the syllables over and over in your mind.

That experience of an energetic presence in the syllables is a sign that the mantra has cracked open for you and that you are experiencing the real mantra, the inner mantra. Ramana Maharshi once said, "Mantra is our real nature. When we realize the Self, then mantra repetition goes on without effort. What is the means at one stage becomes the goal at another." Swami Muktananda used to say something similar: "When you begin your practice of the mantra, it is just a practice. After realization, you discover that mantra repetition is itself the attainment."

This experience can happen quite early in your practice. When you are deep in meditation, you will sometimes feel the mantra dissolving into light, into pure energy, or into bliss. People have "seen" the form of a deity arising out of the mantra. In meditation, one man saw himself riding astride the mantra syllables, which had formed an arc of light that ended in an ocean of radiance. A young woman began to hear *Om Namah Shivaya* sounding like thunder, then saw that within the sound a path of light had taken form. When she followed the path, she came to a gate. Her Guru was standing before it. The Guru opened the gate, revealing a vast blue sky pulsating with love.

When I repeat the mantra *Om Namah Shivaya* with great feeling, I sometimes find that its energy will fill my body, and then seem to turn into a human-sized white *lingam*—the pillarlike form worshiped in India as a representation of the formless Absolute. Then that form will disappear, and I will be left with a feeling of silent, pulsing presence.

When the mantra begins to reveal itself at the deepest level, both the syllables and the feeling of pulsation disappear completely, and we experience only pure Awareness, the mantra as pure silence. This is a *samadhi* state—a conscious state of absorption in love, power, and crystalline Awareness.

If you want the truth,
I'll tell you the truth:
Listen to the secret sound,
the real sound,
which is inside you.
The one no one talks of
speaks the secret sound
to himself,
and he is the one who has
made it all.

KABIR

THE ESSENTIAL BHAVA: FEELING THE PRESENCE IN THE SYLLABLES

The Gurus of the Siddha Yoga lineage have told us that a mantra will work much more quickly if we can remember that the radiance of supreme Awareness is present inside the syllables. This is a core instruction that applies not only to mantra repetition, but also to every practice that we do. It is the ultimate *bhava,* and yet it can seem quite abstract and difficult to practice at first.

The best way to work with this instruction is not to try to eat it whole, so to speak, but to use it as an invitation to investigate our experience of the mantra. Working with an instruction like "Feel the presence of God, of universal Consciousness, in the mantra syllables" confronts you with the gap between the teaching and your experience. It challenges you to understand how pure Consciousness could possibly be present inside a word. The answer you come up with needs to be a real answer, not just an intellectual formulation. For that to happen, you need to question yourself, to inquire, "What am I really experiencing? How do I need to hold myself so that the mantra will reveal its inner essence? How can I get deeper into the mantra?"

Holding this kind of awake, contemplative awareness as you repeat the mantra makes your practice very alive. It keeps it from becoming mechanical. It leads to insight. I recently talked to a man who told me that when he first heard the instruction "Feel the presence of the Self in the mantra syllables," it drove him so crazy that he finally began asking the mantra itself to help him out. "What do they mean when they say you are God?" he asked over and over again. One day the mantra answered him. It began to vibrate waves of ecstasy all through his chest. The feeling of ecstasy expanded, and along with the mantra, the man's awareness and his sense of being began to expand outward until he felt as though his body contained a vast spaciousness.

As mentioned before, one of Swami Muktananda's basic instructions about mantra repetition was that you should do it with the feeling that you, the mantra, and the goal of the mantra are one. He used to say, "If you were to call someone an idiot, his condition would change completely. Because he identifies with the body, he reacts immediately. But since you don't identify yourself with the deity of the mantra, you don't react to the mantra so quickly. If we believe in the truth of the mantric words, they bear fruit instantly."

Again, this instruction is an invitation to contemplation. It is a way to enter into a more vibrant relationship with the mantra. As you think about how to go about identifying yourself with the mantra, you might find yourself discovering a lot about what you are and what the mantra really is. How do you practice identifying yourself with a word? I've asked many people over the years how they practice identifying themselves with a mantra, and I've heard many imaginative responses. One way is to imagine that the mantra is a cloud that surrounds you on all sides. Another is to imagine it as water, or as light, and to see yourself immersed in it. Still another is to bring yourself *as energy* closer and closer to the mantra until you feel that you are inside it. All of these practices help to open up the experience of repeating the mantra.

Don't look for God.
Don't leave your home.
Don't even exert yourself
*   to attain Him.*
With a one-pointed mind,
repeat Om Namah
*   Shivaya.*
O Lalli!
He will instantly speak
*   to you,*
murmuring from within.

LALLA DED

EXERCISE: REPEATING THE MANTRA OM NAMAH SHIVAYA

Sit in a comfortable, upright posture and close your eyes. Focus on the flow of the breath.

Gently and with relaxed attention, begin to think the mantra *Om Namah Shivaya* to yourself. You may coordinate it with the breathing or simply repeat it slowly, again and again, listening to the syllables as you repeat them. Allow your attention to focus more and more fully on the mantra's syllables. Feel that each syllable is softly dropping into your awareness. Let yourself feel the "space" that the mantra creates inside. Allow the energetic space created by the mantra to expand. Feel that you are inside the mantra's energy and that the mantra is pouring through your body until it fills you and surrounds you on every side, like a river of liquid sound or like a pulsating cloud of energy.

THE SPACE BETWEEN THE BREATHS

The Kashmiri sage Kshemaraja, in his book *Pratyabhijna Hridayam (The Heart of Recognition)*, offered in just a few words one of the great mystical secrets, saying that the way to experience the fullness of the ultimate reality is to expand the *madhya*, or the center. *Madhya* is a technical term for the still point between two phases of movement. When a pendulum swings, there is a fraction of a moment at the end of each swing when the movement stops before beginning to swing back. That moment of pause is the *madhya*, the central still point out of which the pendulum's movement arises. All movement, whether the swing of an axe, the movement of the breath, or the flow of thoughts, arises out of such a point of stillness. As we saw in chapter 2, that still point is an open door into the heart of the universe, a place where we can step into the big Consciousness beyond our small consciousness. As the medieval English saint Julian of Norwich wrote,

"God is the midpoint between all things." One of my favorite descriptions of this reality is from the poem "Burnt Norton" in T. S. Eliot's *Four Quartets:*

> At the still point of the turning world. Neither flesh nor fleshless;
> Neither from nor towards; at the still point, there the dance is,
> But neither arrest nor movement. And do not call it fixity,
> Where past and future are gathered. Neither movement
>   from nor towards.
> Neither ascent nor decline. Except for the point, the still point,
> There would be no dance, and there is only the dance.
> I can only say, *there* we have been: but I cannot say where.
> And I cannot say, how long, for that is to place it in time.

Tripura Rahasya, a wonderful text of Vedanta, calls these pregnant still points "fleeting *samadhis.*" Meditators of several different traditions have pointed out that such points exist at many different moments. One of these is the pause between sleeping and waking, the moment when we first wake up before we become fully conscious. Another is the moment before a sneeze or at the high point of a yawn. Another is the space between thoughts. If we focus our attention in one of these gaps, it may open up for us, and we will find ourselves in the *madhya,* "the still point of the turning world," the placeless place where we leave the activity of the manifest universe and enter the emptiness at the heart of manifestation. This is, in fact, the inner realm that Ramana Maharshi, Abhinavagupta, Gurumayi, and other sages of the nondualist tradition have called the Heart. It is the place of ultimate stillness, where the microcosm expands into the macrocosm. It is the Consciousness that underlies all forms. The great Mind. The Self.

One of the most accessible points of entry into the *madhya* is the space between the inhalation and the exhalation, and between the exhalation and the inhalation.*

The exercise below gives us access to the space between the breaths by having us focus on the sound of the breath itself. The secret of entering this space is awareness and subtle, relaxed attention. The space between the breaths is tiny and subtle—so subtle that at first it seems barely to be there at all. So to enter it, we need to pay close attention.

EXERCISE: THE SPACE BETWEEN BREATHS

Sitting in a firm, upright, yet relaxed posture, softly focus your attention on the movement of the breath. Let the inhalation come into the heart region in the center of the chest, and let the exhalation arise from there.

As you breathe, let the breath make a little sound as it passes through the nostrils. You should notice that the sound is something like *hum* on the inbreath and something like *sah* on the outbreath. In Sanskrit, *ham* means "I" and *sah* means "that." The sound of the breath is a natural mantra, as if we are being reminded with every inhalation and exhalation to remember our identity as the Infinite.

Listen to the sound that the breath makes and notice how when it comes to an end in the region of the heart, in the center of the chest, there is an

---

*For a detailed account of this practice, see *I Am That,* written by Swami Muktananda and published by SYDA Foundation.

infinitesimal pause, a tiny "space" of stillness. Focus on that pause. Don't try to lengthen it; just note it.

Then when the exhalation starts, follow the sound of the breath until it comes to an end in the space outside. Again note the pause. Focus softly there, but don't try to lengthen it.

Keep following the breath in this way, gently focusing on the space inside and the space outside. Let the practice itself absorb your attention.

It is very difficult for people to believe in ecstasy. But when you find the space that exists inside and outside — the timeless time, the pointless point — and when it becomes a prolonged space inside and outside, ecstasy is no longer a concept: it is the experience.

GURUMAYI CHIDVILASANANDA

There is no need to worry about whether or not something is happening and no need to feel frustrated if the space doesn't immediately open further. The doorway to the *madhya* opens by grace, by its own will. If you simply stay with it, the expansion will happen.

For me it opened with a tap on the head! In 1977, a few weeks after Swami Muktananda first instructed us in this practice, I was sitting in the meditation room in his ashram in India, trying to feel the space between the breaths. Try as I might, the space wouldn't lengthen. It was so small that it seemed nonexistent.

Suddenly the door to Swami Muktananda's house, which was off the meditation room, opened and he came in. He walked up to me and tapped me sharply on the head. In the next moment, a vast chasm opened up between my inbreath and my outbreath. The breath stopped, and I was inside a huge space, a kind of ocean of Awareness.

Admittedly this is a rather dramatic example of how the teacher's grace can open the inner space. You don't need to get whacked on the side of the head by the teacher in order for the inner space to open. It is enough to sit, to practice the technique, and to wait. In time you will become sensitive to the feel of the space there. Then one day, perhaps at a moment when your thoughts have thinned out and slowed down enough so that you can perceive in a more subtle way, you will notice the space lengthening. You will be able to feel the gap between the breaths and to enter it for a little while—even while the breath continues going in and out.

One way you know that you are entering deeply into the practice is when you begin to feel that your breath is moving "horizontally." Instead of feeling the whole arc of the breath coming in through the nostrils, going to the heart, and moving back out, you seem to be breathing in and out of the chest. Sometimes instead of a horizontal breath, the breath comes in and out in a circling motion that seems to operate completely independently of the body. At that point, you might begin to experience how the space inside the body is connected to the space outside. You'll realize that one field of Consciousness connects both the spaces and that the separation we normally make between inside and outside is nothing more than an illusion.

In general, it is better to let the breathing come in and out naturally—not to hold your breath or otherwise try to force the breath to extend itself. Yet, I've found that at certain times—perhaps at the beginning of your daily practice—the following exercise can help jump-start the process by giving you a feel for the space between the breaths. It recreates the state that we would like to have arise spontaneously, in this case the moment when the *madhya* begins to reveal itself in meditation.

EXERCISE: FINDING GOD AT THE END OF THE EXHALATION

When you come to the end of an exhalation, let the breath stay out for thirty seconds or as long as feels comfortable to you. Rest in that space where there is no more breath. Then name the space "God" or "the Self" or "pure Consciousness." Letting yourself stay in that moment of emptiness at the end of the exhalation is a way of entering into the space of the Self. Notice how in that space you are fully in the present. There is no past, no future, just the experience of now.

MEDITATION ON CONSCIOUSNESS

Meditation on pure Consciousness is usually considered an advanced practice, mainly because Awareness is so elusive and insubstantial that a beginning meditator can have a hard time finding a foothold in it. But once the mind has shed some of its surface agitation and acquired a bit of subtlety, this practice tends to suggest itself naturally. In fact, it often happens on its own.

Any form you meditate on will eventually disappear for you, even if you try to hold on to it. In India there's a saying that a technique is like the car you drive to the temple. When you get to the temple, you leave the car behind. In fact, the "car" of your meditation technique usually gives out long before you get to the temple. At some point, the mantra syllables will dissolve into pulsations of energy, the visual form will melt into the space that surrounds it, and the breath will slow down or stop. Then you will be left with your own bare consciousness, your own feelings and inner sensations, the basic pulsation of your own energy. Some people worry when they get to this point. They think

When you find me
    within yourself,
your own naked mind,
that Single Awareness
will fill all the worlds.
Then the joy of the One
will hold you like a lake.

YESHE TSOGYEL

that they have lost the technique and that something has gone wrong. In fact, it means that the technique is bearing fruit. Once the mind has become centered and relatively quiet, our deeper Awareness naturally emerges and presents itself as the primary object of meditation. To use Emily Dickinson's metaphor:

> The Props assist the House
> Until the House is built
> And then the Props withdraw
> And adequate, erect,
> The House supports itself.

Consciousness, of course, is not a house nor is it any kind of object. It is the eternal subject; it is what Meister Eckhart called the ground of being. Because this technique is so direct, it can create a big shift in our understanding, even if we are only able to hold it for a moment or two.

Most days I begin my meditation practice by working with a form. Sometimes I focus on the mantra; at other times, I follow the breath or look for the space at the end of the inhalation.

At some point, usually half an hour to forty minutes into the meditation session, the thought stream slows to a trickle, the object of focus melts back into the Awareness from which it has arisen, and my attention becomes focused on the subtle, pulsating energy that underlies my thoughts. At that point, my meditation becomes centered directly on the energy field of my own consciousness. For me this is the heart of my meditation practice. Usually I find myself focusing on the pulsation of energy that throbs constantly inside Awareness.

Let's look for a moment at that pulsation. It is one of the most important clues to deeper meditation.

EXERCISE: FINDING THE PULSATION IN YOUR CONSCIOUSNESS

Sit in a comfortable, upright posture. With eyes closed, regard your inner consciousness. You are not looking for anything. You are just observing your own inner world with your inner eye, becoming aware of what your inner eye actually sees when you close your eyes. Perhaps you see blue light or a field of gray, or perhaps you see a haze of darkness filled with tiny points of light, like a pointillist painting. You are looking at what in Sanskrit is called the *chitta*, the mind-stuff, the inner consciousness. This is the energetic ground from which all thoughts, feelings, perceptions, and sensations arise and subside.

Now, notice the dynamic quality of this inner consciousness. Notice how there is a constant shimmer of subtle movement, a kind of vibration or pulsation within it. Your inner consciousness is made of energy. It vibrates, and it is that vibration that gives rise to thoughts and feelings and images.

See if you can become aware of the pulsation of your consciousness. In its physical form, that pulsation manifests as the heartbeat, but if you pay close attention, you can sense a subtler pulsation that underlies the heartbeat.

If you do not immediately feel the subtle pulsation, focus on the throb of your heartbeat.

Stay with the heartbeat until you begin to feel its subtler level, or to feel how its pulsation actually reverberates through the body. Or, if you feel a pulsation of energy somewhere else in the body, focus on that until you gradually become aware of the subtler pulsation that underlies it.

*Thinking of the magnitude
of the sky,
Meditate on the Vastness
with no center and
no edge.*

MILAREPA

In Sanskrit, the subtlest level of this pulsation is called *spanda*, meaning "throb" or "vibration." According to the sage Kallata, the author of the *Spanda Karikas (Stanzas on Vibration)*, one of the key texts of Kashmir Shaivism, the *spanda* is the original impulse of energy that creates all life and all worlds and that keeps them going. When we sense the pulsation inside us, we are sensing our own personal spark of that huge, primordial life force. It is the energy behind the breath, the heartbeat, and the movement of our thoughts and feelings. It is also the source of all our experiences in meditation. When we get deep into meditation, we realize that this throb, this subtle pulsation, is actually meditating us.

Swami Muktananda, in a book of commentaries on Shaivite texts called *Nothing Exists That Is Not Shiva*, spoke of this pulsation as the pure expression of *kundalini*. Quoting a medieval Shaivite text called the *Tantra Sadbhava*, he pointed out that the same power that enlivens a mantra is inherent in the mind of a meditator. It is experienced, he said, as "the throbbing movement of the mind by which a yogi meditates." If we focus on it and follow it, it will lead us to its source, to the ultimate silence of the Self.

Once you sense that subtle pulsation, stay with it. Let it become your point of focus, just as if it were a mantra. When you get out of touch with it, bring yourself back to it. As you stay with the pulsation, it will keep releasing you deeper into the field of your own being.

Of course, there are several other ways to practice directly entering Consciousness. Some of these practices, such as becoming aware of Awareness or being the observer or knower of thoughts, can be found in chapter 2. The one that follows is adapted from the *Vijnana Bhairava*. It is a practice that yogis have been using for several thousand years.

EXERCISE: YOU ARE IN AN OCEAN OF SPACE

Sit in a comfortable, upright posture, close your eyes, and gently merge your attention with the flow of breath coming in and going out through your nostrils. Keep returning your attention to the breath each time it wanders away. Do this until you feel the breath gently slow down and the thoughts become quieter.

Imagine that your body is completely empty. It is as though your skin were a thin membrane, like the skin of a balloon, and inside it is nothing but space. Not only is your body full of space, but space also surrounds you on every side. As you inhale, have the feeling that you are breathing space in through the pores of your body. Exhale with the same feeling. Your skin is a delicate, porous membrane, and you are breathing through it. You are in an ocean of space. With each breath, gently let go into the ocean.

FOLLOW YOUR INSTINCTS

Any one of the practices in this chapter will open up into the Self. All are empowered, infused with the energy of a lineage of enlightened meditators. I suggest you spend some time experimenting with each one. Notice how each practice affects your meditation. If one practice doesn't seem to fit, try another. Of course, you don't want to become a technique junkie, flitting from practice to practice without ever entering deeply into any particular one. However, if you clearly understand that a technique is not an end in itself but simply the doorway into the greater Awareness, you can begin to sense which doorway is going to open most easily for you at a particular moment. Some practices will energize you or pull you out of stagnation. Others will kindle love. Others, you'll find, will help quiet an agitated mind.

Playing with different practices helps us get to know ourselves and what works best for us. Everyone's road is unique, and ultimately no one else can tell us what we need. That's why there aren't any rules about the "best" way to meditate, except that a practice should soothe the restlessness of the mind and make it easier for you to enter the interior silence. You find this out only through practice.

There is one more principle to remember in working with a technique. Nearly always, when people have difficulties going deeper into meditation, it is because they are keeping some sort of separation between themselves and their technique and between themselves and the goal. The antidote for nearly every problem that arises in meditation is to give up the feeling that you and the technique and the goal are separate from each other. The *bhavana* of oneness is so powerful that just thinking about it, even if you don't believe it, will change the quality of your meditation.

CHAPTER 5

Entering
Into Your Experience

Years ago when I was first beginning to meditate, I once found myself swimming in an ocean of light. Experiences like this often come at the beginning of our meditation journey, like gifts or beacons that show us what is possible. Though they usually don't last, they reveal truths about the nature of reality that we can contemplate for years. In this particular meditation, as I sensed the light around me, an inner voice said, with great conviction and authority, "Become the light!" I felt that if I could manage to do that, my journey would be over. But I couldn't. The problem wasn't that I was afraid. I was simply caged, enclosed in the feeling of being "me." My sense of limited personal identity was too stubborn to let go. As I came out of meditation, feeling vastly disappointed in myself, two words arose: "Practice oneness." My inner being was telling me that if I couldn't realize the Truth, at least I could practice it, contemplate it, and remember it. Since then I have become convinced that even if we were to forget every other instruction about meditation, we could never go wrong if we would just remember the teaching that whatever we experience is part of one great field of light, of energy, of Consciousness.

Oneness is the Truth. All the teachers of the great nondual traditions—whether they are Vedantins, Sufis, practitioners of the Shaivite Tantra, or followers of the Buddhist Mahayana or Vajrayana path—say the same thing in their own ways. Jalaluddin Rumi, classical texts of Advaita Vedanta like the *Avadhuta Gita*, the Tibetan teachers of Dzogchen, and the German mystic Meister Eckhart all have told us that there is only one reality, one Awareness in the universe, and that we have never been separate from that. They have also pointed out that all our problems, from fear to craving to feeling abandoned, from selfishness to aggression to loneliness to carelessness toward each other and the earth, arise from the feeling of being separate. So even an instant spent remembering oneness strikes at the root of our human dilemma. Even better is to follow the advice of the Kashmiri sage Somananda, the author of *Shiva Drishti (The Viewpoint of God)*, an important Tantric text. Somananda's position was this: "I am God, and all the instruments of my *sadhana* are God. Being God, I will attain God."

Of course, just to know this intellectually is not enough. One famous Vedantic parable tells of the sage-king Janaka, who used to repeat "*So'ham*—I am That" (meaning "I am the Absolute")—over and over to himself. One day, as he stood by the local river saying "*So'ham, So'ham*," he heard a man on the opposite bank shouting over and over, "I have my water bowl, I have my stick."

First Janaka became annoyed. Then he became curious. "Why do you keep shouting that you have your water bowl and your stick?" he called out. "Who said you didn't have them?"

The man (who, as is often the case in these stories, was actually an enlightened being in disguise) called back, "That's just what I wanted to ask you! You already are the Absolute, so why do you have to keep shouting about it?" The point he was making was that it isn't enough just to practice oneness. We need to realize it, to get it, to let ourselves *be* That.

Still, practicing oneness helps increase our chances of experiencing it. That's the basic law of inner transformation after all: practice creates an inner climate within which grace can reveal the reality we are trying to discover. If we keep feeding the *bhava* of unity into our mind, our intellect, and our imagination, they will eventually respond by generating their own spontaneous intuitions and realizations of oneness. That is one reason why it is so important for meditators to read and study the teachings of realized beings who speak from the state of oneness. Our sense of duality is so tenacious, so deeply ingrained, that holding onto a feeling of unity is not easy. The mind might grasp the concept for a moment, only to skitter off when a really gripping emotion or fear seduces away its attention.

THE SHAIVITE PHILOSOPHERS OF KASHMIR

At this point, I would like to digress for a while to say a few words about Kashmir Shaivism, the philosophical system that is the basis of most of the teachings in this book.

Kashmir Shaivism has a rather remarkable history. Between the seventh

The knowledge of one's identity with the pure Self... sets a person free even against his will, when it becomes as firm as the person's belief that he is a human being.

SHANKARACHARYA

Take a pitcher full of
water and set it down
on the water—
now it has water inside
and water outside.
We mustn't give it a name,
lest silly people start
talking again about the
body and the soul.

KABIR

and thirteenth centuries of the common era, a lineage of yogi-philosophers flourished in northern India. They belonged to a cloistered brahmin community called *panditas,* centered in the city of Srinagar. No one knew of them outside the Vale of Kashmir, though their tradition was linked to schools of nondual teachings in southern and western India, as well as to other northern Indian schools of Hindu and Buddhist Tantrism. The teachers of Kashmir Shaivism were not just theoretical philosophers. Many of them were Siddhas, enlightened yogis, who used the system as a way to clothe their inner experience in words. Their path was a juicy amalgam of metaphysical doctrines, maps of human consciousness, yogic practices, and devotion. They worshiped the ultimate Reality as one great divine Consciousness with two inseparable aspects that they called Shiva and Shakti, the former being supreme Awareness and the latter being its intrinsic creative Power. Since their realization showed them that Shakti *becomes* all the forms, subtle and physical, in this world, they had no trouble loving the absolute Reality as a personal deity, as all-pervading formless Awareness, and as their innermost Self. Shiva, as the ultimate divine intelligence, was also considered the original teacher of the tradition and the ultimate source of its core texts—the *Shiva Sutras,* the *Malini Vijaya Tantra,* and the *Vijnana Bhairava.* These texts were, at the least, inspired by the deep meditational experiences of awakened sages.

The unique quality of the Shaiva system is its radical nondualism. Rejecting the Vedantic view that the material world is illusory, an empty dream, the sages of Kashmir Shaivism saw all forms of the universe as manifestations of divine creative energy, of Shakti, the dynamic female principle. They worshiped Shakti in themselves, in the earth, and in every substantial and insubstantial thing, and they looked for the pulsing heart of divine bliss within all domains of experience. Astute seekers of the tradition knew innumerable pathways for uncovering the experience of the divine. They knew how to extract it from states like terror or pleasure or in the high point of a sneeze; they knew how to find the pulsation of ecstasy in empty space, in fixed attention, and in the sensations that come from swaying or twirling, or enjoying music or the taste of food. But the crucial insight of Shaivism is its recognition that when human consciousness lets go of its identification with the body and reflects back on itself, it is revealed as a perfect, if limited, form of the supreme "I," which is God. By expanding their own I-consciousness beyond its limits, past its tendency to cling to narrow definitions of itself, yogis of the Shaivite path experienced God as themselves.

Because they saw the world as divine, the Shaivite yogis of Kashmir had no difficulty enjoying life in all its different flavors. In this they differed from their Vedantic cousins and from the Madhyamika Buddhists who inhabited the same region of India. Shaivism was not a traditional renunciant's path. Abhinavagupta, the preeminent genius of the tradition, was not only a philosopher and a widely revered Guru but also an aesthetician, an artist and musician, and the center of a circle where sensory experience—including art, music, and drama—was constantly being transmuted into yoga.

It is this insight—that a serious practitioner of yoga does not reject his world, but instead transforms daily experience through his practice—that sets Kashmir Shaivism apart from many Indian yogic traditions and has made this system particularly resonant for our time. Yet Kashmir Shaivism had all but disappeared as a living tradition when a series of synchronous events rescued it from obscurity.

In the early years of the twentieth century, the maharaja of Kashmir had encouraged important local scholars to bring together some of the texts of the tradition. These were printed, in Sanskrit, in a limited edition called the *Kashmir Series of Texts and Studies.* Sent without fanfare to university libraries in India, Europe, and the United States, the books gathered dust, unnoticed until the 1950s. It was then that a few scholars around the world—a Bengali Sanskritist in Benares, a French scholar at the Sorbonne, an Italian professor—picked up some of these texts and began to go through them. Translations began to appear in French and in Italian. Some graduate students traveled to Srinagar to sit at the feet of Swami Laksman Joo, one of the last living masters of the tradition.

Meanwhile, in western India in the early 1960s, Swami Muktananda had found a Hindi translation of the *Pratyabhijna Hridayam,* a tenth-century text by Kshemaraja, one of Abhinavagupta's disciples. The *Pratyabhijna Hridayam* describes the stages by which the divine creative energy (called in Shaivism *chiti,* or creative Consciousness) becomes the world, creating the illusion of separation within its essential unity, descending into the state of a limited human soul, and finally recognizing itself again. (Hence the book's title, which means "The Heart of Recognition.") Muktananda saw his own experience of the postenlightenment state mirrored in this text. When he began teaching in the West, he brought the *Pratyabhijna Hridayam* with him and introduced it to his students. He also became instrumental in its initial publication by the Indian press Motilal Banarsidass.

DISCOVERING THE TEACHINGS

For me, as for many others who discovered Shaivism through Swami Muktananda's casual talks, this teaching created a shift in awareness that was almost as radical as the experience of *kundalini* awakening. From the beginning, just reading some of the aphorisms of the *Pratyabhijna Hridayam* would instantaneously transform my state of mind. One moment I would be out of sorts, worried, and off center. Then I would remember one of the teachings of Shaivism—perhaps "Universal Consciousness manifests this universe out of its own freedom, upon the screen of its own being"—and my perspective would immediately expand. It was like being in a small room and suddenly having the roof blow off to expose the sky. Even to consider the possibility that this could be true, that everything could be made of one Awareness, demanded a complete reframing of my ideas about myself.

I remember, one afternoon in the mid-1970s, overhearing a discussion between two friends. We had just been working with a practice for recognizing our identity with divine Consciousness. This involved looking at our own mental process—in which thoughts are constantly coming into being, staying for a while, then dissolving—as a mirror of the cosmic process of the creation, maintenance, and dissolution of natural forms.

One of my friends had been practicing this understanding with a lot of diligence and inspiration. On this particular afternoon, with persuasive excitement, he began to describe his experiences. He'd realized, he told us, that everything inside him is a manifestation of divine Consciousness—that in every moment and in every mood he could recognize the presence of divine energy, of Shiva, the supreme Lord.

A woman who was listening became more and more uncomfortable as he went on talking about how we are all Shiva, all God. Finally she burst forth with her objection. "But what if you're depressed?" she asked. "How can you be Shiva if you're depressed?"

"If I'm depressed, then I'm depressed Shiva!" he said.

The entire world is the play of the universal Consciousness. One who sees it in this way becomes liberated while in the body.

SPANDA KARIKAS

"No way," retorted the woman.

I could sympathize with her problem. I, too, had a hard time feeling that my unhappy, uncomfortable states were divine, that they were inseparable from the wholeness of Consciousness. Like this woman, I held the deep assumption that I could only be close to the Truth (let alone one with it) when I was "good," happy, pure, and feeling positive about myself. It was difficult for me to understand that divinity could also exist inside feelings like depression and anger. As another friend once put it, "How can I be God when I don't get along with my mother?"

The magic of practicing remembrance of your innate divinity is that it has a way of changing your attitude toward your mother, and also toward your depression. It isn't that negative feelings disappear overnight. Depending on our mental habits and tendencies, they might continue arising for some time. Nor can we let our understanding about intrinsic divinity become an excuse for indulging in anger, greed, and the rest of our darker emotions. (Ramakrishna Paramahamsa used to say that milk and muddy water are both God, but we don't drink the muddy water!) Still, if you can remember that divine energy, pure Awareness, God-ness, is present even in the midst of your fear, anger, and depression, it becomes easier to let these feelings come and go without clinging to them, letting them derail you, or rejecting yourself for having them. There will be times, in fact, when your remembrance of oneness dissolves these feelings entirely. Remembering oneness helps make love arise.

It takes a lot of contemplation and self-inquiry to hold on to the understanding of oneness. Every time we practice it, we see the gap between our intellectual convictions and our underlying conditioning. Over the years, I've repeatedly been humbled by seeing how tenaciously I've clung to identification with my body and my personal agendas, and by my own resistance to the force that wants to expand me.

Yet these obstructions begin to disappear if we confront them. Rather than backing down before the force of our conditioned habits of mind or giving in to our fear of seeing our own largeness, we can simply ask ourselves, "What lies behind this resistance? What deeper feelings might be there?" Once we discover what the resistance is made of, we can do the practice for working with intense emotions on page 128, and let go of each successive layer. We can keep on investigating what the sages meant when they told us that we are not different from Consciousness, that we are not different from God. We can do it every time we sit for meditation with whatever technique we happen to be practicing.

PRACTICING ONENESS

A good place to begin is with one of Shaivism's basic teachings: the idea that when we repeat a mantra, we should understand that there is no difference between ourselves, the mantra, and the goal of the mantra, which is the experience of the Self. Like most high teachings, this instruction sounds simple. The challenge comes when you try to do it. How do you go about identifying yourself—your solid, physical, personal self—with a mantra, with a Sanskrit word? How do you make that instruction real for yourself?

You have to begin by disengaging yourself from your feeling of being a particular personality and physical being. It is hard to identify with a mantra if you are thinking of yourself—even very subtly—as Martha, the 122-pound brunette who grew up outside Louisville, Kentucky; the person who secretly

Whether through
immense joy or
through anguish,
Whether from on a wall
or in an earthen jug,
Whether from external
objects or from within,
Reveal yourself to me,
O Lord!

UTPALADEVA

95

worries about her weight and whether or not she is lovable. On the other hand, if you think of yourself as energy or Awareness, and if you also think of the mantra as energy or vibration, it is a different matter entirely. Then you can begin to bring your own energy into alignment with the energy in the mantra.

How do you do this? You might begin by working with the pulsation in the syllables and in your mind. Feel how the syllables vibrate in your inner space when you say them. Let yourself tune in to the sensation of that energy. Then tune in to your own internal space, your own Consciousness, and feel the shimmer of vibrating energy there. Become aware of the natural energy that is you. Once you mentally bring these two things together, you can feel that the energy in the mantra is no different from the energy of your own Awareness. You can mentally merge your own energy into the energy of the mantra.

So to practice oneness, it helps to let go, at least provisionally, of the idea that you are simply a body. You will need to sense your own energy and to begin to contemplate what it means to identify yourself with energy or Awareness rather than with your body or your thoughts or your personality. Initially this is the best way to make sense of the concept of oneness: realize that it is your Awareness, your energy, and your love that exist as one with others. (Eventually we do come to realize that the body, too, is energy, but in the beginning it is easier to work with the energy whose subtlety we can easily sense.) When you and I are identified with our bodies, we are miles apart. When we are thinking of ourselves as individual personalities, we are wildly different. Only as energy, as Awareness, can we experience our unity.

Once we see and begin to remember that "I" am not a body but a center of Awareness and energy, all sorts of ways to practice oneness suggest themselves.

EXERCISE: YOUR AWARENESS PERVADES THE WORLD

Sit in a comfortable, upright posture, close your eyes, and become attentive to the rhythm of your breathing. Observe the flow of the breath as it moves in and out of your nostrils. When thoughts arise, let them flow out with the breath. Keep your attention on the breath for a few minutes.

Now, shift your attention from the breath to the Awareness that knows you are breathing. As you become aware of your Awareness, notice how everything you are experiencing in this moment is actually contained in this Awareness. It is not that Awareness is inside your head or inside your body. Your body, your breath, and your thoughts are all inside Awareness.

Now, allow Awareness to expand outward. With each exhalation, feel that your Awareness expands more and more. Let it fill the room, then the building, then the surrounding area, expanding out into the sky and into the universe. Let Awareness expand as far as it can go. Rest in the spaciousness of your expanded Awareness.

When, with a one-pointed and thought-free mind, a seeker contemplates his whole body or the entire universe all at once as being of the nature of Consciousness, he experiences the supreme awakening.

VIJNANA BHAIRAVA

ENTERING THE EXPERIENCE

One very potent and kinesthetic way to invoke the experience of oneness in meditation is to practice entering into whatever presents itself to us, whether it is a mantra, a visual image, our own heart space, or the Guru, whether it is a pain in the knee or pressure in the forehead, whether it is the space between the in-breath and the outbreath or a vision. We can change our relationship to whatever appears in our meditation if we enter it.

I like to use an imaginative process to do this. I think of a doorway or an opening, and I take myself through it. I keep on doing this until I have the feeling that I have entered the inner cave of the Self, the cave of the heart, the cave of Consciousness. This often takes several entrances through several successive inner doorways. But if I keep imagining doorways or openings or corridors, and keep taking myself through them, I eventually find myself in the deeper layers of my being. Consciousness seems to recognize this image of the doorway as a signal to release into the subtler and deeper layers of itself. It is an amazingly simple and powerful process. What waits on the other side of the doorway, finally, is the Self.

You can work with this principle in nearly every situation. Whatever appears before you in meditation and whatever technique you are practicing, you can enter it. You can create a "doorway" inside the pulsation of breath as it moves in and out of the heart by imagining an opening in the space between the breaths. Or you can enter the breath or the mantra by imagining that it surrounds you, like a cloud, or that you are immersed in it, like water. Or you can simply remind yourself, "This is a part of my own consciousness."

I often use the awareness of oneness as an antidote to feelings of blockage or discomfort. Sometimes in meditation, I'll come to a point where I can't go further. It is as if an inner wall, an energy block, bars the way. There might be a strong feeling of pressure or even pain. Trying to move past it doesn't work. If I can let go of my resistance to the feeling of discomfort, stop trying to push it away, and instead go into the pain, I often find within it an entryway to a deeper level of energy. Often at that point, the block simply dissolves.

When we practice oneness, we are practicing the Truth. That is why it has such power to change us. Thousands of enlightened teachers from countless lineages have realized this Truth and passed on the experience to their students. Their wish for us to experience it is very strong, and the force of their well-wishing moves through us every time we remember to let go of our feelings of separation. A single moment of remembering oneness connects us to the stream of knowledge that flows from the enlightened ones and opens us to revelation.

Of course, if the understanding of oneness is to be more than an intellectual exercise or a dutiful remembrance of a beautiful teaching, we need to come to terms with our own tendency to create separation. That means coming to terms with the discursive mind—*manas* in Sanskrit—whose innate tendency to rove among thickets of thought and perception effectively blocks us from seeing the unity behind our experience. Like Cerberus, who guarded the threshold of the underworld in Greek mythology, the mind stands vigilantly at the doorway to deep meditation. If we don't befriend the mind, it will never let us enter. That is why the texts of meditation devote so much space, so much attention, and so much effort to the eternal question: How do I deal with the mind?

CHAPTER 6

Working with the Mind:
Part 1

Ever since the artists of the Indus Valley carved their famous statue of the horned god sitting in meditation—back around 5000 B.C.E.—meditators have been grappling with the same basic scenario. We sit for meditation. We focus on the breath or practice mindfulness or begin repeating a mantra. We try to hold on to the feeling of oneness. Then the thoughts come. The thoughts come.

Thethoughtscomethethoughtscomethe-thoughtscome. Fast or slow. Flooding or trickling. Steady or intermittent. Apparently endless. Thoughts about the phone calls you have to make, thoughts about what your son's teacher said to you yesterday, thoughts about your aunt. Thoughts about the thoughts. Thoughts on the order of "Am I really meditating? This can't be meditation. My mind isn't still. And why am I not seeing anything?"

This is a universal human experience—like birth, the first day of school, and leaving the body at the time of death. Even great meditators go through it. We tend to assume that a good meditator, a really successful meditator, never gets disturbed by thoughts. Somehow a real meditator just sits down for meditation and, *wham,* he is in a deep state of stillness, merged in the witness or watching golden lotuses of light waft gently through the inner spaces.

But this is not true. Even great meditators have to wrestle with thoughts. Swami Muktananda once said, "In the beginning, I meditated just as you meditate now. When I sat for meditation with my eyes closed, my mind would go here and there, thinking of one thing or another. But as I meditated more and more, I began to learn the skill of getting into meditation. I found that as I did *sadhana, sadhana* taught me *sadhana.* Meditation taught me meditation."

In fact, one of the most important lessons that meditation teaches us is that it can go on even when there are thoughts in the mind. In other words, the mind need not be completely still for us to experience the state of meditation. Often when we are deeply settled inside, thoughts continue to drift across the screen of our awareness. Even when the actual thoughts slow down, a subtle buzz of mental static might remain. This is only a problem when we don't understand what thoughts are and how to deal with them. Much of the meditator's art lies in knowing how to work with thoughts and ultimately how to let them dissolve into the subtle fabric of the mind.

This much should be obvious: we can't deal with thoughts by taking them out and shooting them. The delicate, intelligent energy we call the "mind"

The
Mind is ever a tourist
Wanting to touch
*   and buy new things*
Then toss them
*   into an already*
Filled closet.

HAFIZ

does not respond well to harshness. There is good reason for this, as we will see further in the next chapter, since the mind is essentially nothing more than a thought-clogged form of the pure Awareness that is the goal of our practice. ("Consciousness plus thoughts is the mind," says the *Yoga Vasishtha*, a text of high Vedanta. "Consciousness minus thoughts is God.") Consciousness filled with thoughts is Consciousness nonetheless, and Consciousness by its very nature is free, powerful, and elusive. That is why when we try to suppress our thoughts or stamp them out, or even when we try to bring our attention forcibly to one point, the mind reacts rebelliously.

Indian tradition compares the mind to a king who has not been given a proper seat. Until the king is seated on his rightful throne, he will be restless, dissatisfied, and even quarrelsome. Once he is seated, however, he becomes calm and begins to manifest his royal qualities. The mind's proper seat—in fact, the only place the mind will be satisfied—is in the Self, in the deep abode of pure Consciousness. The mind's restlessness actually comes from the fact that it is searching for the throne room, looking for the place where it can experience its true grandeur as Consciousness. Our job in meditation is simply to keep it pointed in the proper direction. As we direct it toward its seat again and again, it will begin to settle down into it and eventually go there on its own.

Seating the mind, like much else that we do in our meditation practice, involves equal parts of rigor and of subtlety, practice and understanding. Usually when we first begin meditating and for several years thereafter, we spend most of our time bringing the mind back to an object of focus. A thousand times, our thoughts run us from here to Paris. A thousand times, we bring our attention back—gently, softly, without straining. It is boring and frustrating some-times, but there *is* a reward. In time the mind begins to listen to us. Swami Muktananda wrote, "You must stop your mind from wandering here and there. If it begins to wander to a place ten miles away and you try hard to stop it, it may at first go only nine miles. The next time you try, it may go only eight miles. Eventually it will go only one mile, and finally the day will come when it will remain completely still."

Focus is a kind of mental muscle. When you strengthen it by learning to hold your attention in one place for a while, instead of remaining trapped on the surface, you automatically strengthen your ability to hold subtle states in meditation and to find the inner pathways that lead you deeper. Eventually this basic practice of catching yourself in distraction and bringing your mind back begins to affect your whole life. Not only does the mind become more stable in meditation—so that you can actually sit for a long time in the space of the heart or remain in stillness for longer than a moment—but the mind also acquires a new ability to focus on things like driving your car, writing a report, or perfecting your golf swing. Learning to resist distraction makes you more resistant to boredom, worry, and depression, more grounded and less prone to being driven by untamable fantasies. That is why there is no substitute for this basic practice for dealing with the mind and no way you can dispense with it, any more than an athlete can dispense with his or her warm-ups.

CONFRONTING THE INNER DIALOGUE

Ironically enough, when we begin practicing seriously, the mind often seems to become more troublesome. Some people get scared by this. I know a man

Love your mind. The mind is the friend who leads you by its restlessness to search for God. The mind is the instrument by which you detect the inner world.

SWAMI MUKTANANDA

who actually stopped meditating because he found it so uncomfortable to confront that inner dialogue. "I don't care what anyone says," he told me once. "My mind never used to be this bad. Meditation just makes me more restless. In fact, I feel better when I *don't* meditate."

His mind wasn't getting more restless, of course. It's just that when he sat down to meditate, he noticed how restless it really was. Normally, we aren't aware of the intensity of our inner dialogue. Our attention is focused on what is going on around us, so unless we are unusually introverted or introspective, the wild and crazy scenarios running through the mind generally escape our notice. But when we sit for meditation—ah, then we see them.

Besides becoming more conscious of our normal state of distraction, we may also experience something that we could call "samskaric burn off." *Samskaras* are mental and emotional tendencies, residues of our habitual thoughts and feelings, the ones we replay so often that they have made tracks in the field of our Consciousness. As meditation releases energy into that inner field, those buried *samskaras* rise up and are burned away by the energy of our Awareness, the *kundalini.*

At one point early in my career as a meditator, I noticed that my morning meditations had become fogged with irritation. I was living in an ashram then, with several hundred other people, and in that atmosphere had no way to hide from my mood. Finally I put a question to Swami Muktananda. I asked, "What should you do if meditation makes you irritable?"

"It's not that meditation makes you irritable," he told me. "You have irritability inside you, and meditation is helping you see it so you can let it go."

PURIFICATION: THE INNER STEW

One reason we meditate is precisely so that this can happen. Our personal unconscious is a murky stew, filled with a huge array of tasty and untasty items. All these things have to come out of the stew. Otherwise their presence bubbling around inside us blocks our experience of the pure, clear water, the pure light, that is our real substance. Meditation allows these buried feelings, obstructive ideas, and painful emotions to float to the top of our consciousness, where they can be recognized and removed.

Once *kundalini* is awakened, this work of purification goes on more or less continuously under the surface. However, it is during the time of sitting practice that our inner energy gets a chance to work full throttle. The act of sitting quietly and focusing inward invites the *shakti* to leap into action, churning up the ocean of our consciousness and dislodging whatever is buried there. So naturally as we sit in meditation, we experience not just random, stray thoughtlets, but huge, charged ice floes of heavy emotions and old buried complexes—those tangled webs of memory, belief, and emotion, the tendencies that block our freedom. When these things come up in meditation, it is a sign that they are ready to move out of our system. Our part in the process is to let them go. There is no need to get involved in these feelings or analyze them—at least not while we are meditating. Instead, notice them and breathe them out, releasing them with the exhalation. Or repeat the mantra, letting the *shakti* embedded in the mantra move through the emotions and negativities and melt them away.

As our meditation practice deepens and becomes more stable, we get the strength to stand aside from all these feelings and to witness our own process of purification. In fact, as we will see in the next chapter, the inner witness can become a platform from which we can look at and begin to heal these buried feelings.

But many of us, especially in the early years of meditation, find witnessing too difficult. Our thoughts are too thick, fast, and uncontrollable to allow us to stand back from them for long. This is another reason why the Guru's mantra is so helpful for most meditators.

SWEEPING YOUR HEART WITH MANTRA

An empowered mantra acts as a sort of cleansing force, a subtle but extremely strong broom that sweeps the basement of our subconscious. The yogic texts speak of *kundalini* as an inner fire, a transforming heat that burns up mental detritus and melts away psychic debris. The mantra that comes from a Guru lineage is filled with this transforming fire. When we rub the mantra against our thoughts, it generates an inner friction. The Sanskrit word for this friction is *tapas,* meaning "heat." *Tapas* is also the word for the yogic austerities that refine and purify the mind. The subtle fire in the mantra generates the heat of *tapas* in the mind. That is what cleanses our inner ground.

During the first year after my *kundalini* was awakened, the effect of the inner purification process was sometimes so intense and uncomfortable that I could hardly bear being in my own skin. Some days, the uprush of buried negative feelings—guilt, unworthiness, anger, and the like—would begin the moment I opened my eyes and would roil around all day long. More or less in desperation, I used to repeat the mantra as a way of distracting myself from these feelings. I would begin the moment I woke up and repeat it all day long, whenever there was space from ongoing activities and sometimes even during conversations.

As I kept this up, I began to notice that the emotional charge behind the feelings had lessened dramatically. The feelings still came up, but they didn't knock me over. The mantra seemed to create a counterforce. It released an energy of light, repose, and happiness in my mind that swallowed up the painful feelings. After some time, this layer of deep-seated, painful feelings, feelings that had troubled me all my life, was gone.

Every time we sit with a mantra in meditation, we go through a small-scale version of this clearing process. Little by little, as we cling to the mantra, the combination of our own focused intention and the mantra's intrinsic power dissolves the day's residue of thoughts and images so that the mind can settle into stillness. Once this settling has occurred, then the natural process of meditation takes over. The inner *shakti* begins to draw us inward and to dissolve our ordinary waking mind into pure conscious energy.

This is one of the most important secrets about meditation. In fact, it is a fundamental law of Consciousness. If you just sit quietly with the intention to turn your mind within, and if you keep pulling your attention away from thoughts and focusing it on your chosen practice, the mind will eventually resolve into pure energy. It will reveal itself as the clear field of Awareness within which the deeper experience of meditation can arise.

LETTING GO: THE PRACTICE OF VAIRAGYA

Patanjali, in his *Yoga Sutras,* has told us that there are two aspects to the process of steadying the mind. We have just discussed the first one: *abhyasa,* or practice, the effort to stay with our object of focus. The second part of the process is *vairagya,* or detachment. *Vairagya* is a way of putting the gears of the mind into neutral, disengaging ourselves from the thoughts, feelings, and desires that normally hook our attention.

A few years ago, a young woman was attending a retreat at the Siddha Yoga meditation ashram in New York. She had been planning a trip to Japan, and her mind was already running through her checklist for departure, wondering how many sweaters to take and whether she needed to pack a winter coat. Suddenly a voice inside her mind spoke up loudly. "Drop it!" the voice said. Startled, she let go of her plans and began to focus on her breath. No sooner had she done so than she was overwhelmed by a feeling of sadness. She thought of how much she had received from the retreat and how sorry she would be to leave.

Then she heard the inner voice again: "Drop it." She let go of her sad thoughts. Still, the voice came again: "Drop it." She asked herself, "What shall I drop? What's my biggest block right now? My sense of unworthiness. Okay, I'll drop that." The voice said again: "Drop it." She didn't know what else she could drop. She gave a big sigh—and fell into a deep state of meditation. It was as if a field of bliss had opened in the ground of her mind. She felt as if she were swimming in the oceanic tide of this bliss, lulled on its waves. "Oh, please," she said inwardly, "don't let this stop." Immediately the voice came again: "Drop it." "Drop the bliss?" she wondered. "No, drop wanting to keep it." She let go of her feeling of clinging to the bliss. With that she fell into the deepest, most quiet state she had ever experienced. She felt utterly present, completely loved, and as clear as limpid water.

As you can probably see, this woman's experience points out a pathway we can follow. If we move through the stages she went through, we also can discover how much peace arises when we just drop everything—our plans, our thoughts, our doubts about ourselves, and even our desire to hold on to our beautiful

When we have the experience of letting go, it is called liberation, freedom.

GURUMAYI
CHIDVILASANANDA

experiences. Ultimately, of course, we want to let go of the tendrils of deep-seated identification, attachment, and aversion that reinforce our sense of separation and that clothe our false personality in an appearance of permanence. We want to drop—at least for a while—the feeling of being a particular "me," separate from all others. That is the key, the sages have told us, to entering our own essence. Even the *Vijnana Bhairava* tells us that the experience of our innate wholeness and freedom naturally arises when the ego of separateness has dissolved. Of course, few of us can dissolve the separative ego just like that, especially if we aren't entirely sure that we want to do it. But practice helps.

Here are three levels of *vairagya* that we can practice in meditation:

1. Letting Go of Tension

The first is releasing the tension in the body. As we saw in chapter 3, we can do this at the beginning of any session of meditation by scanning the body, noticing where we feel tight or uncomfortable, and then breathing out the tightness.

Breathing out the tension in the body does more than relax us physically. It also relaxes the mind because every physical tension has its inner counterpart. Sometimes when I work with seasoned meditators, they will tell me afterward that the most helpful part of the process was not the actual meditation instructions, but the time we took in the beginning to breathe out tension. Sometimes this is all we need to do to enter deep meditation.

2. Letting Go of Desire

In the second level of *vairagya*, we let go of the layers of desire and its many offspring—hope, expectation, fear, and worry.

I like to begin meditation sessions by making a conscious decision to leave everything else aside for a while. I mentally set aside my work and all my personal agendas, and I make a resolution not to let myself get distracted. That is the first step. The second step is to keep renewing the intention every time the mind begins to throw up tempting morsels of desire.

Practicing this level of *vairagya* shows us the seams of desire that are layered throughout our mind. As soon as we try to let go of desire, we begin to realize how pervasive it is—and how it derails us. In fact, this is one of the great learnings we can receive in meditation. Each time we sit, we give ourselves the opportunity to come face to face with all the disguises desire takes and with the power that even a simple desire has to throw us off track.

Here is an example: How many times have you been pulled out of meditation by the smell of coffee brewing in the kitchen? Or by the *thought* of the coffee? Your mind is just beginning to get quiet, and then you remember that besides the coffee, you have a croissant waiting in its waxed paper bakery bag and that if you get up from meditation now, you can put it in the oven and heat it up so you can have a hot croissant before work. Before you know it, you are off the mat and halfway to the kitchen.

Desires have a way of filling the mind with wonderful reasons why you should follow their siren song. *Of course* you need to have breakfast now—otherwise you might have to rush to get to school. *Of course* you should get up and watch that video now instead of waiting until later—because, after all, it is better not to clutter the mind with images too close to bedtime. *Of course* you need to write down that terrific idea that just came up—in fact, you need to turn on your computer and start exploring it, since you are feeling so inspired.

Our desires and dislikes are two apes living in the tree of our hearts; while they continue to shake and agitate it, with their jogging and jolting, there can be no rest for it.

YOGA VASISHTHA

111

(Actually, it's not a bad idea to keep a notepad by your meditation cushion, so you can jot down a note to yourself when an idea comes up. Then you can go back to meditation.) Or even more compelling, isn't this the right moment to go and look up the phone number of your high school boyfriend, Timmy, whose face just surfaced so meltingly in your vision? He was surrounded with blue light, and you heard he just got divorced . . .

Even if you resist the temptation to get up off your mat and swing into action behind one of these impulses, letting yourself dwell on them can seriously throw off your practice. (This is just as true when the desire you follow is a subtle one—like those tempting philosophical speculations that some of us enjoy indulging in or the various plans and life scenarios that play like movies through the mind if you don't catch them.) As we meditate, we see this again and again. We learn the penalty, the immediate costs, for getting caught up in desire. On the other hand, each time we drop one of these desires, we lessen its grip on us. Just as focusing in meditation helps us to develop our power of focus in daily life, our practice of dropping desires in meditation trains us in the practice of detachment, which helps keep us from being tossed around by distracting impulses in our waking life.

This kind of letting go is the essential act of the spiritual warrior.

EXERCISE: BREATHING OUT THOUGHTS, DESIRES, AND EMOTIONS

Sit in your meditation posture, paying attention to the grounding of your sitting bones and allowing your spine to elongate. Close your eyes and focus your awareness on the breath until you feel yourself becoming settled and centered.

Now begin to notice the thoughts as they arise. Whenever a thought, a desire, or an emotion comes up, breathe it out. Breathe in, and breathe out the thought. Another thought arises. Breathe it out. A desire, an impulse arises. Breathe it out.

There are variations on this practice. If you like dramatic visualizations, you could imagine a sword made of your subtle will with which you lop off each thought. You might create an inner fire and throw the thoughts into it. (Neither of these are gentle practices, of course, but we are in warrior mode here.) Sometimes I imagine that I have a recycling bin in the corner of my mind, and I mentally drop the thoughts into it.

In this nakedness the spirit finds its rest, for when it covets nothing, nothing raises it up, and nothing weighs it down.

ST. JOHN OF THE CROSS

Afterward contemplate the effect of this exercise. What do you notice about your inner state? What was the effect of this intense focus on dropping thoughts?

3. Letting Go of Identifying with the Thinker

The third kind of *vairagya* is subtler. It involves letting go of our attachment to being the thinker, the one who identifies with the thoughts and desires, the one, in fact, who constantly, if unconsciously, chooses to think. Instead we identify ourselves with the witness, the watcher of the thoughts. We don't try to cast out thoughts. We let them be there, but we pull back from them. We identify with the one who watches the thoughts.

Swami Muktananda used to tell us to look at thoughts as if they were clouds passing in the sky. Clouds don't touch the space of the sky. The sky isn't affected by clouds racing across. It isn't changed if the clouds are big and black and full of thunder or if they pour rain. In the same way, your Awareness—the real you—isn't touched by thoughts. Your Consciousness is completely unaffected by anything that arises.

Becoming the watcher of thoughts instead of the thinker is simply a matter of shifting your perspective. You could do this by working with the practice of becoming aware of Awareness as it is described in chapter 2. Or you might like to work with the image of the sky and the clouds.

Pure Consciousness cannot say "I."

RAMANA MAHARSHI

EXERCISE: WATCH YOUR THOUGHTS MOVE LIKE CLOUDS THROUGH THE SKY OF THE MIND

Sit quietly and close your eyes. You can focus your attention on the flow of the breath as it moves in and out of the body. As you do, become aware of the space inside your mind. Imagine that your mind is a sky, an open space. Thoughts move through it like clouds. Let the thoughts arise and let them depart. You are the watcher, not the thinker, observing the thought-clouds as they move through the sky of your Awareness.

Once we begin to identify with the sky of Awareness rather than with clouds of thought, a great sense of spaciousness arises. We can let the thoughts be there without being caught by them.

From there, it is just a small step toward understanding the great truth about the mind: Even our thoughts are part of that underlying field of Consciousness.

CHAPTER 7

Working with the Mind:
Part 2

Classical yogic mind disciplines—letting go of distractions, bringing our minds to a point of focus, and even witnessing—are basic to all mind training. The only problem with them is that they can entangle us in a subtle feeling of duality. The moment we start trying to discipline our thoughts, we seem to begin seeing them as adversaries. Then meditation turns into a battle between our striving for quiet and the very mind that we are hoping to coax into stillness, and we find ourselves out of relationship with our inner realm.

That is why the ultimate practice for dealing with the mind is to let it be. Not to let it lead us around by the nose, but to let it be, with the understanding of what the mind actually is.

Here's what Swami Muktananda said about meditation and the mind:

> A yogi should ponder the nature of this mind he is trying to
> stabilize. What exactly is it? Of what substance is it made? How
> does it come into existence? How can it be overcome? It is essential
> to grapple with these questions. Awareness of the mind's nature is
> the root of yoga, meditation, and all spiritual disciplines.

What is the mind's nature? The *Pratyabhijna Hridayam* puts it like this:
the mind, it says, is simply a contracted form of the vast intelligent energy, the
great Consciousness, that creates the universe.

In Sanskrit, the word for our individual human consciousness—the
mind—is *chitta*. The word for universal Consciousness is *chiti*. (*Chiti* is also
another word for *shakti* or *kundalini*.) Both words, *chiti* and *chitta*, come from the
root *chit*, meaning Awareness or Consciousness—but not in the limited sense in
which we usually use the word "consciousness" in the West. *Chit* is Consciousness as an absolute intelligence, an intelligence that is unlimited in its knowledge
and creativity, omnipresent, and blissful, with a boundless capacity to do and to
become whatever it wills. It is, in short, Consciousness as the creative force of
the universe.

In Sanskrit, the root of a word describes its essence. The essence of
chitta—the individual consciousness—is the same as *chiti*, the great intelligence
that creates the universe. The only difference is one of scale. *Chiti* is boundless,
free, and omnipotent, capable of creating and dissolving solid planets, stars,
galaxies, sea anemones, and porcupines, capable, as the Book of Job so dramatically reminds us, of setting the waters upon the earth and creating the Leviathan

*You lose sight of the
original mind and,
seeing the thinking,
discriminating mind,
take that as your own.
But that is not your
real mind.*

SUTRA OF PERFECT WISDOM

and manifesting voices out of whirlwinds. *Chitta*, on the other hand, is limited, contracted, and relatively powerless. Nonetheless, *chitta* does exactly the same thing that *chiti* does. Even though it only operates on a small scale, the consciousness-stuff in our mind keeps endlessly creating. Just as *chiti* creates landscapes, people, planets, and solar systems and keeps them going, *chitta* creates ideas, thoughts, fantasies, and moods, not to mention novels, poetry, philosophical systems, designs for buildings, piano concertos, and software programs.

If we could fully recognize this truth about the mind, we would instantly free the mind to expand back into its original vastness. In short, *chitta* would start to emerge from its disguise and reveal itself as *chiti*. The ramifications of this are literally mind-blowing, but we will feel them only if we start to practice this awareness.

YOUR THOUGHTS ARE NOTHING BUT CONSCIOUSNESS

Years ago when I was beginning to practice Siddha Yoga meditation and feeling like a complete victim of my vagrant and uncontrollable thoughts, I heard Swami Muktananda explain this. He did it rather casually, almost as a digression in the midst of a talk on meditation. He said, "Why do you chase the thoughts of the mind, trying to drive them away? This is the road to frustration. Instead of trying to get rid of thoughts, understand what thoughts are. Thoughts are nothing but Consciousness. What you have to understand is that your mind itself is made of Consciousness. The same Consciousness that has become this universe exists in a contracted form as your mind. Just the way that divine *shakti*, that Consciousness, creates universes on the outside, it constantly creates universes in your mind. That is its play. How are you going to fight the

*The Essence of Mind
   is like the sky;
Sometimes it is shadowed
   by the clouds of
   Thought-flow.
Then the wind of the
   Guru's inner teaching
Blows away the drifting
   clouds;
Yet the Thought-flow itself
   is the illumination.
The Experience is as
   natural as sun-and
   moon-light;
Yet it is beyond both
   space and time.*

MILAREPA

117

universal Consciousness, the great *shakti* of the universe? How are you going to make the divine creative energy stop playing?"

How indeed! All of a sudden, I saw why I had such problems in meditation. I had been looking at thoughts as the enemy—especially the negative thoughts, the angry thoughts, and the irreverent, ungodly thoughts. Swami Muktananda was suggesting a radically different approach to thoughts. He would say, "The mind is the Goddess herself. Every thought in your mind is a wave of the great *shakti*. Honor them as *shakti*." He had a delightful way of talking about this aspect of thought. He said, "The horse, the dog, and the camel that arise in the mind are not made of anything material; they are made of Consciousness. . . . The mind-stuff that forms itself into a camel, a dog, or a horse is nothing but a pulsation of the same Consciousness that has formed the universe."

Hanging on to this awareness even for a few minutes had an effect on my meditation that I can only call magical.

First of all, the worried, conflicted attitude that I usually had toward thoughts dissolved. Even more amazingly, the thoughts themselves tended to dissolve. Sometimes after I had been sitting for a while with the understanding of my thoughts as Consciousness, I would have to look hard to find a thought. They would all have melted back into the energy that was their substance.

THE MIND IS THE GODDESS

This practice becomes particularly powerful when we regard our thoughts the way Swami Muktananda and the sages of Kashmir did: reverentially as manifestations of a divine dancer, the Goddess Consciousness. One of the most significant facets of Indian metaphysics is its understanding that divine reality is both utterly formless and impersonal and at the same time totally capable of taking a personal form. Because they understood this, even the most antidualistic sages could relate devotionally to the divine. When we think of the world-creating energy as an abstract force, it might seem awesome but never approachable. Think of that same energy as a goddess, however, and suddenly the whole situation becomes more personal. We can pray to a goddess, talk to her, honor her, and love her. When we think of the energy of the mind as a divine person, we can have a relationship with her. In fact, a relationship becomes imperative.

Try this for a moment: Think of your mind, your extraordinarily powerful mind, as a glorious feminine entity, a goddess who has forgotten she is a goddess and is going around collecting rags and bottles from the scrap heap of thoughts, piling them up and obsessing over them, chewing them like bones and spitting them out at you. She acts a bit wild, but who can blame her? After all, even though she has forgotten who she is, she still knows she is someone pretty important, and she doesn't understand why she is not being treated with the respect she deserves. Can you imagine how such a great divinity feels when you get impatient with her, when you angrily shove your thoughts away, when you treat her as your enemy? Or when you behave like a limp victim of every vagrant thoughtlet or fantasy? Naturally she gets outraged at your harshness, and naturally she runs wild when you meekly give in to her. Both these attitudes toward the mind simply encourage the goddess to demonstrate her creative power in all sorts of unproductive ways.

When you recognize who is dancing in the form of the mind, it is as if you free the goddess to manifest herself as she truly is and to expand back into

O wavering mind,
awaken your upward-
flowing awareness.
Become the sublime
warrior Goddess Kali,
who moves with grace-
ful power through the
vast landscape of
the body....
She is none other than
primordial bliss,
this great swan ever swim-
ming through
the lotus jungle
of the subtle body.

RAMPRASAD

119

her original form. It is like those old fairy tales, the legends of enchanted princes and princesses who are freed by a moment of recognition. It is like the story of the crone Dame Ragnell from the Arthurian Cycle, the legends of King Arthur and his knights.

WHAT DOES A WOMAN WANT?

The story of Dame Ragnell begins with an ambush. King Arthur is traveling alone through a forest when he is surprised by a dark knight. The knight unhorses Arthur, which technically makes the king his prisoner. Instead of holding him for ransom, however, the knight makes a bargain. He will give Arthur a riddle and one week to come up with an answer to it. If the king fails, the whole kingdom will be forfeited to the knight.

The knight's question is this: "What does a woman really want?" Like other men throughout the ages, Arthur hasn't a clue. As he rides away, however, he is accosted by an aged hag who hangs on to his bridle and insists that he stop to listen to her. The crone is shudderingly ugly—hunchbacked, covered in warts, and bald except for a few pathetic gray strands sticking straight up out of the crown of her head. She walks like a duck, and her voice is somewhere between a cackle and a screech. "I am Dame Ragnell," she croaks. "I can give you the answer to the knight's riddle—if you agree to my price."

"There *would* be a price," sighs Arthur. "Still, anything is better than handing over my kingdom to that wretched knight."

"Then promise me the hand of Sir Gawain in marriage," cackles the hag.

Arthur hesitates for a moment, weighing the fate of the kingdom against the prospect of blighting his friend Gawain's life, and then chooses the kingdom.

"If you can solve the riddle," he says, "Gawain is yours."

"Such a simple riddle," Dame Ragnell tells him. "Really, it should be obvious. What a woman wants is to have her own way!"

Sure enough, this turns out to be the right answer. The kingdom is saved. And Gawain, being a loyal subject of his liege, agrees to go through with the marriage.

On the appointed day, he meets Dame Ragnell in the palace chapel. In her bridal gown, she looks like a dressed-up skeleton. The ladies of the court break into tears when they see the woman this noble knight is to wed. Gawain, being the model of courtesy, gives no sign of distress. But after the ceremony, he escorts his bride to her chamber, bids her goodnight, and turns to leave.

"Not so fast," cackles the crone. "You've married me this day and, by God, you shall bed me this night."

Gawain is appalled. Still, his good manners do not fail him. Taking a deep breath, he clasps the old woman in his arms and kisses her. As his lips touch hers, a miracle happens. Dame Ragnell's warty, hunchbacked shape falls away, and she is revealed as a stunning blue-eyed blonde, the very incarnation of a medieval knight's feminine ideal.

"You have saved me," she tells Gawain, looking up at him through long, curling lashes. "I was under a curse that could only be lifted when a gentle knight kissed my lips. Now I am free to be my true self—but only for half the day. Husband, which would you prefer? Would you rather have me beautiful by day or beautiful by night?"

Gawain is in a quandary. If she remains beautiful at night, he will have to look at Dame Ragnell all day. But if she is beautiful only during the day, he will have Dame Ragnell in his marriage bed. "I don't know what to do," he says. "You choose."

"Ah," says his wife, "now you've lifted my curse completely. Because you gave me the choice, you've freed me to be my beautiful self all the twenty-four hours!"

This is what we do for the mind when we recognize the beautiful Goddess Chiti beneath her skin of thoughts. We free her to reveal the beauty and power that lie behind those thoughts. It was Gawain's willingness to treat his ugly wife with courtesy that made the difference. In the same way, our respect for the goddess within the mind allows her to reveal her sweetness and glory.

EXERCISE: SEEING THE MIND AS THE GODDESS

Sit in a comfortable posture and close your eyes. Allow your attention to center itself on the breath. As you do, say to yourself, "My breath is a manifestation of the Goddess, the divine energy of creation." Each time a thought arises, say to yourself, "I honor this thought as an aspect of the Goddess, Consciousness. I honor this thought as *shakti*: divine, conscious energy."

Continue this for at least ten minutes and notice how it affects the flow of thoughts in the mind.

DISARMING NEGATIVE THOUGHTS

It is fairly easy to do this practice with ordinary, random thoughts. It becomes more problematical when the thoughts are of something we desire intensely or when they are negative or unwelcome. Negative thoughts exercise a particular power over us, partly because we tend to judge them more harshly than other thoughts. Most of us have a secret yardstick that we apply to our mental content. Some thoughts we deem acceptable, usually because they fit our image of ourselves as intelligent, mature, kindhearted, *good* people. Other thoughts, however, contain too much negative charge for us or reveal us to be less evolved, detached, or loving than we would like to be. These we judge, deny, and do our best to push away. The habit of judging our mental content is a congenital disease for meditators. It is one of the more insidious manifestations of the inner judge, the fearsome parent figure so many of us hold inside, whose fulminating criticisms we sometimes confuse with the voice of God. That inner judge rises up in self-righteous condemnation of anything that seems weak, immature, or "bad," constantly on the lookout for more evidence of our general unfitness. The inner judge is the one who has us convinced that having negative thoughts makes us bad people.

But, of course, our negative thoughts are also manifestations of *shakti.* Even our ugliest feelings—our jealousy, our anger, and our hatred—are created by the Goddess. Our anxiety, our fear, and our painful memories—all these are waves arising in Consciousness, forms and figures in the Goddess's great dance. If we can realize that a thought or an image—whatever it is—is just a bubble or wave rising out of the sea of Consciousness, then even the ugliest, the most fearful, hostile, frightening, or blasphemous thought need not disturb us.

One deluded thought and we are all dull and ordinary. But with the next awakened thought, we are as wise as the Buddha.

HUI-NENG

123

Consciousness is so creative that she can transform herself in a moment from a state of contraction and rigid negativity to a state of expansion and love. Just as the Goddess Chiti can manifest any thought, she can drop any thought. The moment we genuinely recognize a thought or an emotion as part of our Consciousness, it automatically resolves back into its original state.

Let me give you an example. I am writing this early in the morning after a long session of meditation. Because I'm engaged in this writing process, my mind is busy these days, filled with ideas about what I'm writing and also with a driving compulsion that I recognize as the creative urge. That urge, however, often gets derailed into irritation, anxiety, and fear. This morning as I sat in meditation, I began by focusing on the breath, merging my awareness with the space between the inbreath and the outbreath. Usually after I have done this for a while, the space between the breaths begins to lengthen, and I find myself slipping into a state of spaciousness, a state that I identify as the Self or my own free Consciousness. Today, however, the space felt choppy, like an ocean in a storm. The energy was sharp and uncomfortable, almost unpleasant. Then in the midst of the ocean, a wave of overpowering anxiety arose and took the form of words. They went something like "Omigod, the structure, the structure, I haven't figured out the structure."

At that moment, I experienced a flash of recognition. I saw that the anxiety was just energy and that the words were simply the form that the anxiety-energy was taking. In short, I realized that I didn't have to pay attention to the content of the thought. Instead, I focused my attention on the energy bundle that was the feeling of anxiety and its verbal expression. I regarded it with the feeling that it was simply energy. In that instant the energy dissolved, imploding back into itself, and the surface of my Consciousness resolved itself into a thick, palpably blissful, undulating sea of energy.

Sometimes, of course, the overpowering thoughts that come up in meditation are messages that need attention. If you have a feeling that something needs to be attended to, it probably does. Still, you don't have to let it derail you. Make an inner note of the thought. Promise yourself that you will attend to it later. Then go back to meditation. If it really seems important, write it down; I keep a pen and notepaper handy for insights that I don't want to forget. When they come up, I pick up the pen, scrawl a reminder, then go back to meditation.

WORKING WITH INTENSE EMOTIONS

Once we discover how to let thoughts and feelings dissolve into their own energy, not only have we learned the secret of dealing with thoughts, we also have a way to work with the real heavies: our charged emotional states. Sometimes people say that they are afraid to meditate because heavy emotions come up and ambush them as soon as they close their eyes. Usually it turns out that they have been sitting on a backlog of unprocessed feelings that they find unacceptable and therefore overwhelming. We can make it safe for ourselves to let these feelings come up in meditation if we keep part of our attention on our wider Consciousness, on our "real" Self. On Awareness. Then when strong emotions arise in meditation, we can acknowledge them, hold them in our Awareness, and let our own Consciousness dissolve them. When we are very afraid or grief-stricken, or when we are flooded with anger, jealousy, or anxiety, Awareness can become both a cradle in which we hold these feelings and a cauldron in which they dissolve. It is one of the most important things we can learn in meditation: how to

Wherever the mind goes, whether turned inward or toward the outside world, everywhere there is the divine. Since the divine is everywhere, where can the mind go to avoid it?

VIJNANA BHAIRAVA

125

hold strong feelings in Awareness and how to allow Awareness to dissolve them. Once we know how to do it, we no longer fear our own feelings. There is nothing we can't process.

THE CRUCIBLE OF AWARENESS

A few years ago, a friend of mine was shocked to learn that her husband had fallen in love with someone else and wanted a divorce. She had not suspected there was anything wrong with her marriage. She loved her husband. Feelings of grief, anger, insecurity, distrust, betrayal, and confusion erupted inside her. At times they seemed nearly uncontainable.

Meditation was especially difficult because then she had nothing to distract her from the emotions churning through her mind. At last she decided to sit with her feelings without trying to push them away. She would let herself feel the burning sensation of anger and notice how it made her chest hot and her breathing rapid. She would feel how grief caused pressure to build up behind her eyes, as if from tears wanting to be shed. She observed her own inner recitals of betrayal and revenge until she knew every word of them.

One day as she was sitting in meditation, reeling under the onslaught of feelings, she suddenly became aware of her own Awareness. She could feel how her Awareness surrounded and held her feelings. Then an image arose. She saw a container like an old-fashioned warming pan. She realized that this was her Awareness. It could hold her hot feelings the way a warming pan can hold burning coals.

She let the feelings be there. She let herself feel them and all the physical sensations associated with them. She let her Awareness hold them. After a while, the feelings began to slowly dissolve, as if they were melting into her Awareness. When she got up from meditation, she was free of them for several hours.

Every day after that, she sat in meditation and let her feelings come up, held them in her Awareness, and let them dissolve. As she did, different layers of grief revealed themselves. She saw that this new pain was fueled and supported by ancient griefs, old feelings of loss and hurt and anger. Sometimes her breathing would change as she saw a flash of childhood memory. Sometimes she even saw scenes that seemed to be glimpses of past lives. As she held the feelings in her Consciousness, each layer eventually would dissolve. After several weeks of these daily meditations, she found that not only had she processed her anger and hurt at being left by her husband, but she had also become free of a subtle sadness that had been controlling her moods from beneath the surface. Layers upon layers of old hurt, old anger, and old suffering had dissolved.

Admittedly, this process takes courage. The key to it is to let go of the content of the feelings, the plot of your internal drama, and to focus first on the feeling itself and then on the energy of the feeling. As you learn to do this in meditation, you get to the point where you can do it in action. Anger, jealousy, or grief will come up, and you will be able to hold it in Awareness and let the edges of the heavy emotional energy dissolve into the wide and calm energy of your Awareness.

When you are fiercely angry or feeling joy beyond description, when you are at an impasse, not knowing what to do, when you are in terror or running for your life, know that such intense states of mind are fully permeated with the spanda, the creative vibration of divine shakti. Find her there.

SPANDA KARIKAS

EXERCISE: ALLOWING YOUR CONSCIOUSNESS
TO DISSOLVE INTENSE EMOTIONS

Sit in a comfortable, upright posture, and close your eyes. Focus on the flow of the breathing, allowing the breath to bring your attention into the heart center, the place where the inhalation comes to rest. This is not the physical heart, but a subtle center located in the center of the body, beneath the breastbone, at a point four to five inches, or approximately eight finger-widths, below the collarbone. Let yourself enter the space inside the heart center. Let that inner space of the heart expand with the breathing, softening and widening.

As you hold your awareness in the heart space, remember a situation that is bringing up intense feelings such as anger, grief, pride, fear, or desire. If there is no current situation, see if you can remember an experience that triggers a particularly strong emotion. (Even though it may not be as powerful for you as something current, you can still practice the exercise with a remembered emotion.)

As the emotion begins to fill your mind, let go of the thoughts you have about it. Let go of the story line, the drama of it, and your tendency to obsess on the situation that triggered it. Focus purely on the energy of the emotion, on the feeling of it within your body. Where is the feeling located? Is it in your head, your heart, your belly, or somewhere else? What sensations do you notice? Is there heat? Sharpness? Heaviness? What other sensations do you feel?

As you focus on the feeling-experience of your emotion, become simultaneously aware of the heart space, the field of Awareness that contains the feelings. Hold the emotional feeling within the heart space as though you were cradling it in your Awareness.

Sit with the emotion, feeling its energy while simultaneously keeping your focus opened out into the widening spaciousness of the heart.

Sit until the energy of the emotion dissolves into Awareness.

ALL THINGS ARISE OUT OF YOUR OWN CONSCIOUSNESS

As we practice looking past the content of our negative thoughts and intense feelings, and seeing into the energy that is their essence, we eventually begin to see ourselves in a profoundly liberating way. We realize that everything that appears in our meditation—every single thing—is pure *shakti*, pure Consciousness. Every image, every thought, every feeling—everything is made of energy. The ugliest, scariest thought is Consciousness. So is the most beautiful vision. Ultimately all of it, even our most exquisite inner experience, has to dissolve back into Consciousness.

In the Tibetan Tantric tradition, advanced practitioners are assigned to meditate on a particular deity. They have to visualize the deity, giving it a form inside their own consciousness. The ideal is to get so good at the visualization that you eventually see the deity step outside your mind, as it were, appearing before you in a moving, speaking form.

Your own mind is originally as pure and empty as the sky. To know whether or not this is true, look inside your own mind.

PADMASAMBHAVA

Accomplished practitioners of this difficult and complex visualization report that it is possible to get the deity to actually appear. That is because Consciousness is infinitely creative. When you focus on something with enough intention, it does become a real entity within your mind. The stuff of your mind takes that shape and gives reality to that object of focus. Then depending on what kind of object you are focusing on, you have an experience of it. An entire complex of thoughts, feelings, images, and bodily sensations makes up an experience. When the form you are focusing on is a negative one—the thought of the insensitive remark someone made to you yesterday or the latest news about global warming—you experience feelings of anger, sadness, or fear. Your heart feels hard or your cheeks get tight. You feel pressure behind the eyes from held-back tears or your breath gets choppy with held-in resentment. Your inner consciousness contracts around the feeling much the way your hand contracts into a fist, and before you know it, your whole world is sadness or anger. The negative thought is creating emotions. It is creating tension in the body, even affecting the immune system.

In the same way, when you focus on a mantra, on an inner flame, or on the form of a deity, this form creates its own complex of thoughts and feelings—usually feelings like love, reverence, happiness, relaxation, and fullness. Most of us, of course, prefer the complex that goes with the divine form over the one we associate with negative thoughts.

Yet even the most beautiful image or form eventually has to dissolve back into Consciousness. That is the point of the Tibetan exercise with the deity. Once they have made the deity real enough to actually appear to them, they are supposed to deliberately let it dissolve back into their own Awareness. The ultimate purpose of the exercise is to reveal that *everything*, including the divine forms that religious people love, is actually a manifestation of and within our own Consciousness. As Swami Muktananda used to say, "Everything exists because you exist. Everything is within your Self. That's why I tell you, 'Don't worship God on the outside. Worship God within your own Consciousness.'"

He used to tell us that whatever object of focus we chose to meditate on, however we decided to meditate, we should do it with this understanding: all thoughts, feelings, and ideas are Consciousness, no different from our inner Self. They are manifestations of the underlying energy, the *shakti* that is bubbling up from within us.

Once we begin to acknowledge this truth, we are close to the heart of meditation. In fact, we are ready to begin following Sir Gawain's example.

We are ready to let the Goddess show us how *she* wants to meditate.

CHAPTER 8

Letting the Shakti Lead

A few years ago, a friend asked me to spend an afternoon meditating with her. She had been having a hard time with her practice and hoped that I could help her find a way to give it a jump start.

"What's the problem?" I asked her.

"I don't know. I think it's that my heart feels dry," she said. "There's no energy there."

"Where do you feel energy?" I asked her.

She closed her eyes for a minute, and then reported, "There's a sort of pressure between my eyebrows. It gets stronger when I close my eyes."

"Why don't you try focusing there?" I said. "Let yourself be in that energy, and try to breathe in and out of it."

Half an hour later, she opened her eyes.

"How was it?" I asked.

"Fabulous," she told me. "I kept breathing through the energy, and after a while it opened up. I was in a pasture made of emerald-colored light. The sun was so bright that I could hardly look at it. Then it became huge, and I was just in the light. It was terrific."

At that moment, I felt as if I had been handed the ultimate secret of meditation. "Of course," I thought. "Find out where your inner energy is playing and let it guide you." Let the subtle energy in your body determine how you meditate. That way, the power that is already working will get behind whatever you do and impel it forward.

Like so much of what I've discovered during my journeys through the inner country, this was not a new idea. In fact, it was basic. I had been hearing about it since my very first Siddha Yoga meditation retreat in 1974, when Swami Muktananda described meditation with awakened Kundalini as being like a fast ride in a Mercedes. "Kundalini will drive your meditation," he said. "The energy that has been awakened in you is intelligent. It is the same intelligent force that creates the universe. She knows how to take you where you need to go." I had taken his words seriously and experienced the truth of them many times. Nonetheless, like so many other people, I had rarely thought to investigate exactly how the Goddess Kundalini was working inside me.

Of course I felt her presence, especially when she took over in meditation, dissolving my thoughts into an emerging witness state, pushing me into a *hatha yoga* posture and holding me there, or manifesting such an ocean of happiness that I couldn't help letting go into it. I had noticed how she gave impetus to certain practices and how she enlivened teachings so that they became experience. Yet at the same time I tended to take her for granted, the way when I was a child I took for granted that my mother would be there to cook supper and make my dentist appointments. The one thing that had never occurred to me was to ask Kundalini where she wanted to take me and to follow her lead.

Yet when Kundalini is awakened within us, this is what we are constantly being invited to do: move beyond technique into the sweet and mysterious country of spontaneous meditation. "If you learn how to pay attention to the awakened Kundalini, she continually guides you," Gurumayi once said. "She is a living torch that guides you on your path." Our meditation will deepen and open to the exact degree that we pay attention to the *shakti's* signals and allow it to lead our practice.

What does it really mean to let Kundalini lead? Does it mean becoming passive, sitting back, and waiting for something to happen? Or is there a way to work with Kundalini, to follow her like a dance partner? Beyond following the basic disciplines of meditation—sitting, directing our attention within, and invoking grace—what do we need to do to be in the correct relationship to our own *shakti?*

As usual, it is a matter of attention. *To dance with Kundalini, we need to keep ourselves attuned to the felt sense of the* shakti *as she moves within us.* Kundalini pulsates. Through her pulsations, she is always communicating with us, drawing us inside, and showing us the pathway that will lead us deeper into ourselves.

THE LANGUAGE OF KUNDALINI

The inner *shakti* communicates with us through subtle impulses, feelings, and sensations, through insights, images, and realizations. Some of these communications are obvious, immediately recognizable once we tune in to them. For example, there is the urge to meditate. At different times during the day, we might feel a strong inward pull, an urge to focus inside. It can happen at our desk or on the bus, and it often manifests as a sensation of heaviness or even sleepiness. If we aren't attentive, we may think that we need a nap or a cup of coffee. But what we really need is to give in to the impulse that wants to draw us into meditation—even if it is only for a few moments.

Here are some of the more dramatic signs of Kundalini's workings. Perhaps a light appears in our inner field. Or we find ourselves in a natural witness state, observing our experience. A feeling of love arises and grows stronger as we focus on it. Our awareness begins expanding, pushing aside the energy walls that make us feel confined within the boundaries of the body. The breath speeds up or stops. The head shakes or moves backward or forward. We might feel ourselves dropping or rising to a different level within ourselves. The Awareness that has hovered behind our surface mind seems to move to the foreground. A vision appears.

Other signals of the *shakti* are much subtler. Perhaps we feel a pulsation in the heart, a slight tingling in the forehead, a sensation of energy on one side of the body, or a realization that the mantra "wants" to stop being repeated.

These subtle signals are easier to ignore than the more dramatic ones, so we often fail to pay attention to them. Nonetheless, they are as significant as dramatic manifestations. They are our own personal trail markers, footprints that reveal the direction that our inner *shakti* is opening up for us. We need to learn to recognize them for ourselves, because there is no rule book that can possibly describe each one of them.

You might like to close your eyes at this moment and tune in to the energy within your body.

EXERCISE: SENSING THE SHAKTI

Close your eyes and allow your body to move into a relaxed, upright posture. Turn your attention inward and scan your body. Where do you feel the currents of energy in your body now? How do you experience your inner energy? Do you notice it throbbing in particular areas of the body? Are there feelings associated with the sensation of energy—feelings like tenderness or heartache or longing? Inner sensations like pressure or heat or hardness or softness? Sounds or lights? Notice them and see whether they are familiar to you.

I have realized at last the true nature of prayer and meditation. They are simply your own play as longing and as aspiration.

RAMPRASAD

THE THREE MODES OF EXPERIENCE

Just as we each have our own style of feeling emotions, processing information, and solving problems, each of us experiences inner phenomena in our own way. Until we recognize the validity of our own personal mode, we often doubt our meditation experience, especially when it doesn't conform to the experiences described by our teacher or in the classical texts of yoga. If we have been taught to identify true meditation with a dead-quiet mind or to imagine that good meditation means seeing visions or entering into dramatically altered states of consciousness, we might discount the other insights, subtle movements of energy, and various shifts in mood and feeling that are equally important signposts in the inner world.

In one of the more lyrical passages in his spiritual autobiography, *Play of Consciousness,* Swami Muktananda wrote about the inner sensory experiences that manifest when the *kundalini* becomes active. He described how our desire for visual beauty is satisfied through inner lights and visions. We hear inner music, or *nada,* the subtle sounds that arise when we are in contact with the spiritual centers in the body. We feel sensations of inner touch as the *kundalini* moves through our system. In higher meditation, we may even smell fragrances or taste sweet flavors.

This passage is more than an invitation to subtle sensation. It contains a paradigm of the ways that many people experience the *kundalini.* As we saw in chapter 4, our inner world tends to reveal itself visually, kinesthetically, or auditorially. Some of us even experience all three modes simultaneously. Nonetheless, if we look closely at our meditation experience, we usually discover that we do have a prevailing "style."

Kinesthetically, the *shakti* reveals itself as sensation. We might feel pulsations of energy in different parts of the body, including the feeling of an energy balloon, so to speak, expanding in the heart, a pressure between the eyebrows, or a feeling of fullness in the throat. Tingling sensations might run through the legs or the torso. We feel pressure or even pain in different spiritual centers as the energy pushes through the blocks there. Perhaps the *shakti* manifests as a feeling of love, as a wave of warmth and tenderness, or as a flow of energy on which we almost seem to float. On the other hand, we might feel it as extreme heat or cold.

"The *sadhaka* [spiritual aspirant] feels the touch of Kundalini in his body," Swami Muktananda wrote. "When she is awakened and spreads through the . . . *nadis* [channels that carry *prana*, the vital force], the *sadhaka* becomes aware of her soft, tender, joyous, divine touch. Sometimes her touch is harsh, and then the whole body feels as if it is on fire. Whether her touch is soft or hard depends on the nature of the aspirant. But either way, it is the touch of God."

I'm a kinesthetic person myself, and for me, following the *shakti* usually means following impulses of inner pulsation, sensation, and feeling. The awakened *shakti* first introduced itself to me as a subtle feeling of intense pleasure that moved through my body according to mysterious laws that I did not understand. After a while, I began to notice that the sweet inner sensation ebbed and flowed in response to my state of mind. When I held negative thoughts or feelings, when I spoke harshly to myself or others, or when I did things that contradicted the subtle laws of the universe and my own values, the energy in my body would often become hard and almost painful. If I softened my thinking or my behavior, the energy would also soften. I began using the inner sensations as a compass, a kind of guide to action. To this day, it remains a reliable inner guide.

For an auditory person, the *shakti's* pathway might be an inner sound — a tinkling sound, a murmur as if *Om* were being repeated very fast, the buzzing of bees, or even distant music. Gurumayi described this once as the song of Kundalini: "As she gently moves in and around you, she sings to herself. So listen to the sound she makes." In Sanskrit, these sounds are called *nada.* The texts of *kundalini yoga* describe them as emanations from the highest spiritual center, the *sahasrara chakra.* One of the important practices in the *kundalini yoga* tradition, called *laya yoga,* includes focusing on these inner sounds until they lead the mind to a state of stillness.

One woman told me that for years she had heard a high-pitched ringing sound when she went deep into meditation. She thought she must have tinnitus, a disease of the inner ear. When her doctor found nothing physically wrong, she decided that meditation was causing her ear problems and actually stopped sitting to meditate. Then someone told her about *nada*, the inner sounds that arise in deep meditation, and suggested she read a yogic text called the *Nada Bindu Upanishad*, which describes some of the classical forms of these subtle sounds. As she read the description, she recognized her own experience and began to focus on the sounds in meditation. The *nada* would eventually dissolve into a subtle, delicate pulsation in which she would rest in a powerful, loving energy.

A friend of mine hears poetry composing itself in meditation. Other auditory people hear inner guiding words that direct their meditation or their daily actions. Trying to force himself into a straight-backed posture one day, one man heard an inner voice saying sweetly, "It seems to me that you want to start from some place other than where you are." He relaxed into a less rigid posture and then felt "hands" gently guiding and correcting his posture, lifting his back so that he was able to sit straight without strain. "The hands," he wrote, "were subtle but *real*. They were full of gentleness."

The visual manifestations of the *shakti* hold particular glamour for many people. We understand immediately that a vision of a huge, golden ball of light is important. If we are engaged in an activity and suddenly catch a glimpse of the tiny blue light that the Siddhas call the light of the Self, we feel supported and confirmed in our course of action. When a face shows up in our meditation, or a landscape or a field of light, we pay attention—sometimes more than is warranted. We may wonder if it is real or our imagination, but we do pay attention.

Swami Muktananda, whose meditation journey was highly visual, described many such experiences in *Play of Consciousness.*

Some visions are more important than others. Many visual experiences are simply a kind of downloading of data from our unconscious image bank. Others have universal significance. A vision can give us a teaching or reveal symbolically some truth about reality. A friend of mine had a vision in meditation in which he saw the material universe taking form out of a luminous field of swirling blue energy. He told me later that as he was watching it, he had the feeling that he was having a genuine glimpse of the way matter arises out of the underlying energy source. The ancient sages received insights into the nature of reality—many of which mirror the findings of contemporary physics—through just such visions.

RECOGNIZING THE SHAKTI'S PATHWAYS

All these sensations, whether visual, auditory, or kinesthetic, are manifestations of one particular aspect of the *kundalini: kriya shakti,* or the power of action. For this reason, they are often called *kriyas,* or yogic movements. But *kriya shakti* is not the only power of the *kundalini.* Four other aspects of this powerful inner energy awaken in us when the *kundalini* becomes active, and their manifestations are as significant as those of the *kriya shakti.* The teachers of Kashmir Shaivism described these energies as the power of Awareness (*chit shakti*), the power of bliss (*ananda shakti*), the power of will (*iccha shakti*), and the power of knowledge (*jnana shakti*). These powers are inherent in the universal energy, the *shakti* that creates and supports life; Shaivism tells us that every action that takes place in this universe is performed by one of these powers of the *shakti.*

Now here is the point: When the *kundalini* becomes active in us, all these powers naturally come into full play in our inner world. As they play inside us, they give us experiences. Every experience we have in meditation is brought about by one or another of these five powers.

For example, our experiences of expanded consciousness come from the *chit shakti*, the power of Awareness. *Chit shakti* might manifest as a spontaneous experience of the witness, or as a realization that one Awareness pervades everywhere, or as the experience of pure being, beyond the ordinary sense of body or personality.

Ananda shakti, the power of bliss, unfolds within us as an upsurge of spontaneous love, contentment, and unmotivated joy, the feeling of an ever-expanding heart. The joy of awakened *ananda shakti* is different from ordinary pleasure not just because it is much deeper but also because it is independent of our superficial moods and experiences. "It is not just a certain feeling or giddy emotion," Gurumayi writes. "Joy is the natural state of the Self." Once the *ananda shakti* begins surging, we are capable of feeling a tickling joy not only when things are going well, but even in times of sorrow or frustration.

When the force of *iccha shakti*, the power of divine will, is moving inside us, it enhances our own power of will and makes it easier for us to practice yogic discipline, stay focused on a subtle state in meditation, or even do our daily tasks one-pointedly. We might feel it as a force that pulls the mind inward, drawing us into meditation. Some people say that when their *kundalini* becomes active, an inner force will sometimes bring them fully awake at an hour much earlier than they are used to arising. It is as if the force is suggesting that it is time to get up and meditate. *Iccha shakti* can also manifest as guiding impulses,

The most exalted experience of bliss in any realm of being is directly knowing the universal Mother, the supremely blissful one.

RAMPRASAD

as feelings about the rightness or wrongness of a particular action, as stirrings of conscience, or as powerful intuitions that come both in and out of meditation. One of the ways we learn to tune in to the guidance of the inner power is to follow these guiding signals and observe the results until we learn to distinguish them from the ordinary (and often unreliable) impulses that come from the mind.

Jnana shakti, or the power of knowledge, brings insight, understanding, and a subtle ability to know what is true. *Jnana shakti* reveals the difference between our limited self and our pure I-awareness. It shows the meaning of our experiences and gives us inner instructions, hints, and convictions about subtle truths. *Jnana shakti* is the power that answers our questions from inside and, ultimately, lets us recognize the Truth.

Again, we need to recognize and honor the form in which *kundalini* is manifesting in us. A man once told me that he had always devalued his own experience because it didn't pulse with light, bliss, and drama. Then one day an insight arose almost as though his *kundalini* were speaking to him. It said, "Your way is not the way of the *kriya shakti.* It is the way of the *jnana shakti,* the way of understanding." After that he began to recognize the significance of the subtle realizations that often arose in his meditation. He would focus on them and contemplate them. As he did, his meditation became more centered on his underlying Awareness, and he began to experience powerful, lasting contact with his essential Self. Once he recognized and began following the pathways that the *shakti* was opening up for him, his meditation went deeper than it had in ten previous years of practice.

Why don't more people do that? One reason is that we tend to objectify our experience. We watch our meditation passively, as if we were at a movie. When our experiences are subtle, especially if they are purely energetic, we often ignore them or take them for granted. If they are big and dramatic, we may treat them as spiritual coinage, as signs that something special is happening and that we are succeeding at meditation. In both cases, we separate ourselves from the experience. We might try to hold on to it or push it away; we might get caught up in analyzing it, trying to figure out what it means, or turn it into a kind of trophy.

On the other hand, if we take our experiences as directional signals from the *shakti*, as doorways into deeper meditation, and follow them, any one of them can take us deeper. Suppose a soft glow appears behind your eyes. Very gently you bring your attention to the light. You don't try to hold it, to cling to it, to make it stay. You just softly move your attention close to it. (Often, the best way to do this is not to observe it frontally, but as if you were watching it from the side.) Perhaps you gently breathe into it and let the breath merge your awareness into it. Or you explore it. How does it look? What is its texture? What do you see or hear? You might also try shifting your perspective. Instead of feeling that you are outside this vision, observing it, imagine that you are inside it. With a sound, imagine that you are hearing it all around you.

Letting yourself be with an experience allows you to move much deeper into your own inner field. Perhaps there is a sensation of expanding awareness, but the expansion stops at a certain point. You can let yourself linger on the edge of that expanded awareness, sensing the subtle texture of the consciousness that is expanding, or you can enter the field of consciousness that stretches within you, unreeling itself to the inner senses. The way to enter it is to become it. You think of yourself as Awareness. For some people, this may mean going through a process in which you disengage yourself from identifying with your body, perhaps saying, "I am not my skin, my bones, my blood, or my organs. I am not my senses, my breath, my mind, or my thoughts. I am not my emotions or my sensations. I am Awareness. I am energy." Then you move as awareness *into* Awareness, as if you were a snowball picking up more snow as you roll.

As you focus on and move into the pathway that the *shakti* reveals, the doorway often changes or disappears. The energy sensation widens or diffuses. The light dissolves. The inner sound shifts its tone, becomes a subtle throb, merges into silence, or becomes light. If you stay with the *feeling* of it, the felt sensation of the experience, you can still follow it.

Suppose, for example, you begin by noticing an energy pulsation in the *ajna chakra,* the space between the eyebrows. This, you feel, is the opening that the *shakti* is revealing to you now. So you focus gently on it, breathing in and out of it. Or you remind yourself that it is your own energy and let yourself feel an identity with it. At some point, you might feel that the energy opens and takes you inside. Perhaps you find yourself in a large ball or field of energy, or in a cavelike space. You might sense or see colors or sensations inside the space. As you let yourself be with it, the energy might draw you deeper into itself. It might manifest as forms, faces, or colors, as feelings of love, or as an expanding sensation. There might be a sudden rush of insight.

Then at a certain point, you will probably find that whatever arises—whether it is a light, an inner understanding, or a feeling of love—has dissolved, evanesced, become attenuated into pure energy. As the *shakti* moves us inward, its natural tendency is to dissolve forms—to lead us from the gross to the subtle,

Often when I step away from otherness into myself, I behold a most wondrous beauty. It is then that I believe most strongly in my belonging to a higher destiny.

PLOTINUS

and then to the subtler, deeper, and finer realms of consciousness, where the threads of form disappear into the formless and the surface mind merges into its source. As the landmarks on the *shakti's* pathway melt, you can let yourself melt with them. You can keep breathing out the inner sense of holding in your consciousness, relaxing the tightness of your mental "muscles," and moving toward and into each new space as it opens up. The principle is to keep entering more deeply into the place where the *shakti* is playing. As you do that, it will keep moving you deeper into the inner world. Some people lose their awareness at this point or fall into a sleepy, unconscious state. It's good to try to stay aware, but don't worry if at this point you lose awareness. As your attention becomes more stable, you will be able to hold the state.

INVOKING SHAKTI

Learning how to follow the *shakti's* lead is such a core practice for entering the heart of meditation that in some schools of traditional *kundalini* meditation practice, students are told not to try to practice any technique at all. Instead they simply sit and wait for the *shakti* to take them where it wants to take them. To do this successfully, though, we need to keep ourselves vigilant; otherwise we might wind up suspended on some seductive thought train. The Goddess, after all, has two faces — her "mayic" face, which creates separation and identification with the small self, and her liberating face, which dissolves duality. We want to stay in touch with her liberating face. Ramakrishna Paramahamsa, who was a great lover of the divine Mother, used to pray to the *shakti* the way a child speaks to its mother. He would beg, "Please, show me your liberating face rather than the face of your *maya,* your delusion!" This is a powerful little prayer. I often try it when meditation feels particularly thick and agitated. As I utter the words, I begin to experience a radical shift of perspective. I see how thoughts are taking form out of my underlying consciousness, how they stay for a while and then dissolve. Instead of being lost in thought, I find myself watching the play of the energy of the mind. This instantly frees me from identifying with the thoughts, so I am able to move into a deeper state.

In fact, whenever we want to meditate on the *shakti*, the best way to begin is with a prayer and an invitation. Like the invocations to the Guru that we looked at in chapter 3, our petition can be very simple: "O Kundalini Shakti, please show me how you want to meditate today." It can also be elaborate and imaginative, like the praise-hymns of the devotional poets. "Mother Kundalini," you could intone if that were your mood, "you are the very foundation of inner experience. You shine like the sun within my body and purify the mind. Please be gracious to me. Guide my meditation."

There is also a kind of prayer that is actually meditation. Here we seek out the *shakti's* presence in the depths of the mind, feel it intimately present inside us, and move with it. The most natural and immediate way to do this, I have found, is to meditate on the *spanda*, the inner pulsation that we looked at in chapter 4. You may notice that we keep returning again and again to this pulsation. That's because it is such a direct way of becoming familiar and intimate with our own *shakti*.

The following exercise takes a little time. Before we can discern the subtle inner pulse, we need to give the mind time to let go of its surface busyness.

You are no longer able to conceal yourself or appear distant from me. My very breath and being bond with your potent mystery, and I experience your power alone as my own inviolate strength.

RAMPRASAD

147

EXERCISE: INVOKING THE SHAKTI'S GUIDANCE

Step 1: Settling the Mind

Close your eyes and sit in an upright, relaxed posture, following the steps on pages 62–64.

Focus your attention on the breath. Observe the breath without trying to change its rhythm. Instead of feeling that you are breathing, have the understanding that you are being breathed. The breath is being drawn in and out by the energy within your body. *Kundalini* is breathing you.

As thoughts come up, name each thought as Consciousness, as *shakti*.

Continue this for fifteen minutes, or until you begin to feel the mind relaxing and becoming quieter. Now let yourself rest in your own inner consciousness, the field of your inner experience.

Step 2: Experiencing the Pulsation

Feel for the slight shimmer of movement, the subtle vibration, the pulse of energy that is always throbbing inside your consciousness. Notice where in your inner field of awareness you feel that vibration and focus your attention there.

The pulsation of the *shakti* may manifest as a subtle vibration, a pulsing throb, but it may also manifest as a sound or as a glow of light. You might notice that the pulsation is especially strong in one area of your body—in the heart, between the eyebrows, in the throat, or at the top of the head. If that is the case, gently allow your attention to go to that center. Or focus on the sensation of the heartbeat as it diffuses itself throughout your body.

As you feel that shimmer of movement, that pulsation within your aware-ness, begin to honor it. Say to it, "I recognize you as the inner *shakti*, divine Kundalini in this form. I honor you. I know you as the Goddess, the mother of the universe, who pulses within me. I know that out of you come all my thoughts and all feelings. Out of you comes the mantra, the divine sound. Out of you come visions, lights, and experiences of bliss."

Now speak inwardly to the divine pulsation, this form of the Goddess within you. Ask for her guidance and help. Say to her, "Where do you wish to play today? Where do you wish to take me? In what direction should I follow you? How do you want me to meditate now?"

Once you have asked these questions, wait, with great alertness, for the answers that arise from inside. Wait without expecting anything, without having a program.

An answer may come as an insight, as a verbal direction, as a very subtle feeling, or as an impulse to do a particular practice or focus in a particular way. Don't worry about whether you have the right answer. Trust that what-ever comes up is your answer from the *shakti*.

When an impulse, a direction, a practice, or an experience arises, follow it. Focus on it. If nothing else arises, continue to focus on the vibration, on the *shakti* as you are experiencing it. Allow yourself to feel at one with the pulsation of the *shakti*. Let it draw you deeper and deeper into its shimmering field of vibration.

Holy Spirit,
giving life to all life,
moving all creatures,
root of all things,
washing them clean,
wiping out their mistakes,
healing their wounds,
you are our true life,
luminous, wonderful,
awakening the heart
from its ancient sleep.

HILDEGARD OF BINGEN

PERMISSION TO UNFOLD

Even though I have worked with this process for years, I'm always slightly awed at how much it enlivens practice. The simple act of asking the *shakti* for guidance seems to create space for new openings and deeper meditation. Often these openings come when someone focuses on a phenomenon that they had never even noticed before.

One man asked the *shakti* for guidance, then felt a movement of energy on one side of his head. Ordinarily he would have ignored it, but because he was looking for a signal from the *shakti*, he focused on it and tried to enter it. The energy softened, widened, and expanded. He found himself in a plane of soft, vibrating energy, surrounded by waves of love. It was like resting in subtle water. His sense of being a physical body dissolved, and he realized that he was this expanded body of Consciousness.

A young woman found that the first time she invoked the *shakti's* help, a light field opened up before her. Now whenever she sits for meditation, she experiences this field of light. Another woman felt a strong pressure in her third-eye center between the eyebrows, which resolved itself into a blue ball of light. She focused on the light and found herself in a huge ocean of radiance, where she floated for the rest of the meditation period. After that, the pulsation in her forehead continued to grow stronger. Not only did she experience it in meditation, but she also kept feeling the pressure throughout the day. She described how, along with the sensation of pressure, there was a new clarity in her mind. "Sometimes when I close my eyes during the day, I feel as if I'm looking through crystal. Even when my mind is very busy, there's lightness underneath it."

Other people have reported spontaneous physical movements, yogic *kriyas*, or the feeling of witness-consciousness descending over them. For some there was simply a feeling of sweetness and depth in their meditation. As one meditator put it, "I began to be drawn to meditation in a way I hadn't been before. My experiences became precious to me."

THE POWER OF SURRENDER

This process of invoking and following the *shakti* is powerful because it contains three of the most important practices in the meditation of grace: recognition, worship, and surrender. As we recognize the divinity of Kundalini pulsating within our mind, we free her to reveal her love and her liberating intention. When we worship her by praying to her and invoking her grace, when we give her attention and ask for her help, we enter into a loving relationship with our energy and arouse her compassion. When we surrender—that is, when we genuinely commit ourselves to following her guidance—we give her permission to show us the depths of ourselves and the depths of her love for us. Kundalini cannot do this unless we allow her to act. Before she can fully reveal herself to us, we need to have given her permission to guide the program.

This is not always easy. Most of us have a deep inner need to control things—in meditation as much as in daily life. When the *shakti* presents us with an opening into deeper meditation, there is usually a moment when we want to resist, to move back from the opening. At such moments, we have to consciously remind ourselves to let go or to surrender. Ultimately surrender isn't something we can "do." It's a natural movement of Consciousness, a deep release that happens over time and often only in deep meditation.

Trust the divine power, and she will free the godlike elements in you and shape all into an expression of divine nature.

SRI AUROBINDO

151

Emerging into her
   thousand-petal reality,
O meditator, become the
   Goddess consciously.
She is your essence,
   you her expression.

RAMPRASAD

Yet there are practices that allow us to release our hold. One works with the breath—which, as we have seen before, is the great engine of release in meditation. We breathe in, and then exhale with the feeling that we are breathing out the distracting thoughts, the feelings of resistance, and the sense of separation and limitation. That inner gesture of exhaling resistance not only helps release the mental muscles that create constriction in our breathing, but also releases constriction in the mind and removes our feeling of separation from the *shakti*.

It is important to remember, when we practice surrender, that we are not surrendering to something outside. The *shakti* who guides us into meditation is our own higher energy—the Goddess Shakti. She is the energy of our soul who, out of love, is drawing us toward herself. She compels us by her very existence to stretch, to expand, to grow, and to become our best and highest self. She does this out of love. She does it because she is, truly, our Self.

So as we invoke Shakti and become aware of her signals, as we learn to surrender our meditation agendas and follow Shakti's footprints into the inner world, we can periodically stop to breathe out our feelings of resistance and tension. We can stop to remember the reality of oneness, the seamless congruity between the personal consciousness and the great Consciousness. We can remind ourselves that the energy of the universe is our energy, that the great Awareness is our awareness, and that God's mind holds, contains, and encompasses our own mind and ultimately dissolves all of it into the vastness of pure *chiti*, pure Consciousness.

PART TWO   The Inner Process

CHAPTER 9

Moving Through
the Inner Realm:
The Pathways of Meditation

We have been examining a series of practices for
coming into relationship with our inner world and
various principles that make it easier to swim in its
waters. We have discussed a few of these: devotion,
playfulness, opening to and entering into techniques rather than trying to "do" them, feeling
one with our practice and its goal, learning how to
sense and follow the clues that our inner energy
shows us. As we have seen, when we turn our
attention to the inner world and sit with the intention to sink back into ourselves, we open ourselves
to the natural inward movement of Consciousness.
By now, it should be apparent that this inward tendency is a kind of dissolve. It is a process of allowing the relatively gross, thickened state of our

ordinary mind to resolve itself back into its own ground, into that natural state of clarity and awareness that the Indian tradition calls the Knower, pure Consciousness, or the Self.

This process happens differently for everyone and brings with it a great variety of inner experiences.

Here is where most of our questions arise. First of all, we want to know the meaning of our experiences. We want to understand whether it is important that we see visions of faces, or what that light means, or why our head falls forward onto the chest, or whether the feeling of joy that surfaces fleetingly is the ultimate joy of the Self or some lesser pleasure. If we are going out or seeming to lose consciousness in meditation, we want to know whether or not we are just asleep. If we remain in our normal waking state, we are afraid we aren't meditating. Behind all our questions is the great question, the one we all want an answer to eventually: am I actually making any progress in meditation at all?

Periodically during the years of experimenting with my practice, this particular doubt would seize me. I would begin to wonder whether I was really moving deeper in meditation or simply indulging myself, drifting through realms of dream and moving energy. To deal with these doubts, I began looking carefully at what the sages had to say about the inner realm and comparing my own intuitive sense of the journey with the maps found in different meditation texts.

Fortunately, great meditators from every tradition have left us accounts of their own experiences and pointed to certain experiences as signposts, signals that we are actually moving forward. Of course, the indicators of what the *Shvetashvatara Upanishad* calls "success in yoga" differ in certain particulars in different traditions. And ultimately most of the great teachers of meditation would

Be strong then, and enter into your own body; there you have a solid place for your feet. Think about it carefully! Don't go off somewhere else!

Kabir says this: just throw away all thoughts of imaginary things, and stand firm in that which you are.

KABIR

156

agree with Gurumayi, who says that the most important signs of spiritual progress are revealed in our character, our ability to maintain equanimity, our power to keep the mind clear and still, our compassion and kindness, our clarity, and our capacity to hold our center. Nonetheless, there is value in looking at the maps that different traditions offer us when we are trying to understand where our inner experiences fit and what, if anything, they mean. If we don't understand them, we are liable to discount significant experiences or to short-circuit yogic processes that are not only normal but profound and helpful. Or we can fall into the opposite trap and become inflated about experiences that are only signposts, thinking we have reached the final goal.

One friend of mine often describes an early meditation in which she saw a blazing golden light rising out of her heart. "This is it!" she thought. "I'm enlightened. Now what?" She was musing about her future when she realized that the light had disappeared. Later her teacher explained that her vision, though profound and meaningful, was not by any means a sign that her journey was finished. It was instead a gift, a kind of promise of what she could discover if she persevered. Another woman wrote a book about the painful confusion she suffered after being catapulted into a state of more or less permanent expanded consciousness in which she was suddenly freed of any sense of identification with her personal self. Lacking any reference point or guidance, she assumed that her condition was pathological and suffered for nearly ten years until she met someone who could put it into perspective. So the maps are essential. Even more essential is our own contemplation, our willingness to examine our experiences in the light of the various yogic paradigms.

In the Indian tradition, the most famous map of the spiritual journey traces our progress up the chakras, the spiritual centers that lie along the spinal column. Most practitioners are familiar with the names and locations of the main chakras and are also aware that each chakra is related to certain systems in the physical body and also seems to correspond to particular emotional or spiritual states. In *Shat Chakra Nirupana*, one of the authoritative Tantric texts on *kundalini* and the chakras, the basic paradigm places our lower, more purely human experiences in the heart and the chakras immediately below it*: the *svadhisthana chakra* near the gonads, which is said to be the seat of lust and fear, and the *manipura*, or navel chakra, where our power urges are said to be seated. In the *anahata*, the fourth chakra at the level of the heart, we begin to move into a higher awareness, which becomes higher and subtler when our awareness ascends to the *vishuddha* (pure) *chakra* at the throat, and the *ajna* (command) *chakra* in the center of the forehead between the eyebrows. When awareness becomes stable in the crown chakra, called the *sahasrara* (thousand petaled), we experience divine light, expansion, and unity; we become, according to the tradition, Self-realized.

Another yogic map comes from the tradition of Kashmir Shaivism and traces our movement in meditation through thirty-six *tattvas*, or stages of manifestation. According to this paradigm, the spiritual process is one of ascent from the state where one identifies with the physical body and experiences reality as hard, material, and intensely differentiated to the God-realized state, where one experiences complete unity with the ultimate Consciousness, which is utterly free, blissful, and capable of knowing and doing anything it wills. In this system,

---

*In this text, the *muladhara*, or base chakra, since it is the seat of the sleeping *kundalini*, is described simply as a center of bliss.

progress is measured by our degree of freedom from the feeling of limitation. At the lowest stage, we feel separate, fearful, and limited in our capacities, while at the highest stage, we experience perfect joy and feel all that exists to be a part of ourselves. There are various stages in between.

These two maps are related and actually can be fitted together, the experience of each group of *tattvas* corresponding to a particular chakra. Both are related to the map I will look at in detail in this chapter: the paradigm of the four states and four bodies offered by Shankara, the great teacher of Vedanta. I decided to look at meditation experience along this particular grid for three reasons: because it is simple and easy to follow, because it was the one that Swami Muktananda seemed to use most often, and because it helps us understand progression in meditation as a process of moving inward or, as Gurumayi once said, of "unpeeling" different layers of our being.

THE FOUR STATES AND THE FOUR BODIES

The texts of Vedanta speak of the physical body, the mind, and the other aspects of our being as "sheaths," or bodies superimposed like layers of an onion over the subtle energy of Consciousness that is our core Self. Linked with these are four states they identify as basic to human experience: waking, dream, deep sleep, and the state of transcendental Awareness we experience in meditation. Normally we live in one or another of these states, or, to put it another way, we live in the body that corresponds to that state. So when we move inward in meditation, we actually move through these four bodies, or, if you prefer, layers, each one subtler than the last and each interpenetrating the others.

When we are awake, we are normally grounded in the physical body

In this body... are seers and sages; all the stars and planets as well. There are sacred pilgrimages, shrines, and presiding deities of the shrines....The sun and moon also move in it. Ether, air, fire, water, and earth are also there. All the beings that exist are also to be found in the body. He who knows all this is a Yogi.

SHIVA SAMHITA

(*sthula sharira*). In dreams and reverie, when we are lost in thought or fantasy, or during certain stages of meditation, we lose awareness of the physical body and move into the subtle body (*sukshma sharira*). We experience the causal body (*karana sharira*) in deep sleep. The supracausal body is the place we inhabit when we are fully absorbed in the Self. This state normally reveals itself in meditation, though, as we saw in chapter 2, it can also open out when we are wide awake.

Everything that happens to us in meditation happens in one of these four bodies. Of course, as we look at our experiences through the lens of the four bodies, it is important to remember that the map is not the territory. In yoga all categories, all paradigms, are simply convenient ways of putting names to levels of experience that are so subtle and personal that any description of them can only be partial. We are, after all, in the domain of the wordless, trying to fix in language experiences that are often beyond the reach of language. Because concepts can trap us here, we always need to remind ourselves to take them lightly so as not to allow the limitless world of meditation to be limited by our definitions. The world we enter in meditation has so many corners, so many realms, and so many avenues of experience that we can never describe them all or fit them into any one paradigm.

Another trap to be careful of is the assumption that spiritual progress is linear. Sometimes we imagine that consciousness rises or descends step-by-step, as if we were climbing a ladder or riding an elevator with the operator calling out each floor. In reality we move in a much more random manner. We may experience extremely subtle states during the very early days of our practice, and then ten years later find ourselves completely taken up with a pain in our physical body. When *kundalini* guides our inner process, it moves in the direction and at the pace that is appropriate for us at a given time. It works in different layers of the onion and not necessarily in sequence. However, for the sake of convenience here, we will look at our meditation experiences in the four bodies from the outside in.

MEDITATION IN THE PHYSICAL BODY

One of the most universal meditation experiences in the physical body is pain. When we are first learning to sit in a yogic posture, our knees and hips and back show their resistance to this unaccustomed discipline by manifesting all kinds of mysterious aches and tremors. The body tends to complain every time we try to sit longer than usual or otherwise push it past its limits. So most of us have a rather ambivalent attitude toward our experiences in the physical body, and when we become aware of it in meditation, we often assume that we aren't meditating deeply or that we are stuck.

This isn't true. The pain or discomfort we experience in the body during meditation can be a genuine and, believe it or not, significant meditation experience: it can be a sign that the body is being purified. Because the body is the support of our meditation practice, it needs to be stable, clear, and strong to contain and conduct the energy that pours through us when *kundalini* leads us into the subtler stages of meditation. So when we sit for meditation, the awakened *shakti* will move through the muscles and joints and open them up. The physical body is layered with memories of old wounds, sicknesses, environmental toxins, unhealthy food, and emotional upheaval. The awakened *shakti* removes all of this, along with the tensions, both recent and ancient, that we

The unpracticed one will be pulled out of meditation by the senses, even if he forcefully tries to control them. His meditation may be disturbed by such distractions as cold, heat, pleasure, pain, mental upsets, and mosquitoes, which create bodily pain and cause the mind to wander.

YOGA SIKHA UPANISHAD

161

have accumulated. One friend of mine swears that when her neck gets stiff, not even the chiropractor can do anything with it, but when she sits for meditation, the *shakti* moves her head in circles and lets out the kinks. Other people simply experience a gradual release of tension as they sit. Sometimes the experience of release feels pleasant; at other times, it is rather uncomfortable. But somehow the discomfort seems to be part of the process, because the experience of opening is an experience of learning how to feel. When our bodies are deeply blocked and tense, we often feel fairly numb and may not even be conscious of our physical discomfort. As the surface layers are moved away, we literally open up to the stored pain within the body. We may feel aches that we have never been aware of before—and along with aches in the body, a corresponding emotional pain. This pain is not the pain of sickness but the pain of healing. Though much of *kundalini's* work takes place below our awareness, much of it must necessarily go on within our awareness. By allowing ourselves to feel the spontaneous release that *kundalini* inspires, we learn how to release and open up on our own. We can't do this when we are unconscious. The pains that we experience in the body during meditation help us to become more conscious of what is going on in our bodies.

Many of the physical signals of the *shakti* that we mentioned in chapter 8 are signs of this purification. The intense pressure that some people feel in the forehead or in the crown of the head is a sign that the energy is working to open the spiritual centers in the head. When the energy is moving in the heart chakra, we might feel a heaviness around the heart; one person described it as a sensation of having an elephant sitting on her chest. We sometimes experience heat or a piercing sensation at the base of the spine or at other points along the spinal column as *kundalini* activates the chakras.

When a particular chakra is being activated, we might feel its effects in the organs associated with that center. The spiritual center at the navel is associated with the digestive system, and when it is being purified, some people go through digestive upheavals. (Of course, before deciding that your digestive problems are associated with *kundalini* purification, it is highly advisable to have yourself checked out medically.) When the center at the throat is being opened, we may feel a kind of exaggerated tension in the muscles there or even a sore throat. Swami Muktananda wrote in *Play of Consciousness* about the piercing sensations he experienced in his eyes when the optical centers were being opened.

Understanding the nature of this discomfort helps us to bear with it. Instead of defining it as pain, we can see it as the pressure of the awakening force within. We can realize its benign intention. We can relax into the pressure and move toward it and into it, instead of away from it. Often just relaxing will shift our experience out of the discomfort zone.

For more than twenty-five years, whenever the *shakti* becomes particularly strong in meditation, my head will bend backward and then lock in that position. Sometimes it jams up against the spine. In my early years of practice, I had a lot of tension in my neck, so this posture was excruciatingly uncomfortable. In fact, it sometimes hurt so much that I would try to come out of it—only to find that the moment I straightened my head, it would move right back again. Once, as if to underscore the value of this pose, Swami Muktananda came up to me during a meditation retreat, put his hand on my head, and bent it back into that position! Another time Gurumayi appeared in one of my dreams, pushed my head into that position, and said, "This is the golden posture."

One evening I found myself thrust so tightly into this posture that I couldn't move. I had no choice but to give in to it. It soon became obvious that my resistance to staying in the posture made it more painful than it had to be, but I didn't know how to stop resisting. Then a thought arose: "This posture is a gift of *kundalini*. The divine energy in my body is doing this out of love, in order to free me. Even though I don't understand it, still, it is an act of love." As I held that thought, a great feeling of love washed over me and, simultaneously, something released in my neck. The posture, which had been sharply painful, became easy and sweet. A few minutes later, my head spontaneously straightened up. It was as if my letting go, my moment of understanding and acceptance, had opened the way for *kundalini* to free my neck of its tension.

Later I read in a *hatha yoga* text that this posture is a classical position for opening the heart center. As it spontaneously manifested year after year, the center in my heart did open.

PHYSICAL KRIYAS: THE MOVEMENTS OF THE AWAKENED SHAKTI

Movements like these—called yogic *kriyas*—can range from a gentle swaying of the torso, to wildly flailing circles of the head and neck, to spontaneous *hatha yoga asanas* easily performed even when your body is not used to such positions. Each one of these *kriyas* has both a physical and a subtle effect. As they release tension in the physical body, they also remove subtle blocks. For example, many meditators experience a *kriya* in which the energy causes them to bend forward from the hips and place the forehead on the floor. This posture is called *mahamudra*. It is one of the most important *hatha yoga* postures for activating *kundalini* and opening the central channel, the *sushumna nadi,* in the center of the body. (The *sushumna nadi* is the pathway that *kundalini* takes as it moves through the chakras. Once it opens, our breathing, which normally flows in and out of the nostrils, can begin to flow in the *sushumna*. This is when we are able to go into deep meditative states.)

On a physical level, the *mahamudra* posture opens the hips. When the forehead presses against the floor, it not only clears and opens the sinuses, it also opens the *ajna chakra*, the third-eye center between the eyebrows. That center is the junction point for many different *nadis*, or pranic channels. It is also the seat of one of the inner *granthis*, the yogic knots that block access to higher states of consciousness. The knot at the third-eye center, called the *rudra granthi*, is a kind of inner gatekeeper that prevents our awareness from entering the spiritual centers in the crown of the head. This knot holds us in the illusion of separateness. Once this knot is opened, there is a profound change in our awareness of ourselves. We begin to realize directly, through experience, that our consciousness is not confined to the limits of the physical body. We can know ourselves as much larger and subtler than we ordinarily believe ourselves to be. We stop clinging to ego limitations, fears, and constrictions. We begin to experience our unity with others and our unity with God.

There are hundreds of different kinds of *kriyas*, spontaneous physical movements that the awakened *shakti* performs as she purifies the blocks in your body. For example, you may experience the following:

- Your jaw may make rapid lateral movements, as though it were trying to loosen itself up. These movements are helpful in opening the throat chakra.

It is Her nature to dance with great joy, and therefore there is always a gentle motion, a slight sway in your being, even when you are absolutely still.

GURUMAYI
CHIDVILASANANDA

165

- Your body may rotate from the hips or your pelvis may wriggle in circles or back and forth or up and down. These movements are related to the first three chakras: *muladhara, svadashthana,* and *manipura.*

- Your hands may move in dancelike gestures. Your fingers may spontaneously press themselves into your forehead or your heart—again gestures that help to open these centers.

- Your body may move into a *hatha yoga* posture like the ones mentioned above. You might fall backward into the yogic posture called *supta-padmasana,* a posture that vitalizes the kidneys and digestive organs.

When *kriyas* occur (and not everyone experiences them), it is one sign that *kundalini* is working strongly and that spontaneous meditation is taking place. Usually you have *kriyas* during the early part of a meditation session; at a certain point, the energy will release the body, and you are able to move into a quieter meditation. If possible, it is best to allow *kriyas* to happen—to witness them but not to short-circuit them. However, if a particular movement is extremely uncomfortable or if it is disturbing to people around you, you might try dropping your awareness deeper inside, into the heart or another spiritual center, consciously moving past the physical to a more subtle level. Or you can invoke the *shakti* and ask it to give you a quieter experience.

The discomfort that we sometimes experience when these processes are taking place (and not all of them are accompanied by physical movements) is a sort of growing pain. It is the inevitable pain of opening past our limits, moving through blocks, and releasing tensions. It is a good pain, in short, and the more we can accept it and be with it, the faster our opening will take place.

Being able to sit with the discomfort of growth takes a lot of courage and a willingness to be open to the unknown. There is great nobility in the attitude that a meditator takes: sitting with the intention to experience whatever the inner energy wants to give. It is the attitude of the spiritual warrior, the warrior of yoga, who dedicates himself or herself (at least for the hour of meditation) to going for it—going for the growth, going for the breakthrough, going for the transformation.

At the same time, we shouldn't feel that we need to go faster, or sit longer, than we want to. It's not that anyone is going to give us prizes for endurance or stoicism. We are not in this to get hurt or to prove how strong we are. We are in it for love. So if something feels like too much for now, trust yourself and give yourself permission to back off. Move when your posture becomes stiff, pray to the inner energy to give you a gentler experience, or simply come out of your posture for a few minutes and relax. There are times in meditation when it is right to push through a feeling of discomfort and times when the best tactic is to relax, to back off. As we experiment with our practice, we learn to sense all this and also to honor our intuitions.

ENTERING THE SUBTLE REALMS

Usually after we've been sitting for a while, our awareness of the physical body lessens. If we are having physical *kriyas*, they die down. Gradually, we become more aware of thoughts and images and of the shifting energy currents that move beneath the surface of our being.

The subtle body is made of energy—the energy of our vital force, the energy of thoughts and feelings and perceptions. According to the *Brihadaranyaka Upanishad*, it is the subtle body that transmigrates, leaving the physical body after death and going on to experience the so-called afterlife, as well as life in other physical bodies.

The subtle body consists of

- the *pranas,* or vital energy;
- the so-called psychic instruments—the mind, intellect, ego, and subconscious mind-stuff—along with the thoughts, images, and perceptions generated by the mind and intellect;
- the powers of sensing—sight, hearing, and so on—that act through the physical organs to let us take in information from the outer world and that operate inwardly in dreams, imagination, and reverie;
- the subtle elements of perception called in Sanskrit the *tanmatras,* which create the inner world of images, sounds, tastes, and sensations that we experience when our attention is withdrawn from the outer world;
- the system of subtle channels called *nadis,* which carry the vital energy to the organs and limbs of the physical body and to the chakras, or subtle energy centers; and
- *kundalini* energy.

THE VITAL ENERGY

The energy aspect of the subtle body is sometimes called the *pranamaya kosha,* or "vital sheath." It is truly a kind of sheath, a layer of pure vitality, the energy that powers your life. *Prana* is the name that the yogic sages gave to the life force that becomes the sap in the trees, the radiant currents of sunlight, the negative ions in the atmosphere, and the nourishment in water. Yogic texts say that before becoming this world of matter, the creative energy of this universe evolves into *prana,* a form of energy that is slightly grosser than pure Consciousness and that links the relatively thick and solid physical universe with its subtle essence. In the human body, *prana* forms the bridge between body, mind, and spirit. *Prana* connects all the systems in the body and powers the nervous system, the internal organs, and the muscles. Like a river, it carries impulses from the mind into the muscles and causes movement. It keeps the mind moving out through the senses, bringing in impressions and forming thoughts. When we breathe, we take in *prana* from the atmosphere, and in meditation, we can work with *prana* directly by working with the breath. When the *prana* slows down (a state that yogis try to induce through practicing *pranayama,* or breath control), the mind quiets down in response. That is why following the breath in meditation is so helpful in quieting the mind.

The *pranamaya kosha* interpenetrates the physical body, running through a lacework of subtle channels *(nadis)* that carry energy to all the limbs and organs, giving them power and life. Until *kundalini* is awakened, we are only subliminally aware of the *pranamaya kosha.* We know when we feel energetic or low in vitality, but only occasionally do we become conscious of the way energy flows in the body. Once *kundalini* awakens, its greater force begins to move with the *prana* in the body, and we begin to feel the sensations of that *prana.*

PRANIC KRIYAS: EXPERIENCES OF THE PRANA

The subtle "touch" of the *shakti,* the kinesthetic sensation of inner movement that we looked at in chapter 8, is actually a manifestation of *kundalini*-activated *prana.* Sometimes you experience subtle tingling sensations. At other times, there

Student, tell me, what is God?
He is the breath within the breath.

KABIR

169

is a light sensation of expansion: your field of awareness seems to expand outward to twice or three times its normal size. On the other hand, the *prana* may feel heavy and thick. People say, "I feel as if I'm being knocked out," or "It feels as if I'm sinking underwater," or "It's like I'm being pulled into deep sleep." The heavy-headed feeling, the sense of dancing energy under your skin, tingling feelings in your arms and legs, a sense of superabundant energy, feelings of pressure in the heart or in the forehead—all these are pranic manifestations.

More dramatically, the *prana* can shift our breathing processes in meditation. Sometimes in meditation, the breath becomes very slow or seems to stop altogether. It only *seems* to stop, of course, because as long as we are alive, the breath never really stops. It is just that in yogic states the breath doesn't come in and out of the nostrils, but actually moves within the *sushumna nadi,* the subtle channel at the very center of the body. Ordinarily, the breath moves in and out of the body through two subtle channels, the *ida* and *pingala,* that run alongside of the *sushumna.* When the *prana* moves through these two channels, the mind tends to be outgoing and active. When the *prana* moves into the *sushumna,* it means that the vital force is turning inward. This is an important yogic event because when the breath becomes still, the mind quiets down as well, and one can go into *samadhi.* The first few times this happens, it can feel frightening and unfamiliar. You might be afraid that you won't be able to get another breath. Sometimes you panic, try to take a breath, and succeed in bringing yourself out of meditation.

There is nothing to be afraid of. When your breath slows down or seems to stop, you are actually being sustained from a deeper level of your being by the *prana shakti* itself. You can trust that when the spontaneous process of meditation comes to an end, the breath will begin to move in and out of your nostrils again. The best thing is to let the process happen and to observe how it affects your inner state. Notice how the thoughts become still when the breath is still. Notice how your energy begins automatically to turn inside.

Another classical effect of *kundalini* is spontaneous *bhastrika pranayama*, or bellows breathing—a quick, rhythmic in-and-out movement of the breath, almost like panting, that is accompanied by contraction and release of the abdominal muscles. Again, if this happens, notice the effect on your mind. In traditional *hatha yoga* practice, bellows breathing is a process that is often performed deliberately to activate *kundalini*. When it happens spontaneously, it helps *kundalini* rise in the body, quiets thoughts, and can be the precursor to deeper meditation.

Often as meditation deepens, the *prana* seems to become finer and more expanded. Though the breath may still be moving slowly in and out of the nostrils, we also begin to feel the "inner breath," the gentle rise and fall of energy inside the *sushumna nadi*. As we follow the currents of the *prana*, we find ourselves settling more deeply inside. In this way, the *prana* is creating a bridge between our ordinary waking awareness and the subtler realms. The sensations of *prana* are threads that connect us to the *shakti*. *Prana* is the vehicle we ride as the awakened *shakti* leads us gently through the layers of our subtle being.

MORE ABOUT VISIONS

Meditating in the subtle body often feels like a kind of dream state. Vagrant images pass before our inner eye—a scene, a color, a face, a scrap of landscape, a scene from a movie, or one we have never seen before. Sometimes these images play out as little scenarios, just as they do in dreams. In fact, this is exactly what they are: as we pass through the different stages of meditation in the subtle body, often

During the period of yoga sadhana, one sees mist, smoke, fire, air, fireflies, lightning, crystal, and forms like the moon and the sun in the inner spaces. All these visions precede the light of God.

SHVETASHVATARA
UPANISHAD

we actually enter into the dream state and experience our own inner image bank.

Most of the experiences that arise in this dreamlike state of meditating in the subtle body should be looked on as passing phenomena, like our thoughts. Our subtle body is as filled with stored images as it is filled with thoughts and feelings, and as we move deeper, we literally pass through inner fields of imagery, just as we pass through fields of thoughts.

However, just as dreams sometimes have significance, so at times do the images that arise in meditation. Their importance may be psychological rather than spiritual—that is, they may pertain to issues of our personal histories and psychological growth processes, to work we are doing, or to professional challenges that currently face us. All kinds of learning come to us in meditation, and the messages from our personal unconscious, even though they should not be confused with the transpersonal images that arise from the higher levels of our being, can sometimes be as valuable, in their own sphere.

Here is an example: Several years ago, a young lawyer was meditating before going to court to argue a patent case. In his meditation, the words surfaced: "article 509." Being a longtime meditator, he took this inner message seriously enough to check it out. Before going to court, he stopped in the courthouse library and looked up article 509 in a book on patent law. That day in court, his opponent raised a point that had been addressed by the article, and the lawyer was able to cite article 509 in refuting it. The judge was understandably impressed by his careful preparation, and the lawyer has always felt that his knowledge of article 509 was the thing that turned the judge's decision in his favor.

Another example: In a meditation group, we were doing an exercise that involved dissolving thoughts into Consciousness. One man was surprised when, as his thoughts melted, they were replaced by an image of demons coming up out of a well. He sensed the presence of a higher being near him and asked that being to defend him from the demons. When he contemplated the image, he realized that the demons were deeply buried feelings that were beginning to emerge as his meditation went deeper. Because he was afraid of these feelings, he demonized them. He also saw that he had divine protection within him and that he tended to expect that higher power to protect him by "killing" his negative feelings. Contemplating the image later, he realized that he could take a different attitude toward his "demons"—he could see them as aspects of consciousness rather than trying to kill them. This led to a far more loving and permission-giving attitude toward his inner world.

One reason why it is so important to write down our experiences each time we sit for meditation is precisely because even the apparently silly or nonspiritual images that come up can be important for us. On the other hand, we also need to realize that even when these images are worth contemplating, we should not act on them without a great deal of thought. Until the mind has been fully purified, messages from the inner world are often unreliable or misleading. As a friend of mine says, they are "one hundred percent accurate, fifty percent of the time."

THE TANDRA STATE

Sometimes, however, the images that appear in meditation are of a very different quality. The colors are brighter, and the light is different. The content of the images has a "true" flavor that distinguishes them from the random series of images that ordinarily run across the inner screen when we are journeying through the subtle body.

Swami Muktananda, mapping the territory he passed through on his inner journey, called the realm of visions *tandra loka,* or the realm of *tandra. Tandra,* he said, is an inner realm that is deeper and subtler than the dream or sleep state and is one step before the state of *turiya,* the pure experience of the Self.

He wrote that as he meditated each day:

> Sometimes a very pure intoxication would come over me—what ecstasy that was!—but I did not have the strength to bear it; as I became absorbed in that intoxication, I would fall asleep.
>
> While I was sitting, I would enter *tandra loka,* the state of *tandra.* In this state I would seem to be sleeping, but it was not my ordinary sleep state, for in the sleep from which I awoke every morning, I did not have the same rapturous experiences nor did I have any visions. But the visions I saw in the sleep of *tandra* meditation were quite genuine. I would see something that was going to happen, and it would actually happen. I would see someone come, and then he would come. In *tandra* I would go to some other world and stay there for some time. Over and over again, I gave myself up to the tremendous ecstasy that arose from all this. After meditation I would spend the whole day full of joy and delight and love, and all my body's weaknesses would leave me.

Baba went on to explain that the state of *tandra* is different from ordinary sleep and dreaming:

> It is the state of omniscience. All visions that are seen in this state turn out to be true. Through my own experiences, I have become convinced that our ancient sages and seers were actually clairvoyant and all-knowing.

Our Lord opened my spiritual eye and showed me my soul in the middle of my heart, and I saw the soul as wide as if it were an infinite world, and as if it were a blessed kingdom.

JULIAN OF NORWICH

As Swami Muktananda wrote, in *tandra* the images and visions that we experience tend to be richer, more highly colored, brighter, and generally more objective. The images of the dream state usually come out of our personal unconscious, while the images of *tandra* are true visions* of inner or outer landmarks, scenes, or events. In fact, many meditators enter the *tandra* state not only when sitting for meditation, but also from the state of dreaming sleep. These are the "true" dreams—dreams that seem to come from an inner center of wisdom, from the transpersonal realm. One lovely contemporary example is Antonio Machado's poem:

> Last night, as I was sleeping,
> I dreamt—marvelous error!—
> that I had a beehive
> here inside my heart.
> And the golden bees
> were making white combs
> and sweet honey
> from my old failures.
>
> Last night, as I was sleeping,
> I dreamt—marvelous error!—
> that a fiery sun was giving
> light inside my heart.
> It was fiery because I felt
> warmth as from a hearth,

---

*A true inner vision, according to the yogic texts, is a vision that confirms or is in accord with the yogic scriptures or other texts of a recognized tradition.

In that moment, by divine
favor and the spiritual
assistance of the sheikh,
my heart was opened.
I saw that within me was
something resembling
an overturned cup;
when this object was
stood upright, a feeling
of limitless happiness
filled my being.

TEVEKKUL-BEG

and sun because it gave light
and brought tears to my eyes.

　　　　Last night, as I was sleeping,
I dreamt—marvelous error!—
that it was God I had
here inside my heart.

Gurumayi has often spoken of her own "true" dreams, in which she might become light or travel to distant universes, teach particular students, speak with her Guru, or pass through an experience that later becomes a source of wisdom. Awakened meditators of many traditions have left us accounts of such visions and dreams and of the inner lights and sounds that can appear in meditation. Experiences like this can bring insight that changes people's lives forever. Often they are harbingers of a great inner shift in perception, way stations on the path that transforms an ordinary person into an individual capable of holding the light of the truth inside her. From the prophet Mohammed's famous account of his night journey to the heavens, to Saint Teresa of Avila's inner visitation from the angel carrying a golden, fire-tipped lance that pierced her heart and sent her into ecstasy, to the visions painted by Hildegard of Bingen of blue-tinged divine beings and egg-shaped lights, we see how much power these experiences have to inspire not just the person who went through them but also those who hear or read about them.

When meditation is empowered by awakened *kundalini*, experiences like these are available on a scale that convinces us that mystical experience is a natural realm of human life. Not only saints and mystics have these experiences. So do people like you and me.

Here is how a man described an experience at a meditation program with Gurumayi:

> As I sat listening to her instructions, envisioning the white ocean she described, *kundalini* was released. I could feel a sensation at the base of my spine. It began to spiral up my back, and as it did, that area of my body was filled with *shakti.* As it rose, I became more and more aware of the *shakti.* At first I laughed, the sensation was so wonderful. As *kundalini* rose further, I began to weep. Who can contain such an experience? Soon I was filled with *shakti.* I was *shakti.* I stayed in meditation in this state, and the experience was indescribable. I soon found myself on the shore looking out over a vast white ocean. It was the whitest white you can imagine. I began to wade into the ocean until I was completely submerged. I began to experience a freedom beyond anything I've known. I was free. Free from all limitations. I was swimming and rolling in the ecstasy of the ocean.

This vision, the man said later, created a shift in his sense of self, his priorities, and his understanding about his life. Not all meditation visions have such a powerful effect. Some are merely curious or odd. Yet all of them reveal the incredible variety of the inner world.

A woman meditating in a Siddha Yoga retreat feels herself rising out of her body into the center of the universe, where she sees the form of Jesus, whom she has loved all her life.

A New York man sees in his meditation an undulating pattern of energy circling around a core. That morning he sees the same pattern on the weather channel—it is the energy pattern of a hurricane that is making its way along the Atlantic coast.

A woman in Hawaii sees a wall of blue light rising before her eyes. In it she sees two women who are making breakfast in the next room. She can see everything they are doing and later is able to confirm it.

A woman taking a Siddha Yoga meditation course was instructed to meditate on the witness. She later wrote:

> I heard the teacher of the course say, "You are the eternal witness." Each time I focused on the word *witness*, I would slip behind my thoughts to the place that was listening. I kept dropping back further, further, and further into a deep, deep silence. It was all-encompassing and infinite, so full and peaceful that the thought arose, "If I can be here, why act?"
>
> As if in answer, I had a vision. First, there was the infinite space of the night sky—full yet empty, full of energy yet formless. Then, from this endless space, many hands were reaching down to the earth. The hands were performing an infinite variety of actions. Sometimes the hands were alone, sometimes together. Sometimes they would become entangled and fight with each other.
>
> As the image unfolded before me, these words arose: "No matter what actions you do, they all arise from the same place, they arise from the Infinite."

DIVINE MOODS: THE RASAS, OR FLAVORS, OF THE INNER WORLD

Most of our meditation experience is in the realm of subtle feelings. Harder to categorize and describe than visions, yet often even more fulfilling and transforming,

The soul is not in the universe; on the contrary, the universe is in the Soul.

PLOTINUS

they are the spontaneous moods *(bhavas)* and flavors *(rasas)* of the inner world. Some people's entire meditation experience is in the realm of mood and feeling. "After I've been meditating for about twenty minutes, this tremendous feeling of peace comes over me," a man told me. "It's my baseline experience. Occasionally I'll see a vision or something. But I treasure that feeling of peace because I can take it with me when I leave meditation." A woman related to me that she will often experience a transformation of one feeling state into another while she is sitting. An initial feeling of depression or anxiety will begin to break up into shimmering particles of light that seem to float away from her, leaving her in a state of serenity. Other people have described how at certain moments they will feel a spontaneous sense of surrender to God or trust in the benevolence of the universe, knowing, "Everything is all right. I'm taken care of. I'm loved." Or they might fall into a sense of unity-awareness—a realization that the world around them is a part of them or that they are fully connected to every being in the world. Insights might arise: "All that matters is love" or "I can forgive" or "This is how to deal with the situation." Often the content of the insight is neither new nor startling, but it comes with a certainty and an energy that give it transformative power. As Gurumayi once said, "You are *in* the knowing."

Looking back over our meditation experience, we often realize that insights like these have had a powerful long-range impact on our lives. That is because the deeper insights that arise in meditation actually come from the realm of pure Consciousness, the realm of the Self. The way of the Self is to teach us from within. Once we see in meditation that the source of love is within us, we are no longer quite so liable to get caught in emotional dependency. Once we realize that by inwardly blessing an enemy we can melt our own anger and resentment, we no longer feel like such victims of our feelings. Meditation insights can change our lives.

The realm of the subtle body is huge and contains an almost endless storehouse of experiences. It is a vast universe in itself; in fact, the texts of yoga assert that everything that can be seen in the outer universe can be found within the subtle body of a human being. Many of us linger for years in the different corners of the subtle realm. And yet, there are other meditators who seem to bypass it altogether and move straight to the next level of experience, the state called the causal body, or the state of the void.

THE CAUSAL BODY: MEDITATION OR SLEEP?

Sometimes in meditation, we seem to lose consciousness altogether. Describing the experience afterward, we can only say, "I closed my eyes, and the next thing I knew, the alarm was ringing," or "I don't know where I went," or "I just went so deep inside that I didn't know anything; I wasn't even conscious." If we try to remember how it felt to be in that state, we recall nothing but a feeling of rest, of peace, of ease. We sense that we could have stayed there for hours, perhaps with the head dropping forward onto the chest or backward against the wall and the breath calm and even. It is like being asleep, but we aren't exactly asleep. Perhaps we see a velvety blackness. Or perhaps we see nothing. But it feels good.

At the same time, it can be disconcerting to spend so much time in meditation in a kind of void. We wonder whether this is really meditation—especially if we find ourselves immersed in this void state day after day for months or years.

It *is* meditation. It is meditation in the causal body, the *karana sharira.*

This is a layer of our being composed entirely of darkness—but a deeply contented darkness. We ordinarily inhabit the causal body only when we are deeply asleep, in the state of dreamless rest. One fascinating hallmark of the causal body experience is that it is a place of great bliss.

The causal body is close to the Self. That is why meditating there can bring us such contentment. Often when we have been meditating in that state of profound blackness, we come out feeling refreshed, happy, and rejuvenated. That is the gift of the causal body. But it is not the final state. The causal body is unconscious, while the state of the Self is a state of super-consciousness, super-awareness.

The causal body got its name for two reasons. First, it is the part of our subtle system that lodges the collection of impressions, tendencies, desires, beliefs, and concepts about reality that actually cause our lives to unfold as they do. Second, the causal body is home to the primordial darkness of *maya*, the veiling power that keeps us from seeing our essential unity and light. *Maya* is also a powerful energy, the force that gives rise to our experience of limited existence. *Maya* causes us to experience ourselves as individuals, and it causes us to experience the world as an object outside ourselves. So *maya* is the "cause" of our existence as individuals. This makes the causal body a very powerful place.

Only when the veil of *maya* lifts can we experience the world and ourselves as they really are: pure light, Awareness, and bliss. To reach the state beyond *maya*—the numinous realm of super-consciousness—we must journey through *maya's* darkness. This is not just a symbolic journey. The causal body literally is a "body" of darkness—the darkness of the deep sea of the collective unconscious often described in Jungian psychology, the darkness of the void from which all form manifests, the darkness of deep sleep.

*Darkness within darkness.
The gateway to all
understanding.*

LAO-TZU

At a certain point, we might experience this body of darkness as a velvety black light, the light of the void, and if we meditate on this light, it will take us very deep. Even when we find ourselves in the causal body in a relatively unconscious state, something very significant and necessary is happening.

Here is why we need to experience meditation in the causal body. As we know, one of the main functions of awakened *kundalini* is to clear the accumulated karmas, past impressions, deeply lodged memories, and embedded fears that lurk in every part of our subtle system, but especially in the causal body. Most of us have been around for a long time, and we've been through a lot. In some ways, we are a bit like that pair of boots you bought ten years ago and have been wearing every winter since then. You get them patched and retreaded because you like them and they're comfortable. But they are pretty beat up. They have nicks, scratches, tears, worn places on the toes, and worn patches in the lining. We are the same way. We have been retreaded and recycled many times, and although we are holding up, there's been a lot of wear and tear.

The time of meditation is the time we give *kundalini* to melt, sweep, dust, chisel, and scrub away not only the tensions in the physical body but also all the subtle causes for these tensions: the accumulated layers of old forgotten thoughts, opinions, and feelings that we have acquired over years and even lifetimes. Just to give you an idea of how much cleaning there is to do, think about all the opinions you have had in your life. Remember how you used to think that getting onto the soccer team was the most important thing in the world, or that people who practiced other religions besides your own were somehow deluded, or that a particular political position was worth fighting over? Remember the person you were in love with at fifteen, and how that person looked when you saw them ten years later? All this is lodged in your subtle system, along with every song you ever listened to and all the insensitive things you ever said to the people who loved you, not to mention the things they said to you. All your good and bad ideas are there. Your dreams. Your hopes. The shame you felt when you were caught stealing candy from the luncheonette at age four. The pain in your throat after you had your tonsils out. Your sympathy for the kid everybody picked on, and the exhilaration of riding your bike downhill, and the grinding feeling in your heart when your marriage was breaking up.

Kundalini will root out every last one of those old memories and send them out of your system if you encourage it to do so by sitting for meditation every day. That doesn't mean you will become a mindless idiot. You will still be able to remember the names of your children and what you ate for breakfast Saturday morning. In fact, your memory will be even sharper. What will be gone is the charge in those memories. The emotional baggage attached to those things. Their power to hurl you off the emotional cliff. Actually you probably wouldn't mind so much if some of the memories themselves got cleaned out, too. Who wants to remember the mean things you and your best friend said to Louise Frankovitch when you were in junior high school? Some things are best eliminated entirely.

All these memories and impressions, or *samskaras*, are lodged in different parts of your subtle and physical system. But the bulk of them are in the causal body. That is where the really deep layers reside, the *vasanas*, or tendencies, that rule you from within. I once dreamed that I was living in a huge mansion. In the cellar lived a man who never came upstairs. He was the one who ran the place. He made all the decisions, took care of the maintenance, and subtly imposed his will

Everything depends on this: a fathomless sinking into a fathomless nothingness.

JOHANNES TAULER

on everyone in the house. This is exactly what these buried *samskaras* do. They rule us from inside, and because they are so familiar to us, we befriend them.

When we meditate and allow *kundalini* to work inside the causal body, it roots out the influence of our undercover tyrants.

So this is why at times in our meditation practice it is important to let ourselves go into that state of deep rest, that state where we are "out," lost in a realm that feels much like sleep. At such times, we are entering the sleep state consciously, as meditators. Years ago a friend of mine habitually used to fall into a deep, unconscious state. Eventually he decided to take steps to stay awake, so one morning before meditation, he drank a cup of coffee, and, sure enough, he stayed "conscious" throughout his meditation. Just at the end of the hour, he saw Gurumayi's figure, which seemed to be sweeping out his heart. She looked up and spoke to him. "What are you doing awake?" she asked. "This is my time to do my work. That's why I always knock you out." Reassured, he went back to his usual pattern. Some time later, his meditations moved out of the causal level, and he began having a more conscious meditation. However, since the journey of meditation is not necessarily a straight line, a seamless progression that leads us from one realm of the soul to the next, but more of a one-step-forward two-steps-back zigzag, we may find ourselves revisiting this deep and apparently unconscious state again and again through the years.

THE SUPRACAUSAL BODY AND THE EXPERIENCE OF THE SELF

When all is said and done, however dramatic or quiet our meditation, we must finally come back to the seer, the pure "I" that is the goal of our practice. In any given meditation session, we might pass through all three of the bodies we have just described. When we first sit down, we usually spend some time settling the posture, breathing into tension, perhaps observing the movements of the *kriya shakti* as it shakes the head or sways the torso. After a while, as we follow the *shakti* to a deeper, subtler state, we might find ourselves witnessing the dream-like images of subtle-body meditation or moving through the currents of energy. A profound vision may burst upon us—a sudden glimpse of light or an insight. And we may spend some time in the velvet darkness of the causal body, completely unaware of where we are until we emerge.

Yet in any of these states, and at any moment, there is always the possibility that the pure I-awareness, the ever-present experience of the Self, might emerge. It can happen in many ways. We might find ourselves lifted into a clear field of Awareness, the thoughts left behind or chattering faintly somewhere beneath or below the expansive, peaceful sky where we are sitting. Perhaps the thoughts dissolve into a well of deep contentment. Perhaps our feelings of being a small personal self disappear into a larger, expansive sense of being. We might be engaged in some act of remembrance—asking ourselves "Where is my Self in all this?" or "Who is the *real* I?"—and gradually becoming more and more aware of a witnessing presence, surrounding and containing the body-personality-self or poised above our head, slightly behind and to the left, watching without commentary, simply *there*. When the pure "I," the great Awareness, shows its subtle face, all we have to do is be in it. Merge into it. Allow ourselves to become it.

The texts of Vedanta call the state of being in or with our supreme conscious Self *turiya*, meaning "the fourth"—that is, the state that is beyond waking, dream, and deep sleep. Jnaneshwar Maharaj, the Siddha poet, described it as "the eye of your eye, where the void comes to an end." It is the farthest shore of human experience, the place where the human and particular recognizes itself as spacious, impersonal, and divine. And though the full experience of this state is an experience of limitlessness and formlessness, the sages of the Siddha tradition have told us that this boundless state also has a "body," or a form. To experience this fourth body is one of the most sublime and secret realizations a meditator can have.

Jnaneshwar described how this transcendental body can actually be seen as a sesame-seed-sized blue light, darting quickly in and out of a meditator's field of vision and sometimes even appearing when he is not meditating. Swami Muktananda called this light Neeleshvari, the blue goddess, or Neelabindu, the blue point or Blue Pearl. Following in the footsteps of Jnaneshwar, he described the Blue Pearl as the "body of the Self":

> The Lord of the universe . . . has made His dwelling place in a house as small as a sesame seed. Just as a huge spreading tree grows from a tiny seed, the nourisher of all, who manifests Himself in an infinity of forms, shapes, and sizes, has a tiny seed for a house. . . .
>
> The *bindu*, which is as small as a sesame seed, is the house of the Self. God is inside it—God who is the perfect form of the Self. If you have a vision of the *bindu*, then you should understand that within it lies your Self.

Swami Muktananda's explanation of the *bindu* follows the understanding of the Shaiva and Shakta Tantras. When these texts describe the process by which the material universe manifests within the great field of being/Awareness that is its source, they speak of a moment when the entire creative energy of the

Gaze intently into the blazing heart of joy and you will perceive my blissful Mother, matrix of all phenomena... burning down conventional barriers, pervading minds and worlds with light, revealing her exalted beauty... where lovers merge with Mother Reality, experiencing the single taste of nonduality.

RAMPRASAD

universe, the power behind manifestation, gathers itself into a tiny point, a *bindu*. Out of this point of intensely concentrated energy, the universe eventually springs forth. (You may notice that this view of creation has a certain correspondence to the Big Bang theory of physics.) When we have a vision of the Blue Pearl, we are seeing this point of primal, intensely concentrated energy. Since the sages who wrote these texts based their metaphysics on their own mystical visions, we can assume that they themselves must have seen this *bindu*, this tiny point of energy. In fact, the image of a blue orb of immense power can be found scattered throughout spiritual literature. Hildegard of Bingen painted the blue point. Perhaps Jesus was referring to it when he spoke of the mustard seed. The sages of the Kashmir Shaivism tradition and the householder-saints of Maharashtra mentioned it in their poetry.

Swami Muktananda wrote and spoke extensively on the blue point, which meditators in his lineage quite often see in and out of meditation. He also described, as have other meditators before him, visions of the personal form of God, whom he, like Hildegard, saw as a being made entirely of blue radiance. Based on this vision, he never doubted that the ultimate reality can appear in a form; when people insisted that the divine is only formless, he used to say, "If supreme Consciousness can manifest this universe, why wouldn't it be able to manifest itself in a particular form?"

Yet he also made it clear that the blue point is the *body* of that formless reality, not its essence, and that to experience the goal of meditation, one must, as he said, "enter" that body, thus entering into the state beyond all forms.

"The experience of God is something that is not seen, that doesn't move; it is just there," he once said. "That state is free from all forms. Before you reach that state, many things will take place. You will hear *nada,* the divine sound; you will see many lights. Nonetheless, your goal is to reach that center, that space. Even if you have these experiences, it is not enough until you reach that space."

That space is pure Consciousness, pure knowingness, pure being—the state of immersion in the seer, the Self. To enter that state is also called *samadhi,* the state of complete absorption, or s*amavesha,* the state of merging into your own Consciousness. Of course, there are several levels of experience of *samadhi.* In the first level, called *savikalpa samadhi,* or absorption in a form, one has a sense of merging with an object, however subtle—becoming completely absorbed in a mantra, or becoming one with a light, or merging into a subtle feeling of bliss. In this *savikalpa* state, thoughts can remain. But in the deeper state called *nirvikalpa samadhi* (absorption in the formless), there are no thoughts, only complete stillness—an experience of emptiness that is at the same time utterly full and blissful. "*Nirvikalpa* is *chit*—effortless, formless Consciousness," wrote Ramana Maharshi. He continued:

> To some people whose minds have become ripe from a long practice in the past, *nirvikalpa* comes suddenly as a flood, but to others it comes in the course of their spiritual practice, a practice which slowly wears down the obstructing thoughts and reveals the screen of pure Awareness, "I"—"I." Further practice renders the screen permanently exposed. This is Self-realization, *mukti.* . . .
>
> *Samadhi* alone can reveal the truth. Thoughts cast a veil over reality, and so it is not realized as such in states other than *samadhi.* In *samadhi* there is only the feeling "I am" and no thoughts. The experience of "I am" is "being still."

Swami Muktananda wrote in *Play of Consciousness:*

> As my mind became stabilized in the Blue Pearl, Witness-consciousness would come to me. This kind of meditation can be called *samadhi.* In it one remains fully conscious. The movement of the breath becomes very soft and slow, but it does not cease as in full *kumbhaka.* This is the *samadhi* of the Siddha path, where Witness-consciousness remains fully active. It is not an unknowing, blank *samadhi* where there is no awareness. The realm of Consciousness is that of knowledge, so Witness-consciousness should therefore be present in true *samadhi.*

There is a paradox about this state, perhaps the greatest paradox of human life. The transcendental state, the seat of the soul, the place of the Self, is both *beyond* our normal consciousness and *within* it. On the one hand, it transcends time and space. It is untouched by thoughts, by the feelings and ambitions and confusions and limitations of vision that we experience in the waking state. The evanescent images of the dream state don't touch it, and it is unaffected by the causal darkness of the void. It is a state of total Awareness—Awareness so subtle and so fine that it reduces all matter to its essence and reveals a universe made of radiance. It is, in short, an utterly "extra-ordinary" state.

At the same time, the supracausal body, the transcendental state, is totally and constantly accessible because it pervades every experience and every state of human experience. That is because it is nothing other than our own awareness. It is the Consciousness—the light of Awareness—that illumines our experience and that also turns back into itself and reflects on experience. It is the ever-present witness of all our thoughts and feelings—and even of our state

Eye cannot see it, ear cannot hear it nor tongue utter it; only in deep absorption can the mind, grown pure and silent, merge with the formless truth. He who finds it is free; he has found himself; he has solved the great riddle; his heart forever is at peace. Whole, he enters the Whole.

MUNDAKA UPANISHAD

189

of deep sleep. As Gurumayi wrote: "The *turiya* state is the throb of primordial Consciousness, in which there is the steady awareness 'I am That, I am That.' This is why whenever your mind is free from thoughts, even for a few seconds, you should cherish it, because you are experiencing the transcendental state."

What this means, as we have seen earlier, is that we can experience the supracausal state at any time. We don't have to be in meditation. I know a woman who regularly "wakes up" at night to find herself in a state of total blackness, without thought or sensation. The experience of being "awake" in deep sleep is an experience of the ever-present witness.

Many of us have our first glimpse of our true reality in a flash and in the waking state, as if the fabric of reality turned inside out to reveal itself as a unity. A friend of mine called it "supermarket *samadhi*" because she first experienced it in Ralph's Market in Petaluma, California, when the breakfast cereal packages on aisle 10 began without warning to glow with light, revealing that a single intelligence, sparkling with love, was somehow awake within the stacks of dry goods, the shopping carts, the fluorescent lights, and her sleepy daughter nodding in her stroller. In a commentary on one of the *Shiva Sutras, Udyamo bhairavah*, "The divine flashes forth," Kshemaraja described how the divine Consciousness, the highest state of intuition, the witness, can suddenly emerge as if out of hiding, flashing forth and taking over our awareness. In meditation we experience this in the moments when the underlying Awareness, the self-knowing knower, the clear spaciousness called witness-consciousness, suddenly swallows up our ordinary consciousness. "My mind melted like a hailstone into the ocean of the supreme Absolute," wrote Shankaracharya in a famous passage in *Viveka Chudamani*. A contemporary meditator described how in meditation he'll be lifted up from his mind until he seems to be sitting above himself, poised in a wide, calm awareness, observing the ordinary mind chattering away as if at a great distance, very small and faint.

So the transcendental state, the state of the Self, enters our meditation in many ways, and it can enter our meditation at any time.

It can come as a feeling of deep bliss or love. Gurumayi wrote:

> Drinking this love, sometimes I drown,
>   sometimes I soar.
> Yet there is no touching bottom
>   nor reaching the top.

We can experience it as a field of light. A longtime meditator, asked to describe her experiences, said, "When I sit for meditation, I feel myself going into a peaceful, quiet space. After a while, that space becomes infused with blue light, a wide field of light. Then within that field, different manifestations occur. Sometimes I'll see a burst of white radiance so bright that it blinds me. It's like looking at the sun, only brighter."

Teresa of Avila wrote of these inner lights:

> The light that is now revealed is so different from any earthly light
> that, by comparison with it, the brightness of our sun seems quite
> dim and we never even want to open our eyes again to look at it.
> It is as if we were to look at a very clear stream in a bed of crystal,
> reflecting the sun's rays, and then to come out and see a very muddy
> stream in a bed of earth overshadowed by clouds. The inner light
> is a natural light, and all other kinds of lights seem artificial by
> comparison. It is a light that is never followed by darkness. And
> nothing can ever disturb it. No one, no matter how powerful his

Again the light blazes for me. Again I see the light clearly. Again it opens the skies; again it drives away the night. Again it reveals everything.

SYMEON
THE NEW THEOLOGIAN

191

intellect might be, could ever, in the whole course of his life,
imagine what this inner light is like.

Sometimes simply reading an account like this can trigger an experience of the light, the Consciousness that underlies material experience. So can a practice like meditating on light, perhaps by imagining that a field of blue radiance fills your mind, or through the exercise that follows.

EXERCISE: THE LIGHT OF CONSCIOUSNESS IS BEHIND MY EXPERIENCE

Close your eyes and focus for a few moments on the breath. Silently say to yourself, "Behind my thoughts is the light of pure Consciousness. My thoughts come out of that light and merge back into that light. Behind my breath is the light of Consciousness. My breath arises and subsides in that light. The sensations in my body come out of that light of Consciousness. It is the light of Consciousness that allows me to perceive, and that light of Consciousness is in whatever I perceive, whatever I feel, whatever I hear."

As thoughts come up and as perceptions arise, be aware that they are all arising and subsiding within the ground-light of pure Consciousness, the divine source. When you open your eyes and begin to look around, have the feeling that it is the light of Consciousness that allows you to see and that appears in all that you see.

When *turiya* arises for me, it often comes as a gradual melting of boundaries between inside and outside until I am experiencing everything, within and without, as a part of my own consciousness. This happens most often in meditation, but occasionally I have experienced it with my eyes open. Once sitting with Swami Muktananda in a room full of people, I experienced a sudden shift of vision. Instead of seeing the room around me and sensing myself as being within the room, the entire room was within me. The sounds were happening inside me. The air itself was a pulsation inside me. Swami Muktananda was inside me, and when his hands moved, they seemed to tickle my awareness. When a woman approached to speak to him, bringing a dish of food for him to taste, I could feel her presence inside myself and taste the food. Later, I read in the *Shiva Sutras* that one of the experiences of the transcendental state is the sensation that one's body has become the universe. In our tradition, a perfectly Self-realized being is said to live in this experience all the time, whether in or out of meditation, always aware of the world around her as an emanation of her own blissful Awareness.

Sometimes intense longing or focus can catapult us into the *turiya* state. One morning in meditation, a man began to wonder what Gurumayi's inner experience felt like. As his inner questioning intensified, he heard a roaring sound, and his awareness was pulled backward until he found himself in a realm of blue light. Waves of light undulated around him. The sensation of energy increased until he felt his consciousness vibrating intensely. The roaring sound got louder. Then, abruptly, the movement of the ocean stilled. The roaring sound resolved itself into the pulsating of an awareness: *I am. I am. I am.* Out of that pulsation, waves upon waves of love coursed through him.

Like all experiences of the transcendental state, this one contained elements that we can recognize from the yogic texts and the writings of the sages. The blue

God alone reveals Himself to Himself, the knower being that which is known.

MEISTER ECKHART

*My I is God,
and I know no other
I than this my God.*

CATHERINE OF GENOA

193

ocean appears in many of the *abhangas,* or songs, of the Maharashtrian poet-saints, and Ramakrishna Paramahamsa often spoke of how he experienced Goddess Kali, the form of the divine he worshiped, as a limitless field of blue. The roaring sound was probably an experience of the *megha nada,* or thunder sound, that the texts of *laya yoga* describe as the sound that ushers us into *samadhi,* the experience of merging in the Absolute. The awareness "I am," known as the *purno'ham vimarsha,* or perfect I-consciousness, is described in the writings of the sage Abhinavagupta and others as the ultimate experience of divine subjectivity; it is the *paravastha,* or supreme state, spoken of in the *Vijnana Bhairava* and other texts.

Gurumayi writes about entering this state while meditating on her Guru:

> As I went still deeper into you,
>   form itself dissolved;
>   nothing remained but light—
>   boundless, radiant light!
> No color, no sound, no touch,
>   no smell, no taste survived.
> Beyond the grasp of the senses,
>   nothing was left to describe;
>   the sole reality
>   was the experience of God.
> Once again, an incredible thing happened—
>   as I came to, the light of God
>   condensed into your form.

In his book *Secret of the Siddhas,* Swami Muktananda described in metaphorical language the ultimate paradox of this state, where nothingness contains everything, and the absence of external experience allows the fullest experience of the inner vastness:

> When camphor begins to burn, one can see a flame. When
> both the camphor and the flame vanish, only space remains.
> When one subtracts one from one, nothing is left. In the same way,
> when one discards one's ideas about what exists and what does not
> exist, of what is present and what is not present, all
> that remains is Truth and infinite bliss. . . . In this state, even
> such words as the Absolute, the Self, and God obstruct one's
> bliss; there is not even any room to say, "Nothing exists here."
> This is the state the Siddhas have attained.

No wonder the saints have resorted to metaphor to describe this state —like Saint John of the Cross in his poem "Dark Night of the Soul" describing how, to reach the place where one experiences everything, one must go by the way of becoming nothing. Jnaneshwar Maharaj described that same state, saying:

> For a while, the Self appears as an object of perception. But when
> the seer and the seen unite, both of them vanish. Then the seen is
> the same as the seer, and the seer is merged in the seen. Both van-
> ish, and only the Reality remains.

We recognize this state by the profundity of its joy and peace, and by the immensity it encompasses. We know it because though it is beyond anything we have experienced, it has the complete familiarity of our true home.

The supracausal state is not something we climb into or attain. It reveals itself by itself, through grace. Yet as we have seen before, we can "attract" it because it is always present. When *kundalini* is awake, that state can and does

I do not know where the "I" is, nor do I seek it.... I am so plunged and submerged in the source of His infinite love, as if I were quite under water in the sea and could not touch, see, feel anything on any side except water.

CATHERINE OF GENOA

arise periodically. Many of the practices in chapter 2 help us to cross the bridge between ordinary consciousness and that *samadhi* state. Here is another one, a simple exercise that we can practice with eyes open or closed.

EXERCISE: GOD IS IN EVERYTHING

Sit in an upright, comfortable posture and close your eyes. Take a few moments to relax your body by breathing into any feeling of tightness, then breathing the tightness out.

Focus your attention on the breath, feeling the slight coolness of the breath as it comes in and the slight warmth as it leaves the nostrils.

Have the following awareness: "God, the scintillating, blissful energy that gives life to all, is in my breath. God is in my thoughts. Wherever my mind goes, God is there. God is in my physical body. God is in the air. God is in the chair I sit on. God is in the clothes I wear. God is seeing through my eyes and thinking through my mind. Wherever my thoughts turn, wherever my attention goes, God is there. That which sees is God; that which hears is God; that which I call 'I' is God." After a while, open your eyes and look around with this awareness.

Though an exercise like this may not give us a full experience of the transcendental state, it can open doors in our awareness and make us ripe for the emergence of the full experience. Even one such experience can forever change our sense of who we are—especially if we recall it, hold it in our awareness, and return to it in memory.

As we accumulate experiences of this state, we also begin to realize that there is more, that the journey of meditation doesn't culminate in the experience of indrawn *samadhi*. There are states beyond *turiya*. In the Siddha tradition and in the tradition of the Kashmiri Shaivites, true Self-realization is the state that the Siddha poets call *sahaja samadhi*, or natural *samadhi*. In the *sahaja* state, your awareness of oneness never changes. You experience the whole animate and inanimate world as divine, as full of light, and as alive with Consciousness— even those parts of it that are supposed to be insentient. And you experience it as part of yourself, a part of your own Awareness. At this point, as Ramana Maharshi says, your *samadhi* is unbroken, whether you are meditating, eating, sleeping, or walking.

The poet-saints described it best. Kabir said:

Ever immersed in bliss, having no fear
in [my] mind, [I] keep the spirit of union
in the midst of all enjoyments.
The infinite dwelling of the Infinite Being is everywhere:
in earth, water, sky, and air. . . .
He who is within is without:
I see Him and none else.

Swami Muktananda, in a passage that shimmers with enticement to meditate, described how he saw the world after the culmination of his own meditation journey:

Even now when I meditate, as soon as I am absorbed in
meditation, I see the mass of the blue rays of the Light of
Consciousness and, within that, the Blue Pearl. I see this soft,

*He who without hesitation
Views all this tangible
    world as your form,
Having filled the universe
With the form
    of his own self,
Is eternally joyful.*

UTPALADEVA

197

gleaming Consciousness pulsating so delicately and shining
in all my states. Whether I am eating or drinking or bathing,
it comes and stands before my eyes. . . . Now my vision is neither
dual nor nondual because that radiance is in both. There is no
longer any demarcation between space, time, and substance. The
blue light, subtly spreading everywhere, pervades my own being
as it does the whole universe. . . . Now I really know that my
Self pervades everywhere as the universe.

Meditation's ultimate promise is that it will reveal to us this state of
sahaja, the open-eyed experience of the world shimmering with a single flavor,
the taste of bliss. That is why, as time goes by, we realize that it isn't enough to
experience peace or joy or the taste of our own pure Awareness in meditation.
We want that state to seep out into our days, to fill our awareness even in the
midst of the comings and goings of life. In other words, we want to know, from
our own direct experience, what the sages meant when they said that the Self is
always present, that the *turiya* state, the state of *samadhi,* pervades our waking
and dream life, and even our deep sleep. So we begin to pay attention to the
first moments after meditation and to the ways we can carry that awareness
into the day.

*It is told of one master...
that when he wanted to
contemplate individual
things he had to put on
spectacles in order to
subdue his spiritual sight,
for otherwise he saw all
the individual things
of the world as one.*

MARTIN BUBER

198

CHAPTER 10

Coming Out of Meditation: Contemplation, Recollection, and Journal Writing

It is early morning. I'm sitting in a pool of stillness that opens out from the region around my heart. The longer I sit, the more it expands and the softer it becomes, until my body disappears into it and I'm resting delicately in its smooth vibrant waters. Then the alarm rings—too loudly. It jars me so much that I jump, bumping myself out of meditation, back to a consciousness of the chair and my body and the need to hit the alarm button. Clumsily, I get to my feet and walk to the window. I'm fumbling with the shade when I notice that I'm staggering, that I'm not really in my body, and that I need to go back and redo the entry because if I don't, there will be too much disjunction between meditation and the rest of my day.

A person looks,
The blossoms look back:
Plain heart seeing into
plain heart.

SUN BU-ER

It took me a long time to learn about reentry, to realize that even when we don't feel that we have gone deep, we still need to take time to come out of meditation slowly. When we do, surprising things often happen in the afterglow. One friend of mine says that if she sits for a while when her meditation session is officially done and then opens her eyes, she sees the world around her emerging out of a pinpoint, recreating itself before her eyes as if for the first time. She knows what it really means to say that everything rises and subsides within one's own Consciousness. These moments after meditation are often the time when we pluck the fruit of an hour of "work," of focusing and letting the thoughts slow down. These moments are the time when we feel the peace and taste the bliss. At the very least, they give our awareness time to fully come back to the waking state. If you sometimes feel irritable or oversensitive after deep meditation, it is usually because you haven't given yourself enough time to return to waking consciousness.

We need this time for another reason: it is in the moments after meditation that we begin the process of integration, the process of learning how to bring the stillness of the inner world into our day.

If the great question for a beginning meditator is "How do I get into it?" the question for a person who has meditated for a while is "How do I hold on to it?" Often at the end of a meditation course or workshop, someone will say to me, "I feel great when I'm meditating. But then I open my eyes, and life caves in on me, and before I know it I'm buried in activity, and it's all gone, almost as if I hadn't had the experience at all."

Most of us have our own version of this complaint. It is another of those universal meditator's frustrations: to rise out of deep meditation and enter our day only to watch the peace and stillness of meditation disappear into our daily mind.

Of course, all experiences, whether they are sweet or painful, exalting or depressing, come and go. Part of what we learn through meditation is to allow one state to give way to the next. We have all known people who tried to stay in meditation all day long. They can usually be recognized by their slightly glazed eyes, their air of being not quite focused on the gritty reality of dishes and parking spaces and stop signs, by their tendency to forget where they are, and by the way they do everything very slowly and take a long time to answer simple questions. I vividly remember my own space-cadet or bliss-bunny phase in the mid-1970s, when I once drove a friend's van thirty blocks before realizing that the emergency brake was still on because I was trying to stay in meditation while on my way to the grocery store.

So there is bound to be a difference between our states of meditation and our states of ordinary waking consciousness. In fact, we can trust that even when we forget what happened in our meditation, the inner process that began during that indrawn hour is still alive in us, still working its alchemy in our consciousness. In *kundalini*-inspired *sadhana,* inner work goes on constantly beneath the surface of awareness. The inner intelligence, our own Consciousness, naturally integrates our meditation experiences, weaving them into the fabric of our waking state without our even realizing that it is happening.

At the same time, one unmistakable sign of spiritual maturity is the ability to live from the fulcrum of that inner state—to hold the clear spaciousness of Awareness like a pool of rejuvenating nectar that we can dip into at will. In fact, if our meditation practice is to be more than an escape, a kind of inner calisthenics, or something we do to soothe ourselves, we will eventually need to discover how to maintain our Self-awareness through the day. That is how we

A great yogin is still full of
the samadhi state even
when he is in normal
consciousness, because
even then he beholds the
entire mass of things to
be dissolving in the sky of
Consciousness like a bit
of cloud in autumn.

KSHEMARAJA

practice for living in a state of wakefulness. One difference between an enlightened being and a person on the path is that the enlightened being has learned to
hold on to his inner experience and make it a part of the fabric of daily life.
The skill of merging our inner with our outer worlds is one of the great arts of
spiritual life.

How do we do this? The first step is to get into the habit of consciously recollecting and contemplating our meditation experiences with the
help of a journal. The second step is to learn how to return to our meditation
experiences by bringing them into future meditations, even dwelling on them
between meditations.

COMING OUT OF MEDITATION

Gurumayi once said that in *sadhana* we try to relive the ecstasy in each moment.
She spoke of how we can pause, gather up the particles of ecstasy, and move on.
Here is how you might begin to gather up the particles of your own ecstasy, your
own stillness, at the end of meditation.

Before you sit, set your timer (if you use one) so that it goes off ten minutes before you know you have to get up from meditation. When it rings, sit quietly for a few minutes or slide gently into what *hatha yogis* call *shavasana*, the
corpse pose: flat on your back with your arms near your sides. This is a good
time to begin recollecting your experience.

First become conscious of how you feel at this moment. Notice your
state. How does your heart feel? What are the sensations in your mind? How is
your energy? Is your body relaxed? Energized? Sleepy? Take an inner photograph
of all this. Then go back over your meditation. Recall its quality, its moods, and

its texture, noting any unusual occurrences or simply noting the sequence of your inner experience.

Then embrace your postmeditation state with your awareness. Have the feeling that you are holding it in awareness. As you slowly let yourself ease back into your ordinary state, try to keep a part of your awareness touching the felt sense of meditation.

At first you may not be able to hold this awareness for more than a few minutes. Through practice, though, you will find that even after you have fully entered waking consciousness, you can feel the presence of your meditative awareness for longer and longer periods. The inner photograph of the meditation state stays with you. Each time you take that photograph anew, you strengthen the impression of it. As you recollect the experience again and again, you eventually learn how to reenter it by remembering it.

RECORDING YOUR EXPERIENCES

The best time to write in your meditation journal is in those first moments after coming out of meditation. If you write as soon as you open your eyes or after you have taken a few minutes to recall and hold your experience, you will still be in touch with the state of meditation, and the feeling of that state will come out onto the paper. Meditation experiences are quite often so subtle that if you don't capture them in written form, they will disappear almost before you open your eyes. Yet these subtle realizations can be life-transforming if we can hold on to them. When we reread our journals months or years later, we realize that the experiences we have recorded are treasures that we can return to again and again.

*Let the Truth flash forth
and then hold on to it and
contemplate it. In this way,
instead of living in your
mental projections, you
will learn to live in the
experiences of the Truth.*

GURUMAYI
CHIDVILASANANDA

The challenge in recording these experiences lies in finding the language to capture their subtlety on the page. When you meditate, you are in the realm of the mystical, and that means you are moving in an arena where language does not reach. This may be one reason why so many of the available descriptions of spiritual experience are descriptions of visions, voices, or other concrete manifestations of the inner world. It is a lot easier to describe the glowing star that appeared to your inner eye than it is to describe the sense of an all-encompassing, loving presence or the feeling that you are pushing through veils in your awareness, moving from a thick, rather gross, and contracted state into a state that feels light and clear. Sometimes there are no words to describe these energy shifts and subtle sensations. If you want to avoid falling back on the old standbys like "sweetness," "inner nectar," "deep peace," "bliss"—words that have become tired from overuse—you will need to search for new ways to capture your inner experience.

The effort we make to find words for the spiritual world is profoundly worthwhile because it actually fixes our experiences in the mind. It is simply a fact of human life that what we put into words becomes real to us in a way that the unarticulated often does not. It doesn't matter whether your words are beautiful or even whether they have meaning for anyone but you. You aren't writing for anyone else.

Besides writing down what happened in meditation, I also like to remember and record the process by which I got there. Was I repeating a mantra? Watching the breath? Do I think the technique propelled me toward a shift? Or was it a *coup de foudre,* a pure act of grace? Maybe I think nothing happened. But what did that "nothing" feel like? Was there a moment or two of separation from the thoughts, a little space that opened up between them? Did I feel the energy change? Did an insight come up or a feeling of comfort? Or did I become hyperaware of some lingering anxiety or problem? Was there a moment when my awareness seemed to become sharper, brighter? All these things are worth recording.

Here is a typical entry from my meditation journal:

A swelling love in the heart, and the mantra began to repeat
itself from out of the feeling of love. *Om Namah Shivaya* as if love
were repeating it. Each syllable pregnant with a soft pulsation of
shakti—sweet energy in the heart. A sense: This energy is me. . . .
I offered mental flowers to the *shakti* in my heart, then waved a
light. Offered imaginary gold coins. Worship your Self. Is this
what it means, to worship the energy pulsating in the heart?

When I reread this passage a year later, during a day when meditation hadn't been so sweet, it took me back to the devotional feelings of that other time. The words reminded me of my connection with the divinity inside me—and that it is always there even when I don't happen to be feeling it.

Another meditator wrote his insight in the form of a poem:

Become embodied now!
On the inbreath, the All.
On the outbreath, love.

In this meditation, he realized that only by being "in" the body could he experience the feeling of love. The practice of breathing in the universe and breathing out love had arisen naturally as a result of his insight.

WORKING WITH EXPERIENCES

Once we write down our experience, we have the material not only for contemplation but for going even deeper into the experience itself. Looking at the experiences above, it is clear that though they were very subtle, there was much to contemplate in them: realizations arose in them that created one more tiny shift in the sense of self. Each time you realize something more about your true subtlety—say, that you are actually energy, or that the energy you experience in an enlivened mantra is the real you, or that you are being breathed by a greater force (rather than being the one who breathes)—you let go of another atom of attachment to the limited self. Each tiny realization or insight arising in meditation creates a new pattern in your consciousness that you are free to revisit at any time. The memory is there, and it is a memory of freedom. You will deepen the new pattern each time you return to it. In fact, the experience of one meditation can become a focus for practice in your next meditation.

FOLLOWING THE PATHWAYS

This was how the sages discovered the classical techniques of meditation. As they sat in meditation, a vision or realization would arise spontaneously and lead them to a deeper state. Later they would retrace their steps along that same meditation pathway, except that this time they would do it deliberately.

It is very powerful to use your own experiences as techniques for practice. Suppose you are filled with the intimation of a divine presence during one meditation. In a subsequent meditation, you could invoke that remembered presence, let yourself be with it, rest in it. You could perform inner worship to it, offering flowers into the sensation of the presence or inwardly offering salutations or prayers.

Or suppose you have the experience that "I am being breathed by a greater force." In another meditation, you could recover that insight and practice it. As you train your awareness on your own breath, recall the sensation of being breathed. Feel for the presence of the greater force that brings the breath in and out. To do this, it is enough simply to remember the existence of that larger presence and then attune yourself to it. Be in it. Explore it. Open into it. A meditator who one day had the insight that she was being breathed later sat for meditation and held the awareness: "The whole force of this universe moves through my every breath." I have practiced for years with the *dharana* "God is breathing me," which came out of an actual experience I had in meditation.

Each meditation experience suggests new avenues for meditation. When you feel dull, in need of inspiration, or simply adventurous, it is there in your journal for you to explore.

Eventually you will begin to notice that your practice of staying in touch with meditation insight is affecting your experience in the waking state. The impressions of unity and love will become more firmly fixed in your awareness. They will start to be there for you when you need them, rising up as natural antidotes to feelings of anger or sadness. That is when you will begin to see real transformations inside yourself, real changes in your way of seeing. In fact, that is when many meditators begin to realize that the skills they have learned in meditation are transferable. In other words, you begin applying what you learn in sitting meditation to daily life.

Learn to listen to the voice within yourself. Your body and mind will become one, and you will realize the unity of all things.

DOGEN ZENJI

CHAPTER 11

The Daily Life of a Meditator: Holding Inner Attention

Meditation practice, most of us discover sooner or later, is not just what happens when you are sitting on the mat. Eventually it radiates outward until your whole life becomes an ongoing training in living from the center. As the intrinsic alchemy of meditation works its subtle changes in your consciousness and character, it simultaneously challenges you to take action on what you are becoming—to bring your meditative skills, insights, and experiences into the rest of your life. The strength of your practice is tested in every single moment and interaction. Are you, in Gurumayi's words, bringing the bliss of meditation into your actions? Are you able to stay in touch with Awareness when you are working,

While you live, practice meditation. Do not meditate only hidden in a dark corner, but meditate always, standing, sitting, moving, and resting. When your meditation continues throughout waking and sleeping, wherever you are is heaven itself.

HAKUIN

when you are moving house, or when someone you love disappoints you? Are you speaking and moving from that deeper level of being, or are you on automatic pilot, perhaps even doing the right thing but with no sense of contact with your deeper being, no access to its inspiration and love?

Certainly there will be times when the inner world with its inspiration and broader vision seems to be at your fingertips, moments when love sweeps over you all on its own. You may suddenly find yourself in the state called "flow," acting unerringly without any apparent effort and with a quiet mind. The witness may rise up in the midst of an argument or a crisis, holding you steady and poised in a situation where you would ordinarily go off the emotional deep end. You might have mornings when the world shimmers with sacredness, when you find meaning in the blown leaves on the sidewalk, when the newspapers in the gutter seem to pulsate with the overflow of your own happiness. You will experience the ongoing magic of synchronicity, when a conversation overheard on the bus or a message seen on a billboard seems to give subtle spiritual teachings. At such times, work is transmuted into worship, and a walk in the woods turns into a processional up the nave of a cathedral.

Yet there will be other moments, many of them, when the gifts of meditation are there only if you work for them. The mere fact that you meditate will not suddenly make you immune to psychological pain. It won't eliminate mood swings, feelings of inadequacy, or problems with other people. In fact, people who meditate can be just as subject to ups and downs as anyone else. The major differences lie in their *attitude* toward their moods and tendencies and in the resources they have to deal with them. When sadness, anger, and frustration arise, they have learned how to separate their intrinsic sense of self from their moods and feelings. They know that a core part of them is untouched by the emotional weather. Not only that, they have learned some skills in meditation that can help them through a difficult encounter or a mental traffic jam. They have more choices about how they deal with their feelings, how they work with the desires, fears, and crises that might otherwise derail them.

Living from our own center takes effort, but it is also exciting. When we see life as an ongoing spiritual training, we live inside a view that lends significance to even the most ordinary interactions. We don't think so much in terms of winning or losing, success or failure. Instead there is only the training, the consistent effort to come back to the love and lucidity we carry inside and to bring the values of the inner world into our outer actions.

This, then, is the second level of practice: the waking practice of staying in touch with our center, cultivating our character, contemplating and learning from the situations life presents to us, and discovering the techniques, teachings, disciplines, and forms of open-eyed practice that will allow us to live from the developing awareness of the Self.

MAINTAINING INNER ATTENTION

In the Shaiva yogic tradition, an enlightened being is said to live in a state called *shambhavi mudra* in which, even when her eyes are open, her attention is centered in the inner field of unchanging luminous Awareness. This is a powerful depiction of the enlightened state; it is also a key to open-eyed practice. Open-eyed practice is a kind of "as if" game. You are practicing to be an enlightened being by acting and thinking as you would if you were actually in that state. I have always liked something that Swami Muktananda once said on the subject: "The essence of *sadhana* [spiritual practice] is the constant remembrance of the goal of *sadhana*, the Self. You do everything with the Self in mind." In other words, you maintain a steady current of attentiveness to your inner Self—to the aware, loving part of yourself—that you can come back to no matter what you are doing. Like most essential practices, this one is extremely simple without being at all easy. Inner attentiveness has a frustrating way of dissolving at crucial moments, when you are worried, excited, or under pressure. Even on ordinary days, you naturally move in and out of it, since that essential Awareness tends to be experienced in flashes, in glimpses that come and go. That is why it is helpful to work with different practices at different moments. At times you will face directly into the light of Awareness. At other times you will approach it sideways, through the breath, a *bhavana*, or even a physical posture.

To maintain inner attention in a steady way demands a threefold effort.

First of all, you need a quiverful of practices for inner focus or remembering the Self. They should be practices that work for you, and you need to do them regularly.

Second, you need to be doing character work, examining your motives and attitudes and learning how to express the qualities of the Self—compassion, gentleness, kindness, steady wisdom, truthfulness, and the rest. (For instruction in this type of practice, I recommend Gurumayi Chidvilasananda's books: *My Lord Loves a Pure Heart, Inner Treasures, Enthusiasm,* and *Courage and Contentment.*)

Third, you need to develop the habit of checking in with yourself to monitor your state so that you can recognize when you have slipped off center and discover how to return.

*The true man of God
sits in the midst of his
fellow-men, and rises
and eats and sleeps and
marries and buys and sells
and gives and takes...
and yet never forgets God
even for a single moment.*

ABU SA'ID IBN
ABI'L-KHAYR

OPEN-EYED PRACTICE

Many of the practices described in the preceding pages—practices like mantra repetition, awareness of Awareness, focus on the witness, attention to the breath, seeing thoughts as energy—are also meant to be practiced in day-to-day situations. So are the different *bhavas*, the spiritual attitudes you work with when you meditate. Just as you begin meditation by offering your practice to God, to your Guru, or for the upliftment of humanity, you can also offer your daily actions as service and see how that simple act shifts you out of self-centeredness and unknots the tendency to grasp at outcomes. Your sitting practice of becoming aware of Awareness, being the witness of your thoughts, or seeing the whole content of your meditation experience as *shakti* can become an inner baseline that you return to during the day. It helps you move out of heavy emotions, distractions, or neurotic thinking patterns. Remembering oneness, holding the understanding that the seemingly solid world is essentially energy, will let you act in the world with a sense of openness and fluidity, and sense your kinship with others, with nature, and even with inanimate objects like your computer or your car.

It can be helpful to create set times in your schedule when you practice mantra repetition, awareness of Awareness, or remembering oneness. You could make offering your actions, thoughts, and feelings a daily ritual at the beginning and end of the workday. You could make a habit of remembering to place your attention in your heart once every hour, or you could set your wrist alarm to ring five minutes before the hour, and then use that five minutes to bring to mind a teaching you are contemplating or to spend a moment asking yourself "Who am I?" or "Where is my Self in all this?" You might work with a different practice every day until you find the practice or practices that feel like yours, and then spend some time exploring them deeply. As you practice this open-eyed meditation, you will see its effects. First of all, you should feel more integrated. There will be less of a gap between sitting meditation and the rest of your day. It will be easier to go into meditation when you sit; you should need to spend less time "deprogramming" yourself from the stresses of the day. Then, during your waking, working hours, there should be a certain sweetness to life, a sense of openness and space in your world. You'll find yourself feeling closer to others, less afraid, calmer, and more inspired. During anxious moments, busy days, and periods when life seems to be caving in on you, these practices can become a real refuge. They help you stabilize your state.

RECOGNIZING WHERE YOU NEED WORK

Few of us can practice for long without noticing how life has a way of confronting us with situations that test how steady we have managed to keep our inner state. Perhaps you get sick and have to stay in bed for a few days. One of the first things you may notice is how cranky you feel without your usual occupations—and also that you can't seem to step out of your crankiness! Perhaps your teenager says, "Mom, you're screaming at me again!" or a co-worker asks you pointedly if you have meditated recently.

Such a moment of recognition is extremely valuable, especially if you resist the impulse to kick yourself across the room for not being more together. Not only does it show you where you need to work, but your very awareness of an unconstructive mood or behavior is actually the first step in changing it. *In other words, the awareness that allows you to recognize your state is also the source of the energy that can transform it.*

Most of our more disturbing emotions or behaviors come from areas of our psyche where we have chosen to remain unconscious. In Hindi, the word for these unconscious, immature qualities is *kacha,* meaning "unripe" or "unbaked." All of us are partly *kacha.* We become *pukka* (ripe) through our practice, specifically through *tapas,* the process of yogic heat that *kundalini* ignites and that our practice stokes to blazing. However, the kind of practice that ripens us is not a mechanical accumulation of rituals and focus exercises. It is practice *with* awareness and practice *of* awareness that actually transforms the texture of our consciousness. Awareness itself, with its clarity, its impersonality, its spaciousness, and its capacity to hold everything within itself, is the fire that will cook or ripen our immature feelings and behaviors. Just holding these feelings nonjudgmentally in Awareness—being their witness—is often enough to change their quality from raw to baked.

Gurumayi wrote about the power of Awareness to transform negative experience:

> When someone directs actions towards you
> > that are of a *tamasic* [negative] nature,
> > let them burn in the light of your awareness.
> Only the pure essence of those actions will remain.
> You will benefit from it.

This principle holds true for any situation we face, whether internally or externally generated. Because our awareness is a small-scale version of the great Awareness that underlies all that is, when we direct attention nonjudgmentally toward something that causes suffering either to ourselves or to others, we are actually bringing that state or mood or behavior into the light of the great

*To attend to the moment
is to attend to eternity.
To attend to the part
is to attend to the
whole.
To attend to Reality
is to live constructively.*

PIRKE AVOT

215

Awareness itself. Awareness not only illumines the dark corners of our psyches but can also transmute the strange energies and raw feelings that dwell there. Then the energy that has been tied up in them is freed to become available for more creative endeavors. We are spiritually ripe, baked, when all our knotted energies and feelings have been freed and rechanneled to manifest as wisdom, power, and love. How this happens is one of the mysteries of Consciousness, but our act of turning Awareness toward our inner moods, states, and feelings is *the* great tactic for setting that alchemy in motion.

SELF-INQUIRY

The sages of Vedanta gave the name *atma vichara*, or self-inquiry, to this act of becoming aware of ourselves.

Vichara is not just thinking about something, nor is it the same as psychological self-analysis. It is a yogic practice of self-reflection in which we hold our attention on inner phenomena in a steady, focused fashion without going into meditation. There are two basic types of *vichara*. One is the contemplation we do to get in touch with our deeper wisdom, to open the space of revelation, to understand a spiritual teaching, or to touch our Self. The classical inner question "Who am I?" (taught by Ramana Maharshi and others) is an example of this type of *vichara.*

The other type of self-inquiry is contemplation of what blocks our experience of the Self. When we feel out of sorts, instead of giving way to the feelings or getting lost in the story we are telling ourselves about them, we focus our attention on the feelings themselves. We let ourselves fully experience the feelings. We notice the thoughts that accompany them. We observe the state of

216

our energy, the sensations in our body. At times it can be helpful to trace a feeling back to its source, perhaps to discover the frustrated desire or fear or expectation that may have triggered it. But the most important thing is to keep noticing our inner feelings and the state of our energy until it becomes second nature to notice the symptoms of being off center.

Only when we can recognize and identify the actual inner sensations of being out of alignment with ourselves can we get back in touch. Without that recognition, we only know that we are uncomfortable, and we have little chance of adjusting our state.

SELF-INQUIRY IN ACTION

Imagine the following scenario. It is early morning, and you have been up late working on a project that is approaching its deadline. You need to get to the office early to meet with your team to finalize some important loose ends. As you are putting the coffee on the stove, your ten-year-old daughter announces that she feels sick. She has a high fever and a bad cough. She needs a day in bed and a trip to the doctor. You realize that there isn't anyone you can get to stay with her at such short notice. You will have to stay home and take care of her. Yet if you don't keep your appointments at the office, your project hasn't a chance of being completed in time. The thought of what this will mean sends you into a rapid spiral of panic. "Why do things like this always happen to me?" you hear yourself thinking. "My life is so impossible." Fear, frustration, anger, and despair rush through you, filling you with adrenaline and depression simultaneously.

At this moment, you make a crucial yogic choice. Instead of letting yourself career into acting out of your panic and anger, you consciously pause.

*The more awareness
one has
The closer to God
one is.*

RUMI

You make up your mind to pay attention to your own state and to deal with it before you try to take action.

You take a couple of deep breaths, and then you check in with yourself. You scan your body and notice the rhythm of your breath. You discover that your breathing is choppy—in fact, you are actually holding your breath. You notice a clenched sensation in your diaphragm and stomach muscles and a tightness in your chest. You realize that your heart is also feeling tight and closed and that there are threads of fear shooting through it. Your energy is alternately fluttering and sinking, sometimes rushing through you in waves of panic, sometimes flattening out as depression and a feeling of helplessness. Your thoughts are all about victimization: "It's so unfair. Why can't someone besides me take care of things for a change? Why is this always happening?"

This moment of stopping, turning inside, checking yourself out, noticing how you feel, and observing your thoughts without buying into them is a profoundly significant moment of yoga. It will give you the power to act from a more resourceful, skillful place, rather than simply reacting to the difficulties in the situation. Now instead of blocking your discomfort or trying to distract yourself, instead of overriding your emotions and plunging ahead regardless of how your inner energy feels, instead of letting your strong reactions overwhelm you so that you blow up at your daughter or paralyze yourself with resentment or paranoia, you use these feelings as a signal to stop and return to yourself.

Once you have recognized your own state, you can begin to work with it. For this you have a number of different options.

TAKE REFUGE IN THE BREATH

The first thing I do when I find myself getting caught up in anxiety, hurry, or desire is to silently remind myself, in a reassuring, steady, and deliberate voice, to pause and breathe. Sometimes I actually say it to myself like a mantra: "Pause. Pause. *Breeaathe. Breeeaathe.*" The breath automatically connects the ordinary mind to the deeper Self. When we grab hold of the breath and center our minds on it, it will eventually draw our awareness inside to the heart. So when we want to center ourselves, we always begin with the breath.

You can begin by simply following the breath with your attention, taking a natural inhalation and letting the exhalation be long. Breathe to a count: four heartbeats in, eight heartbeats out, or four in, hold for four, eight out. Do this for five minutes, or practice an *ujayi* breath. Breathe in with the feeling that you are filling your lungs in three sections: the lower third first, then the middle third, then the upper third.

PULL YOUR ATTENTION TO THE HEART

For me this is the second step. Once I have recovered my wits through a few rounds of steady, deliberate breathing, I drop a sort of inner plumb line inside to the area of the middle chest, beneath the breastbone, and I let my attention rest there until I feel the inner heart space relax and expand. When energy is stuck in the head, your thoughts tend to go in circles and you come up with rote, uncreative solutions to your issues. Once your attention moves into the heart, you are automatically in touch with your intuition. You are in one of the essential centers of spiritual wisdom and awareness. Resting in that seat in the heart, you can do whatever other practice is needed.

A heart resolved on abiding in the pure space of the heart is continually refreshed and renewed by this deep intention.

GURUMAYI
CHIDVILASANANDA

EXERCISE: ENTERING THE HEART

Focus your attention in the heart center. As we've seen, this subtle spiritual center is located inside the body, beneath the breastbone, at a point about four or five inches (or approximately eight finger-widths) below the collarbone. You may want to place your hand there as you begin this exercise, to help anchor your awareness. Breathe in and out of the heart space until you feel centered. If you find it easier to center yourself by breathing into the center below the navel, you can breathe into a point in the center of the body, about three finger-widths below the navel.

If the energy in the heart area feels blocked, imagine an opening in the energy block, and let your awareness move through it. Keep moving through openings in the energy until you feel the block begin to disperse.

Putting your attention in the heart will almost automatically loosen the grip of the superficial mind, with its tendency to worry, get attached to results, and look for small wins and short-term solutions. When you contact the heart center in your own body, you open the door into the great Heart, the core of being, the Consciousness that is the source of your fundamental love, inspiration, and wisdom. If you are feeling emotionally overwhelmed, you can actually hold your emotions in that heart space and allow the power of Consciousness to melt them back into their essential energy. Or you can ask your intuition—which for most of us is more easily accessed through the heart center—what is the best thing to do.

But these are just two of your available options. You have others. You might decide that you need to spend some time soothing yourself, perhaps by replacing your agitated thoughts with the mantra. You would then bring your attention to your mantra and hold it in the forefront of your awareness until you feel the mantra soothing your inner energy field.

You could also choose to work directly with the energy behind your feelings of panic, anger, and frustration. First remind yourself that behind the content of the feelings is pure energy. Fear is simply a particular kind of energy. Anger has its own energy, and so does despair. Let yourself feel the energy as energy by letting go of the *content* of the feeling and focusing on the *sensation* the feeling creates in your psychic space and in your body. Notice the energy within the feeling. As you do, be aware of the background energy, the awareness within which the feeling arises and subsides. Let the feeling be there without trying to stop it, act on it, or make it go away. Hold the feeling in Awareness and notice how the fearful or angry energy naturally dissolves into the underlying Awareness, the Consciousness that is its base.

TAKE REFUGE IN THE TRUTH

Another thing you can do is remind yourself of the Truth. I mean the great Truth—the Truth of oneness. If your daughter begins to whine or act cranky, try remembering that the same Self, the same energy, the same Consciousness that has become *you* has also become her; remember that her mood, your frustration, and everything else are simply forms of one energy. Holding this *bhavana,* even provisionally, can have a global effect on your state—opening you up to your compassion, eliminating the sharpness of fear, and allowing you to act resourcefully—simply because you no longer feel so overwhelmed by the world's seeming refusal to work the way you want it to.

Certain spiritual teachings will have particular relevance to a situation or will carry a special resonance for you. One woman was having a difficult season while chairing her university department. During meetings, a hostile colleague kept undermining and harassing her. She got through it by reminding herself, "You are in the peaceful mind of God." A man with a tendency to lose his temper during moments of frustration works with a famous yogic technique called "Practicing the Opposite" from Patanjali's *Yoga Sutras.* When he notices rage surging up inside him, he takes time to become aware of the thoughts associated with the feeling, and then fills his mind with counterthoughts like "I have great tolerance and respect for these people." Even though it isn't always true, holding the positive thought calms his mind enough to make him less reactive. For me, a line from the *Bhagavad Gita,* "You have a right to the work alone, but not to its fruits," often comes up when I'm caught in desire for a particular outcome. Contemplating this resonant, mysterious teaching helps me detach myself from my fears, my wants, and my expectations so that I can act more objectively.

So once you have paused, checked yourself out, and recognized the way it feels to be out of your center, you have many options for beginning to come back to yourself. As you keep working with this threefold process of recognition, self-inquiry, and practice, you learn to navigate your own rough waters and to find the harbors that are always there.

At some point, you may recognize that you need to process the emotions more directly or to discover just what the issues are that are creating anxiety

If you don't realize the source,
you stumble in confusion and sorrow.
When you realize where you come from,
you naturally become tolerant,
disinterested, amused, kindhearted as a grandmother,
dignified as a king.

LAO-TZU

or fear. For this you will need to set aside some time to sit quietly. Then you can work with the practice for dealing with intense emotions that we discussed in chapter 7 (pages 128–29), or use the following variation, which also works with the mantra.

EXERCISE: PROCESSING EMOTIONS IN YOUR OWN HEART

Once you have centered yourself in the heart (see page 220 for instructions on this), bring the emotion into the heart space, holding it there and letting it be surrounded by the heart energy. Still focusing on the heart, expand your awareness so that you are conscious of the entire field of Awareness in which your experience is taking place. Hold the entire room, including your own body, in your awareness. Simultaneously, keep holding the emotion in your heart space and maintain your sense of a field of Awareness that surrounds and contains your body.

Feel the energy in the emotion. Become aware that the emotion is actually a bundle of energy. Then imagine an opening in the energy bundle and move through the opening. Keep doing this, noticing how your state shifts.

If you prefer, you can mingle the mantra with the emotion, letting the energy of the mantra begin to break up or dissolve the heavy feelings. It is important here not to create a sense of opposition between the mantra and your emotions, not to use the mantra as a club to beat back intense feelings. Simply bring the mantra into the emotion and let the mantra work its alchemy in whatever way this happens, without trying to force anything.

The mountain is the
mountain,
and the path unchanged
since the old days.
Verily what has changed
is my own heart.

KUMAGAI

Some rather miraculous side effects flow from this practice of noticing when we are off center and going back into the heart. Everything we do becomes a lot more fun. It seems to take less effort to achieve results. We feel closer to our intuitive wisdom and more likely to trust and follow it. We are not so impatient with ourselves and others. Responsibilities seem less burdensome and routine not so dull. So naturally it is easier for other people to be around us. As we keep turning toward our center and acting from it, we find we can take strength, understanding, and love for granted. We have access to them because we are being fed at the source. That is when meditation truly begins to change our lives.

CHAPTER 12

Troubleshooting

Obstacles are important. B. K. S. Iyengar, the *hatha yoga* master and author of the classic *Light on Yoga,* has written that most of his innovations in therapeutic *hatha yoga* practice came from working with his own injuries and obstacles. His own obstacles taught him how the body works. Obstacles are our teachers, and meditation is a perfect laboratory for learning from them. Most inner blocks that come up when we meditate are versions of quite familiar obstacles. Fear, frustration, dullness, and distraction plague us not only in meditation but also at work, in love, in our family lives. It is just that much of the time we have learned to override these feelings, to distract ourselves, or in some other way to keep ourselves from confronting them.

When we sit on the meditation mat, though, our tendencies and obstructions sit right in front of us, challenging us to look them in the eye and move through them.

Fortunately, there is no block, obstruction, or challenge we can face in meditation that hasn't been faced by the sages. We are deeply fortunate that so many determined men and women have traveled before us on the inner path and left us records of what they did when they came up against the problems that we face. The questions below come from the students in my meditation classes. The answers are based on the advice of the Siddha Yoga meditation masters as well as on my own experience.

QUESTION: How can I keep myself from sleeping in meditation?

First of all, make sure you are getting enough sleep at night. If your body is tired, it will use the time of meditation to snooze.

Next, you need to determine whether you are really sleeping. There are levels of deep meditation that seem like sleep but are actually yogic states. As we saw in chapter 9, when your meditation enters the causal body, you go into a dark and apparently unconscious state. Here you rest while the energy of meditation clears out your deepest limiting *samskaras*, or buried impressions. This process is a significant part of the inner journey.

However, meditation in the causal body leaves you refreshed and energized. If you come out of meditation feeling groggy and dull, you have probably been snoozing and not meditating.

Sometimes we simply can't help falling asleep. As *kundalini* becomes active during a meditation session, your mind begins to turn inward. At this point, you will be drawn out of the waking state and into a subtler state—which, depending on the strength of your focus, will be either sleep or meditation. If your inner will isn't trained to stay alert when the force of meditation is very strong, you will fall asleep. Swami Muktananda wrote in his autobiography that when his meditation was going to a deeper level, he passed through a period where he slept a lot in meditation. Then at a certain point, it was as if his "muscles" for entering the new level became strong enough so that he stopped sleeping and entered the deeper state.

Most of us, when we first begin meditation, are in that situation. We aren't used to surfing the inner world, so we don't know how to stay afloat in it. That is why there is so much emphasis in the meditation texts on learning how to focus the mind.

Focusing, as we've said before, develops a kind of subtle will, so that the mind can hold steady and enter meditation instead of sleep. This subtle will can be developed in different ways. One is to practice keeping your attention focused during those moments in the day when you tend to space out or fantasize. While in the car, on the bus, walking, or washing dishes, notice where your attention is wandering and keep bringing it back to the situation at hand. Keep focusing on your actual tasks—the act of walking or the movement of your hands over the dishes.

Another way to develop strength of focus is to work with a mantra. Keep repeating your mantra even when the energy of meditation is pushing you into sleep. At first, you will feel that you are fighting sleep. After a while, though, you will find that you are able to keep the mantra going even when you are "out." Eventually it becomes automatic for you to keep a part of yourself alert

Whenever the unsteady mind wanders away, He should bring it back to control in the Self.

BHAGAVAD GITA

and focused. Then as the mind turns inside, it will move into *samadhi* rather than into sleep.

OTHER SOLUTIONS

Certain practices can help you conquer your tendency to fall asleep. Most of those listed below are explained in more detail throughout the book.

- **Sit in a strong posture.** Keep your sitting bones grounded and steady, your spine elongating, your shoulder blades down and back, and your heart lifting upward. Refresh the posture periodically during meditation.

- **Do a few *hatha yoga* postures before meditating.** Besides helping you become more flexible, *hatha yoga* shifts the energy in the body so that you become simultaneously calmer and more alert. See the suggested reading list on pages 337–43 for a text or, better yet, consult a teacher of *hatha yoga*.

- **Ask for grace.** When you invoke your Guru before meditation, ask, "Please allow me to focus deeply and to remain conscious during my meditation today."

- **Have a strong intention to stay awake.** Make a bargain with yourself: "Today, for just this hour, I'm going to stay conscious." Then keep your focus on the object of meditation very strong and sharp. Try doing each repetition of the mantra as if it were going to be your last thought on earth.

- **Reread chapter 4 and choose a new focal point or doorway to bring you into meditation.**

QUESTION: What does it mean when I feel sick or nauseated during deep meditation?

Unless you have the flu or some other acute physical disorder, nausea during meditation is often a sign that the meditation energy is working more strongly than your body can handle right now. *Kundalini* is a powerful force, and in order to integrate it, we need to have strong, stable bodies. When the body isn't strong enough, it signals us with feelings of weakness, spaciness, and nausea. If your sickness or nausea happens only during meditation and disappears when you get up, this is probably your problem.

When people around Swami Muktananda showed symptoms like this, he would often tell them to cut back their meditation time. Sometimes he would counsel them not to meditate at all for a few days or a week, or he would have them meditate for only a few minutes at a time while they built up their strength.

When we meditate deeply, we tap into our vital energy reserves. In Sanskrit this energy reserve is called *ojas.* According to Ayurveda, the traditional system of Indian medicine, *ojas* is a subtle fluid located in the bone marrow. Intense activity, especially sexual activity, depletes it. So do irregular eating and sleeping habits or too much talking, thinking, and worrying. Many modern people have depleted *ojas* reserves.

The traditional way to replenish *ojas* is to eat foods that nourish it. Protein drinks such as milk or almond milk are helpful. So is a moderate amount of fruit and natural sweets, like raw honey. Check to see if you are protein deficient; some vegetarians suffer from *ojas* deficiency, especially when they have been on an extremely low-protein diet.

Moderate physical exercise, especially *hatha yoga* and walking, is good for building up strength.

Sometimes symptoms like nausea or sickness are signs of yogic purification, signs that a latent illness is coming up to be expelled from your system. When this happens, you might feel sick or very hot, or you might feel flulike symptoms for a brief while. If your symptoms are the result of yogic purification, they will be short-lived. They will arise intensely and be gone within a few hours or a day. When I was first meditating, I used to get high fevers from time to time. The fever would rise to 102 or 103 degrees Fahrenheit, last for an afternoon, then drop to normal. No one could ever find anything organically wrong with me. When the fever left, I would feel refreshed and light, as if something had been lifted. That is one of the classic signs that purification has occurred: a feeling of release, of lightness, that follows the episode.

QUESTION: What can I do about the fact that I don't seem able to stay in deep meditation? I will be deep inside when suddenly I shoot back up to an ordinary waking state.

This is quite normal. In the course of an hour, we may go in and out of meditation over and over again. We go deep for some time. Then our consciousness might rise again to the surface, only to turn inward and sink again. One quite advanced meditator once counted the number of times he came out of meditation in the course of a single session and discovered that it happened nearly ten times.

The secret is to accept the rhythm of your meditation experience and allow it to be what it is. When you feel yourself pop out of meditation, remain sitting in your posture. If you need to shift your legs or stretch, do it slowly and

Yoga is not eating too much, nor is it absolutely not eating, and not the habit of sleeping too much, and not keeping awake either.

BHAGAVAD GITA

gently. Relax and let yourself experience how it feels to sit in this posture. Be aware of how your body feels. Be aware of the breath. Repeat your mantra or practice the technique you were using at the beginning of meditation. Gradually you will sink inside again—and often go deeper.

QUESTION: I have been meditating for two years, and I never seem to stop thinking or to get into meditation. What should I do?

Even experienced meditators go through periods when meditation is nothing but hard work. It is like rowing against the current. You field the thoughts and you try to focus, but there is no release into your deeper Self, no experience of your state shifting from "waking consciousness" to "meditation consciousness," no feeling that the *shakti* is embracing you and bringing you inside. Though we can take comfort in Gurumayi's statement "When you sit for meditation, whatever happens is meditation," still we wonder: "Why is it like this? What's the matter with me that I don't have any palpable experiences?"

The short answer is, "Nothing." If you were learning tennis, you wouldn't expect to have an effortless serve after three weeks of lessons. You would surrender to practicing your serve for hours, to making bad shots, and to trying again. You would train until the technique became second nature and you began to feel tennis playing you.

Meditation is also a skill. It takes time to develop our inner "muscles" of focus and to learn how to let go into the inner world. It takes practice to discover how to let yourself move along the pathways of the inner *shakti*, to stay aware without thinking, and to hold an inner state when it arises.

If you have a hard time getting into meditation, the best solution is to set aside a longer period of time for each meditation session. Each of us has a natural point when thoughts automatically slow down and a meditative state emerges. You just have to be willing to sit long enough for that point to arrive. For most people, that automatic entry point occurs between forty-five minutes and one hour into meditation. If you have a very busy mind, it might take longer. Most people will have their best meditations if they allow an hour to seventy-five minutes for any given session.

I know a man who complained for years that all he did in meditation was sit and think. To make matters worse, he was married to a woman whose meditation had caught fire immediately and who used to swim ecstatically through realms of light every morning or sit peacefully in the velvety blackness of the void, emerging with a starry and beatific light in her eyes. Her husband felt like a spiritual deadbeat by comparison.

He persisted. Like many other mentally active people, he discovered that sitting for over an hour worked magic. He began entering a state of soft, blissful energy during meditation. His mind became calmer, and after a while he noticed that meditation was beginning to affect his outer life. A feeling of frustration over his unsatisfied ambitions cooled down, and paradoxically the professional recognition he had been missing began to come to him.

Ten years went by—ten years of daily meditation and steady inner growth. Then one day during a meditation workshop, he had a vision of a temple half-buried in the earth. He saw that the temple had once been completely buried. He realized that this is what his inner work had done. It had cleared away enough of the layers of "dirt" around his inner being so that he could now begin to see it.

One thing I always did was to sit in the meditation posture for the full period, even if I couldn't meditate or if my mind was unable to concentrate itself. I benefited a lot from this.

SWAMI MUKTANANDA

This man had a deep interest in meditation, and so he stayed with it. He experimented with different techniques, attitudes, and disciplines. It was his continued steady effort that brought breakthrough for him—and when the breakthrough came, he had earned it. He owned it, so to speak. His inner experiences are his earnings as well as gifts of grace. So he was able to hold them and to incorporate them into his days.

QUESTION: What can I do to keep the mind from commenting on my meditation? It's driving me crazy.

This is one of the mind's tricks. When your mind realizes that you aren't going to pay attention to its mundane chitchat, it starts commenting on your meditation. "Am I doing this right? Wow, I'm having an experience!" You can treat spiritual chitchat like any other chitchat. In other words, try to avoid getting seduced by the message. Remember that all thoughts are made of Consciousness, of energy, and let them go.

If the comments bring you out of an experience, try focusing on the place in your consciousness where you felt, sensed, or saw the experience. Often just by placing yourself there and remembering what occurred, you can go back into deep meditation through your memory. If not, let it go. There will be more.

QUESTION: I keep getting to a point where I really feel that I'm going to merge into a sort of inner sky. Then I get terrified and I bring myself back. I'm furious with myself because I feel that I could have made a huge shift, but I was too scared. What can I do about the fear that comes up in meditation?

Can you coax your mind from its wandering and keep to the original oneness?...
Can you cleanse your inner vision until you see nothing but the light?...
Can you step back from your own mind and thus understand all things?

LAO-TZU

233

There is probably no one in the world who, at some point, hasn't pulled back from what could have been a profound experience out of fear. Part of this is inevitable. We all have pockets of fear inside us, and just as we pass through other states in meditation, we also pass through fear. We also tend to become frightened when we don't understand what is happening to us. An example: Sometimes the breath stops in meditation. If you don't know that this is a profound yogic *kriya* that can lead into the state of *samadhi,* you will be afraid that the breath won't come back. In the same way, when your consciousness expands for the first time, you may not realize that you are experiencing the original state of your own Awareness, which actually encompasses all things. Understanding the meaning of a particular experience can sometimes eliminate the fear.

Another reason we become frightened is because the ego—the part of us that identifies "me" as the psychophysical self—is out of its depth and is trying to bring us back to a state in which it feels comfortable.

Let's look at the relationship of the ego to meditation. The ego performs an important psychic function. Its job is to make sure that we don't forget our identity as an individual being. If we are going to function in the world, remembering our name and where we are supposed to be at ten o'clock, we need the ego to keep reminding us of small details of our personal identity, like "You look good in beige" and "Remember there's milk in that, and you're lactose intolerant."

Unfortunately, the ego tends to extend its portfolio until it feels as though it is the sole protector of our life. That's one reason why it gets into trouble in meditation. Initially, the ego enjoys spiritual practice. It likes the idea of self-improvement, which of course it defines in its own fashion. The ego wants to get better at its game—faster, smarter, humbler, purer, or whatever our particular ego seeks. It hopes that meditation will help it carry out its agenda.

The problem for the ego occurs when meditation begins dissolving its boundaries. If we were to truly experience God, the ego wouldn't be able to come along. There is no room for the feeling of being a small, limited person in the ocean of Consciousness. And the ego knows that. So whenever our boundaries of body, mind, feelings of doership, and so forth look as though they are losing their grip, whenever it looks as if our identity is about to expand a bit, the ego recognizes that its territory is being threatened and throws up its first line of defense. The fear you experience is actually the ego's terror that you will turn out to be bigger than it, bigger than the carefully delimited territory of memories and opinions and affections and aversions that the ego thinks of as "me."

Rather than being afraid of your fear, you might see it as a signal that you need to take care of and reassure your small self. Then it will have an easier time integrating your expansion experiences. And it will let you move forward.

The first thing to do with the fear is to name it. Sometimes I say to my fear, "Hello, fear. I know you are just my ego talking." This alone might be enough to dispel it. If it isn't, here are some antidotes.

You could remember that whatever is frightening you and the fear itself are all aspects of your own Consciousness. There is nobody in there but you. As you may have noticed, the understanding "All that I experience in meditation is a manifestation of my own Consciousness" solves many meditation difficulties. Why? Because it returns everything to its source. This understanding puts us back in touch with our true Self, which is ever present and which is the fabric

How could we forget those ancient myths,… the myths about dragons that at the last moment are transformed into princesses? Perhaps all the dragons in our lives are princesses who are only waiting to see us act, just once, with beauty and courage. Perhaps everything that frightens us is, in its deepest essence, something helpless that wants our love.

RAINER MARIA RILKE

of our whole life as well as of our meditation. When we are in touch with our truth, we are also in touch with our natural courage.

Another thing you can do is face your fear and become its witness. This is the warrior's method. Here is how it works. You start to move deep inside. You feel fear come up. You notice your tendency to move away from the fear—to run before it, so to speak, and to let it chase you right out of meditation. Instead of giving in, you linger on the edge of your fear and look right at the fear. Notice how it feels. Where is it in your body? Do you feel it in your heart? What words is it saying to you? Does it have a color? A shape? Stay close to the fear, but at the edge of it, observing. Notice that as long as you are observing your fear, there is a part of you that is not affected by it. The observer is untouched by the fear. Keep watching the fear, remembering to identify yourself with the observer rather than with the fear.

An alternative to this is to enter your fear and feel its energy. Fear is nothing but an energy. You can actually ride that energy to a deeper state.

A man who did this exercise said:

> As I entered the fear, I felt almost overpowered by it. Then I noticed that it wasn't just fear I was feeling. There was also resistance, a feeling of holding back. I stayed with it, letting myself feel those feelings. For a moment, I was just filled with fear energy. Then I sort of dropped deeper into it, and it was just pure, strong energy. A knot of energy. I stayed with the energy, and at a certain point, the hard knot began to soften. Then it expanded, and I could feel a soft pulsation, expanding outward from my heart.

In the *Spanda Karikas,* one of the advanced yogic texts of Kashmir

Shaivism, a verse refers to the state of fear as a state filled with potential for higher Awareness. It says that the pure experience of the *spanda,* the pure creative energy of the universe, is particularly present "when one is in the state of terror or running for one's life." Fear is a condition of intense, focused energy. As we enter the energy, it takes us to its source.

Finally, you can take refuge in your Guru. Your Guru is fully present in your inner universe. When you call out, you will discover how firmly that protective presence can support you. This is one reason why you *have* a Guru: so that when you feel scared or out of your depth, you can pray for help and guidance.

Here is a prayer I have used when I've felt my inner process moving too fast for comfort: "This is too much for me. Please cool my meditation down; make it a little gentler."

Notice the wording. You are not asking for the experiences to go away. After all, you don't want these expansion experiences shut down. You just want them to be a bit less intense.

Sometimes we wonder what is really happening when we call out to the Guru. In what sense does the Guru hear us? Is it really a personal intervention from the Guru that we are asking for? Or is it a kind of trick we play on our unconscious to access our inner source of strength and courage? My experience is that when we call on the Guru, we are actually accessing the Guru-*shakti,* the protective, grace-bestowing force of the universe that is in us as much as it is in everything else. It is not a personal energy but neither is it "other." Though it is called forth through our connection to a particular teacher, it is actually an aspect of our own *shakti,* or awakened *kundalini* energy. Many people have had the experience of discovering that the physical Guru "knew"

All the rough edges that confront you won't hold you back. If you persevere, they will actually help you to go further, to travel deeper into the ocean of knowledge, the ocean of love.

GURUMAYI
CHIDVILASANANDA

when they called or prayed: Self-realized beings are connected via the heart essence to all their students. Yet it is actually our own *kundalini shakti,* which is not different from the Guru-energy, that transforms our inner state in answer to our prayers.

QUESTION: Something in me just resists sitting to meditate. Even when I do it, as soon as I start to go deep, the resistance becomes so strong it actually pulls me out.

Like fear, resistance is a normal manifestation of the ego. When fear of going deeper doesn't work, the limiting mind comes up with other strategies to keep you under its control. It reminds you of all the other things you could be doing. It points out that you never have interesting experiences in meditation. It tells you that one hour is too long and that if you stopped a half-hour earlier, you could make some of the phone calls you need to make. There is nothing arcane about these voices. They are simply signals from your mundane mind. After a while, if you pay attention, you should get to know them well.

Resistance often arises just at the moment when you are about to go deeper. It arises as an impulse, almost a need to retreat back to the familiar and the known. That membrane of resistance, that deep, conservative desire not to go forward, is extremely tenacious and persuasive. It can hurl you right out of meditation. "Many people," Gurumayi once pointed out, "when they are finally ready for the curtain to drop within themselves, quit."

The best thing to do when resistance arises is to stay put. Just sit. Keep your body on the mat, no matter how much you may want to get up, and keep your awareness focused, without judgment or aversion or fear, on the feeling of resistance.

You don't have to do anything else. If you can sit with awareness of your resistance, your Awareness itself will eventually dissolve it.

You might also contemplate your resistance. Here are two ways to do it:

■ **Ask yourself, "What is behind my resistance to going deeper?"** Write down what comes up. Then ask the question, "Is there anything more?" Keep asking until you feel you have gone as deeply into the question as you can go. Look at the answers you get, then ask yourself, "Is there anything behind this?"

■ **Sit quietly and summon the feeling of resistance.** Let yourself be with it for a few minutes. Then ask your resistance, "What do you have to tell me? What are you resisting?" Write down whatever response arises in your mind, no matter how odd or irrelevant it may initially seem to you.

Fighting and peacefulness both take place within God.

RUMI

A woman who asked herself this question came up with "People who meditate are weird." Going deeper with it, she came up with "I'm afraid that if I let myself go, I won't be able to function." Going even deeper, it was "Suppose I lose my personality?"

A young man came up with "I need to hold on to my thoughts because they're important." Deeper than that, he found the feeling "I need to be doing something. Meditation is a waste of time compared to the work I have to do."

When you have discovered your specific resistances, then you can address them. You can answer them. You can reassure yourself.

For example, "Rather than making me less able to function, meditation gives me a base to function from." "Look at X, X, and X (insert the names of any great teachers or long-term meditators you've met or read about). They have very strong and definite personalities." An even more powerful answer to the fear of being weird is the stance of global self-acceptance: "It is all right for me to be weird."

Another way of inquiring into your resistance is to speak to the feeling directly as if it were a person, and ask your resistance how to work with it. One young woman summoned the feeling of resistance and asked, "How can I learn to let go of you?" From inside she heard, "Just keep turning back to your mantra. The mantra will dissolve me."

Even if you examine and understand and answer the content of your resistance, you might also need to work on an energetic level (as on pages 128 and 239) with the feeling of resistance itself—to hold the feeling in Awareness until you feel it dissolving into pure, contentless energy. Nothing is more powerful in dispelling blocks in your consciousness than pure Awareness.

QUESTION: Nothing ever happens in my meditation. What can I do?

I can't tell you how many times I have heard people say this. Usually, their meditation is much richer than they think. Their problem is that they have concepts about what constitutes a proper "meditation experience," and their actual experience doesn't match their ideas.

This is something that meditators need to contemplate carefully. It may be that the type of meditation experiences normally spoken of in your spiritual tradition actually represent only a part of the spectrum of inner experience. Every path has its own language for describing spiritual experience, and no matter how universal that path may be, most spiritual communities tend to emphasize certain kinds of experience over others. Usually they are the ones that the teacher encountered on his or her own journey. The teacher describes these experiences for the benefit of his or her disciples, to inspire them or to show them some of the landmarks on the path. Though Swami Muktananda wrote extensively about his experiences in *Play of Consciousness,* he said that he had described only a small fraction of his experiences. In fact, when you read his writings on meditation, it is quite apparent that he described only what *could* be described and that many of his most powerful meditations could not be spoken of because they took place in the realm beyond language.

Yet no matter how many times the teacher reminds us that the inner world is limitless, disciples tend to assume that their teacher's descriptions encompass the whole range of "acceptable" spiritual experience. If their own experience is different, they conclude (if they are the self-deprecating type) that they are failing at meditation or going the wrong route, or (if they are the arrogant type) that their teacher is wrong.

Many people suffer confusion because their experience isn't described in the texts of their particular tradition. In her book *How to Grow a Lotus Blossom,* Jiyu Kennett-Roshi described how she experienced doubts about the authenticity of her visions because in her school of Zen, visions are neither admired nor encouraged. When a Catholic contemplative experienced a state of inner emptiness in which her personal self seemed to disappear, her Catholic spiritual director was unfamiliar with the experience and doubted its authenticity. One Siddha Yoga meditator was drawn to focus on an inner field of energy with the feeling that God was present in that energy field. The only exact description he could find for this experience was in a Christian mystical text

*I have a feeling that my
     boat
has struck, down there in
     the depths,
against a great thing.*

*And nothing
     happens! Nothing...
     Silence...Waves...*

*—Nothing happens? Or
     has everything
     happened,
and are we standing now,
     quietly, in the new life?*

JUAN RAMÓN JIMÉNEZ

called *The Cloud of Unknowing*. Yet this did not make him a Christian meditator any more than the Catholic meditator was a Buddhist just because her experience was described in Buddhist texts.

The truth is that we have no idea what *samskaras* we have, what spiritual practices we did in the past that are now bearing fruit, or what country of the inner universe we have entered into. We also have no way of knowing how much inner purification needs to be done before we begin having obvious "experiences." The *Pratyabhijna Hridayam* says that from the point of view of the ultimate Reality, every philosophical position and every type of spiritual experience is simply a stage on the ladder to ultimate oneness. The Splendor, in short, can appear in any way it wants to—and does. It often appears in the form of life changes that become apparent only after you have gotten up from your meditation cushion.

If you feel that nothing is happening in your meditation, the first thing to do is to examine the quality of that "nothing." Before you write off your meditation as dull or static, investigate your inner state, both during and after meditation. The state of blankness or dullness, or the experience of thoughts lingering, does not necessarily mean that something is wrong. It may simply be an invitation to enter your own inner field and to work with it, as described in chapters 1 and 4. Maybe now it is time to explore your own bare Awareness or to see thoughts as *shakti*. If you go into the inner emptiness that you think you are experiencing, you may discover that what seems like "nothing" is actually immensely full, pregnant with Awareness and creativity.

EXERCISE: INVESTIGATING NOTHINGNESS

Close your eyes. Focus on the empty "space" that appears in front of your eyes. Look at the emptiness, the field in front of you. How does it look? Perhaps you see a field of gray shot with little streaks or points of light. Perhaps it is black. Perhaps it is blue with streaks of gold.

This field is the field of your consciousness. It is the background consciousness within which all your experience rises and falls. Let yourself be with it. If thoughts come up, allow the thoughts to be there within the field of your own consciousness. Keep your awareness focused on the space itself, on the inner "nothingness" that you see when you close your eyes.

When you are ready, have the feeling that you are moving through this inner field of nothingness. It is not your body, of course, that moves through it, but you as attention, as Awareness. Allow your awareness to float, swim, or sail through the field of emptiness. Notice what you encounter. Notice the different energy fields that rise and fall within your field of consciousness. Explore your consciousness—all the while understanding that this emptiness, this space within you, is Consciousness itself. This very field of emptiness is the Self, the ultimate reality. In time it will reveal itself to you.

Think of the empty space enclosed by a jar.
When the jar is broken into pieces, the jar alone breaks, not the space.
Life is like the jar.

All forms are like the jar. They constantly break into pieces.
When gone, they are unaware.
Yet He is aware, eternally.

BRAHMA BINDU UPANISHAD

Here is another clue to look for in evaluating subtle meditation. Pay attention to the perceptual shifts that come when you get up after meditation. Even if you never stopped thinking during your time of practice, you might notice when you get up that you feel lighter, as if something has been lifted. Perhaps your mind, which might have seemed so busy when your eyes were closed, is noticeably clearer. Maybe you feel calm and happy. Maybe something you were worried about has been resolved.

Perhaps your vision has shifted and enlarged, so that you can see the world with deeper, more wonder-filled eyes. Maybe your dreams are becoming more lucid—or perhaps the glimpses of deeper states, the heightened awareness, and the numinous feelings and visions that you seek in meditation are happening in your dreams. Many meditators have such dreams. Often we can recognize them by their light and their colors, by the fact that they are pervaded by a numinous brightness that is clearly a glimpse of another world. These, too, are meditation experiences—it is just that they are coming in the dream state.

When you meditate sincerely, it will always create shifts in your life. It will always, ultimately, transform you.

PART THREE   Breaking Through

CHAPTER 13

The Three-Week
Breakthrough Program

The decision to go deeper into meditation is not made just once. We make it again and again, at deeper and deeper levels, knowing that no single intention will carry us forward forever. This month's strong resolution becomes next month's malaise unless we keep renewing the resolution, reinventing it, refocusing ourselves on it. At best, we renew our intention daily and remotivate ourselves as well—reminding ourselves of the shortness of human life, of the opportunity it offers us, of the speed at which everything in this world changes, of the suffering we experience when we're out of touch with our own center, of the sweetness of the inner world, and of the benefits of stable awareness. Yet, everyone has periods when practice is strong, as well as times when it is less focused. And sometimes we will notice that we have simply fallen asleep to ourselves, that we have begun taking our practice for granted, that we are stuck in a routine. This is one good reason to set aside time to strive for a breakthrough.

Another reason we might decide we are ready for breakthrough is that we hear the call of the inner Self, the pull of the inner world. We sense that the walls in our consciousness are ready to come down, that the doors are ready to open. So we commit ourselves to making a greater effort. We say, "This week, this month, this year I am going to meditate more seriously. I am going to have a breakthrough."

Everyone who has ever made a successful raid on the forces of inertia knows that the decisive gesture is the gesture of commitment. As soon as you are willing to direct your full intention toward a plan, a project, or a goal, the universe begins to shift in your favor. Pathways open up; events conspire to help you. This is especially obvious in meditation, where you are dealing with the infinitely fluid and expansive inner universe. Because your inner Consciousness is so endlessly creative, a single strong intention can have an almost miraculous effect.

So the first step in breakthrough is your intent, and the more passionate and serious your intention, the more powerful an instrument it will be.

Traditionally, people who want to go deeper into meditation go away on retreat. The program that follows can certainly be done on retreat—and if you are very busy or have small children, you will probably need to set aside time for retreat in order to follow it. In fact, those of you whose days are so packed with responsibilities that it is hard to find more than a few minutes for sitting

Greatness exists like an ocean within you. Why do you want to act like a fish out of water, wriggling on the sand under the scorching sun? Look! The water is just one millimeter away! Jump in!

GURUMAYI
CHIDVILASANANDA

practice might consider doing it on a retreat day once a week or even once a month. For those who can do it, this program has been designed to fit into daily life, and there are great advantages to integrating it into your routine. Meditating on retreat is relatively easy. We are outside our ordinary context, free of at least some of our daily commitments, and we may be in a place that is especially quiet and conducive to meditation. Yet any retreat, no matter how deep and quiet, inevitably comes to an end. Then we are faced with integrating our retreat life into our ordinary existence. The farther we have taken ourselves away from ordinary life, the harder it can be to import our practice into the routine of busy, crowded days.

The pearl is in the oyster. And the oyster is at the bottom of the sea. Dive deep.

KABIR

When you do your breakthrough program at home, you create a retreat atmosphere inside your ordinary environment. You create a new routine, and the habit of it remains in the atmosphere, spurring you forward even after the program is done.

MAKING THE COMMITMENT

To begin the breakthrough program, you will need to make a commitment to:

1. **Meditate daily—if possible, for one and one-half to three hours per day.** This can be in one session or two. If you are simply too busy to sit for an hour of meditation at a time or if you have young children or a very demanding job, please feel free to adapt the program to your needs. The principles of it will help you even if you only meditate for ten or fifteen minutes at a time, and as you establish a continuity of practice, you may start to find that your situation opens up in unexpected ways. Another way to do this is to set aside times during the week when you

do give yourself a full forty-five minutes or an hour to meditate.

2. **Keep a meditation journal in which you write down whatever happens, and set aside some time each week to read through your experiences and contemplate them.**

3. **Spend at least ten minutes a day reading from a book that induces meditation and inspires love for the inner world.** A list of recommended books appears in the Suggested Reading section.

It might seem daunting to think about spending that much time in meditation every day, especially if you are very busy. That is why the breakthrough program is set up to last only three weeks. If they plan ahead, even people with very crowded lives can usually find three weeks to commit themselves to meditating strongly.

For breakthrough in meditation, continuity of practice is important. When we meditate twice a day, it bookends our day in meditation and also gives us the opportunity to consolidate states we may have experienced during the previous session. As we have said before, most people need to sit for about an hour to significantly deepen their meditation simply because it takes time for the outgoing mind to settle, reverse its normal tendency to rove through the universe, and begin to sink back into itself. The more active we normally are, the more time it takes to digest the residue of our day's impressions. But if we sit long enough, Consciousness will naturally begin to emerge from the layers of thoughts that stir up its surface, revealing its own quiet depths.

SETTING ASIDE TIME

All of us have our own best times of day to meditate. Not always is this in the early morning. Each period of the day has its own particular energy, which affects your own energy field. Traditionally the most powerful times of day for meditation are the *sandhyas*, or junction points. The *sandhya* is a period in the day when there is a shift in the atmospheric energy. There are three *sandhyas*. The early morning *sandhya* is the period of dawn, just before and just after sunrise. The midday *sandhya* marks the switch from morning to afternoon and lasts from about eleven-thirty until approximately twelve-thirty. The late afternoon *sandhya* begins just before sunset and lasts until darkness falls.

Just as the space between the inbreath and the outbreath is an open doorway to the *madhya*, the center of Consciousness, these spaces between one part of the day and another are like cracks between the worlds, times when our inner energy shifts in rhythm with the energy of the day and creates a natural opening into the inner world.

This doesn't mean that we can't get into meditation at other times. However, many people find that their energy naturally turns inward during the *sandhyas*. Observing your own daily rhythms, you may have already noticed a tendency to get "sleepy" during these times. It is not low blood sugar; it is actually the power of the *sandhya* drawing you inside.

So it is very good to experiment with meditating at different times of day. You may have been assuming that early morning is the best time for you when actually you meditate as well or better in the late afternoon or even at lunchtime.

Once you have discovered the best period of the day for meditation, make sure that you set aside enough time during that period to let yourself go

We must, then,... even in the midst of occupations, withdraw within ourselves.

TERESA OF AVILA

251

deep. In general, have at least one time during the day when you meditate for at least an hour, with perhaps some open space at the end in case you want to sit longer. Your second period, if necessary, can be as short as one-half hour.

YOUR BREAKTHROUGH PROGRAM LIFESTYLE

When you are seeking a breakthrough in meditation, your lifestyle matters. Of course, it is not necessary to follow a monastic schedule, to become vegetarian or celibate, or to overwhelm yourself with yogic discipline. However, certain core disciplines will make a distinct difference in your experience of meditation. Here are some of them:

1. **If you intend to meditate in the early morning, go to bed early enough so that you can comfortably get up in time. Before you go to bed, read something uplifting or repeat mantras.**

A friend of mine always says that the decision to meditate is made the night before. If you are going to get up for meditation, you will need to be in bed at a reasonable hour and with your mind clear. This is one of the great secrets of early morning meditation. If you watch television or read the newspaper or a stimulating novel before bed, it not only affects your sleeping patterns, but also programs the way you wake up in the morning.

You can experiment with this. Notice what you are thinking about when you go to sleep. Then notice the first thoughts that come into your mind when you wake up the next morning. Unless you have had a strong dream that stays with you on waking, the thought you wake up with will almost always be the thought you went to sleep with. If, in the moments before sleep, you are thinking about your problems at the office or the project you are working on or the Lakers' chances of making it to the play-offs, there is a fair guarantee that you will wake up with the same issue on your mind.

However, if before you go to sleep you have been reading the poetry of Rumi, a book by your Guru, or some other spiritual book, that is what will come into your mind when you wake up. Even better, if you go to sleep doing a practice, you should find that the practice is with you when you wake up.

2. **Repeat a mantra or focus on the breath before you go to sleep and when you wake up.**

3. **In the morning, get up immediately.**

If you lie in bed, you give the inner dialogue time to start, and you risk going back to sleep.

4. **Shower or wash your hands, face, and feet immediately before meditation.**

Washing before meditation does more than cleanse the body and wake you up. It is also a way of cleansing your mind. As the water pours over your body, you can mentally repeat your mantra or imagine the water as a shower of light that is washing your inner body of its accumulated thought-dust.

5. **Observe moderation in eating.**

The real key to a yogic diet is not to overeat. This doesn't mean you should fast. The ideal is to get up from the table before you feel full. Eating to fullness strains the digestive system and uses up energy that you could use for meditation. Many meditators prefer a vegetarian or mostly vegetarian diet. Still, make sure you get enough protein. Lack of protein makes many people spacy, and even though this might feel like a pleasant state, ultimately it will make it harder to integrate your experiences.

Try to eat at regular times and create a pleasant ritual around your meals. If possible, eat at least one of your meals in silence. It is better, when you eat, not to read or watch television, but to focus fully on the act of eating. Chew your food well—at least fifty times per mouthful. Not only does this make the food easier to digest, it also helps you to focus on the eating process. You become more conscious, more mindful, and more centered as you eat. And you eat less. Repeat the mantra or keep your awareness focused on the breath while you are eating and, if you cook for yourself, while cooking. The energy of the mantra will mingle with the food and will give you subtle as well as physical nourishment.

6. Regulate your social life.

Ask yourself now, "Without abandoning my family or depriving myself of normal human interaction and appropriate social nourishment, what unnecessary engagements can I eliminate during my meditation break-through program?"

It is partly a matter of time. When there are only so many hours in the day and you want to devote some of them to spiritual practice, the easiest way to make that time available is to take it out of your social or leisure-time schedule.

But there are other reasons why you might want to look at your engagement calendar during this period. The people you spend time with influence your inner state profoundly. Though it may not be possible to surround yourself entirely with uplifting people who support your meditation practice, you

For one who is moderate in food and diversion, whose actions are disciplined, who is moderate in sleep and waking, yoga destroys all sorrow.

BHAGAVAD GITA

can certainly stay away from the people and events that will unnecessarily draw you into states of mind that agitate you or make it harder to go inside.

Of course, this presents certain challenges if the people who distract you are the people you live with! Perhaps your housemates, spouse, or children make quiet time difficult to find. Or maybe the people close to you—your spouse, partner, roommate, or children—feel threatened by your practice. Maybe they think it is taking you away from them. Maybe they feel jealous. Maybe they think meditation is stupid. Or perhaps they give you support but find it hard to help create a meditation-friendly atmosphere. One weekend when I was first practicing meditation, I went to stay with a friend. This was during the seventies, when meditation seemed a strange practice to many. Every morning halfway through my practice, my friend would begin loudly rattling dishes in the next room. "Are you through meditating yet?" she would call periodically. My annoyed reaction to her was just as distracting as the interruption itself.

Even if your dear ones are enthusiastic about supporting your practice, it is still a good idea to take time to discuss it with them. Tell them what you are trying to do and why. Tell them what you require in terms of time and privacy. Ask for their support. Then give them a chance to say how *they* feel about it and what they need from you in order to be comfortable and supportive. Be willing to engage, within reason, in whatever process you need to go through to make it all right with them.

7. **Regulate your reading, television watching, and film going during this period.**

*All this talk and turmoil
and noise and movement
and desire is outside the
veil; inside the veil is
silence and calm and
peace.*

ABU YAZID AL'BISTAMI

The images, ideas, and impressions in your mind determine your mood, your inner state, and your feelings. You already have a huge bank of images, ideas, and impressions boiling around inside your unconscious, thickening your consciousness, and creating subtle barriers between yourself and the inner world. The clearer you can keep your mind during your breakthrough program, the easier it will be to meditate more deeply.

Many serious meditators when on retreat give up all reading matter that isn't related to meditation. If you can do that during your breakthrough program, so much the better. It may be professionally impractical for you to ignore the morning paper or the evening news. In that case, decide on the minimum amount you need in order to keep well informed and try to cut down on unnecessary reading.

You might find that your information/entertainment "fast" creates such a welcome space in your mental atmosphere that you want to keep it up after the three weeks of the program. Many of us live with an addiction to information—to movies, novels, and magazines. Sometimes we unconsciously use reading or television watching to barricade ourselves against feeling an underlying depression or looking at life questions we want to avoid. We may even associate quiet with boredom.

But the price of such avoidance is steep. When we fill our inner space with noise and color, with story and distraction, we also cut ourselves off from the natural joy and insight that arise from simply being with ourselves. So take advantage of this opportunity to experience the power of quiet, even if it means that you have to listen to the mental static you have avoided or experience the buried feelings you have hidden from yourself.

8. **Inject practices such as mantra repetition, contemplation, or yogic breathing into the spaces in your day.**

Whenever your mind is unoccupied with work or other essential interactions, for example, when you are walking, during drives or bus rides, or while cooking or cleaning, turn your awareness toward the inner world. Do the mantra with a feeling that you are calling out to your inner Self. Perform your tasks in rhythm with the breath. Do an exercise in awareness—imagine that you are surrounded by a blanket of divine love or look into someone's eyes with the awareness that the same Consciousness is looking out of their eyes as looks out of yours. Walk with the feeling that you are walking into the vastness. Offer your actions to God, to your Guru, or to the ever-present inner Self. Become aware of the witnessing Awareness at different points during the day.

THE BREAKTHROUGH PROGRAM SCHEDULE:
The Day Before You Begin

Set aside some time when you can be alone and do the following process of inner examination.

EXERCISE: INQUIRY INTO YOUR MEDITATION PRACTICE

Ask yourself:

What are the strengths of my meditation practice?

Where do I think there could be improvement?

Why do I meditate? What do I hope to gain from it?

What are my short-term goals in meditation?

What are my long-term goals?

When have I most enjoyed meditation?

What was going on in my life at those times?

Still looking at the times you have most enjoyed meditation, ask yourself whether there were any practices or attitudes that contributed to your enjoyment.

Which practices have helped you most in getting into meditation?

Spend as much time as you need contemplating all these questions and write down your conclusions.

Now write in your journal the following promise to yourself (which you may reword if the language does not suit you):

I, (name), promise myself that I will make my meditation practice a major priority during the next three weeks. I will arrange my schedule to give myself time to meditate regularly for (number) hours a day. I will also live my life during this time so that my diet, my sleeping schedule, and my social life support meditation. I offer this promise to my own inner Self and for the benefit of all beings, and I ask that the supreme Self, living within me and within all things, give me the grace to carry out my promise.

The Meditation Program

During each meditation session of your three-week program, it is suggested that you follow the same sequence of preliminary steps. These are given below. The sequence is designed to help move you out of ordinary, mundane awareness and into the subtler state of awareness that leads to meditation.

ENTERING MEDITATION

Set your timer for one hour.

PRELIMINARY PRACTICES

1. Offering Salutations

Light a candle. If you have an altar, focus on it for a few minutes. Bow to the altar or simply to the space in front of you. As you do, have the feeling that you are bowing to your inner Consciousness, the supreme spirit within yourself and within the universe. Now bow to each of the four directions—north, east, south, and west—moving in a clockwise direction. As you make each bow, have the feeling that you are offering your salutations to the divine Consciousness that resides in every corner of the universe.

2. Taking a Posture

Sit in an erect and relaxed posture, making sure that you are physically comfortable. (See pages 62–64 for the basic points of meditation posture and the method of relaxing the body in the posture.)

3. Stating Your Intention

Formulate to yourself a clear, strong intention. For example:

"I am meditating on my inner Self. I regard whatever arises in meditation as a form of Consciousness. I let go of distracting thoughts or emotions, and immerse myself in my own pure Awareness (or 'in the energy of the mantra,' or 'in the heart')."

4. Invoking the Grace of the Guru

Imagine that your Guru, or a great teacher or saint to whom you feel deeply connected, is sitting before you. Feel that a ray of energy, or a current of love, connects your heart to the teacher's heart. Imagine that streams of grace and blessings are coming from the Guru's heart to yours.

Feeling that heart connection, speak to the teacher in your own words, offering your salutations and asking for blessings to enter deeply into meditation. You might ask for blessings to meditate with focus, or to immerse yourself in the Self, or to enter the heart. You might simply offer the meditation to the Guru. Feel that the Guru hears and grants your request. Allow yourself to receive the blessings that flow from the great teacher's heart.

Once you have done the preliminary steps, you can practice any of the techniques in this book or follow the instructions given below. These instructions are intended to give you a framework for your own process. They are models for practice that you can experiment with and build on. Feel free to try them out or to use whatever practice opens up the inner space and helps you go deeper. It is important to remember that we use these techniques to quiet our

God must act and pour himself into you the moment he finds you ready.

MEISTER ECKHART

mental energy, to calm our thoughts, and to help our attention move inside and stabilize itself. They are doorways into meditation, not ends in themselves. Once your thought stream has calmed and slowed down, you can begin sensing where the inner energy wants to take you. At that point, you might want to let the technique go and follow the inner pathways that your own *shakti* suggests. If thoughts arise, if you become distracted, or if you lose touch with the feeling of the *shakti*, come back to the technique.

Once you have decided how long you intend to meditate during a given session, it is important to stay with your meditation until the session is over. No matter what your mind does, keep your body on the mat. (It is fine to move in your posture or to stretch if you are uncomfortable.) Your steadiness in staying on the mat is essential for going deeper. It creates the container, the framework, within which a state of meditation can arise.

Of course, it may happen that you come out of meditation once, twice, or several times during the course of a session. This is normal. Simply sit, tune in to the energy in your body, and return to whatever technique or centering practice you have been using until you feel your attention turning inward once again.

A THREE-WEEK MEDITATION PRACTICE SCHEDULE

For each week, two to four practices are offered. You might choose one and work with it all week, or you might experiment with different sets of instructions. I would also suggest that you work with the practice described on pages 148–49, "Invoking the Shakti's Guidance," at least once or twice each week.

You might like to make your own tape of some of these instructions that you can play before meditation.

Week One

The Heart of Meditation

Suggested Focus:

Meditation on

Entering the

Inner Pulsation

Week One

Suggested Focus: Meditation on Entering the Inner Pulsation

Meditation Instructions 1:

MEDITATE ON THE PULSATION OF THE MANTRA

Perform preliminary practices 1–4 (pages 259–61).

Begin to repeat your mantra, coordinating it with your breathing. Focus on the energy, the pulsation within the syllables—not the meaning or the syllables themselves, but the pulsation inside them.

Now imagine yourself surrounded by the mantra. You are inside the mantra. You might imagine a door inside the mantra pulsation and enter the doorway. Or imagine the mantra as a cloud that surrounds you and holds you within itself.

When you feel truly immersed in the mantra, let go of the syllables and focus on the pulsation of energy that they have created in your mind. Understand that the pulsation *is* the mantra. That pulsation of energy is the *shakti* of the mantra. It is filled with grace, with divine Awareness, with insight, and with love.

Allow yourself to rest in the pulsation of energy. Imagine an opening or a doorway inside the pulsation, and feel yourself gliding through it. It is not your body that enters the pulsation. It is you as energy, as a point of awareness. As you enter the pulsation, you are entering deeper into your own consciousness, your own inner energy field.

Rest there. If thoughts arise, understand that they are energy, *shakti*.

At any point in this meditation process, the *shakti* of your own inner consciousness may shift your state or guide your meditation in some way. Remember, inner experiences that arise in meditation—subtle feelings, lights, sounds—are all expressions of *shakti*. Let yourself open to the process, allowing the energy to carry you deeper inside. If thoughts arise, remember to regard the thoughts as pulsations of *shakti*. If you should become distracted, return to focusing on the pulsation within the mantra.

VARIATION

Once you've centered your awareness on the inner pulsation, you may want to ask the *shakti* for guidance in meditation, as in the practice described in chapter 8, pages 148-49. Focusing on the pulsation inside your awareness, honor it, recognizing it as a pulsation of the *kundalini*. Then ask the *kundalini* to guide your meditation, to show you how it wants you to meditate, or simply to give you whatever experience of meditation is right for you today.

Meditation Instructions 2:

ENTERING THE HEART

Begin with the four preliminary steps (pages 259–61).

Follow the rhythm of the breathing, focusing on the space where the inhalation dissolves in the heart region and where the exhalation dissolves outside. Have the understanding that the thoughts that arise and subside are made of Consciousness, and let them dissolve into the breath.

Become aware of the inner heart space. It is located at a point four to five inches below the collarbone, inside. (This is not, of course, the physical heart, but a subtle center of Consciousness, a center where we can directly experience the inner Self.)

When you let yourself become quiet, when you settle into the breath, you find yourself in the heart....As you become accustomed to this practice, you can simply sit on your meditation mat and walk into your own heart, the subtle heart, the innermost core of your being.

GURUMAYI
CHIDVILASANANDA

Let your awareness, with the breath, center itself in the inner heart space. Be aware of the energy in that space, the energy inside your heart. How does it feel? What do you sense there? Let yourself explore the space of the heart. See if you can feel the subtle pulsation, the throbbing energy within the heart space. The heartbeat is there, but there's a subtler throb, the throb of your deeper energy, the throb of the heart. As your awareness explores the heart space, have the feeling that there is an opening, a doorway, within the energy of the heart. It's leading inward. You may imagine the opening visually, or simply feel the presence of an opening. Allow your attention to move inward through that opening, deeper into the heart space. It's not your body that moves through the heart space, it's your attention. As you rest in this deeper heart space, let your attention merge with the energy there.

When you are ready, imagine another opening within the heart space. Let your attention move through it, entering deeper into the heart until you come to the place where your attention wants to rest. Rest there, in your spacious heart. As you breathe in, feel that you breathe in pure conscious energy. As you breathe out, allow the pure conscious energy to expand the energy in your heart. Your breath is pure conscious energy. Your thoughts are pure conscious energy.

It may happen during this exercise that the energy draws your attention to another spiritual center such as the space between the eyebrows or the crown of the head. If this happens, let yourself go with it.

Meditation Instructions 3:

ENTERING THE SPACE BETWEEN BREATHS

Begin with the four preliminary practices (pages 259–61).

Focus your attention on the movement of the breath. As you breathe in, feel that you are breathing pure, subtle Consciousness. With each exhalation, feel that you are breathing out your thoughts.

At the end of the inbreath, notice the place where the breath dissolves in the region of the heart. Focus gently in that space, not straining or forcing yourself to hold your breath, simply noticing the space when it occurs. In the same way, focus on the place at the end of the exhalation where the breath dissolves outside the body.

Sometimes as you practice this *dharana*, you will find that the inner and outer spaces become one. You realize that your body is no longer a barrier between inside and outside. You can simply rest in that space.

As you become more and more centered in the space between breaths, imagine an opening at the end of the exhalation. You may visualize it as a doorway, or simply feel it as an open space. Enter that opening. It is not your body that enters it, but yourself as awareness, as attention. Hold your awareness in the space you sense there even as the breath continues to flow in and out naturally. You are not holding your breath. You are simply letting yourself rest in the space at the end of the exhalation.

Keep moving deeper into the space at the end of the exhalation. Meditate on that inner space. If thoughts arise, remember that they are made of Consciousness, of energy, of *shakti*.

AFTER MEDITATION

Take some time to come out of meditation, and let yourself sit long enough to savor the subtle feeling that remains. If you have space, you can lie down on your back in the corpse pose (as described on page 202) for a few minutes. Sometimes those few moments of rest after meditation bring you all the fruits of meditation. The shift into the Self that may have eluded you during your sitting meditation practice may come all on its own when you relax in the moments after meditation.

As soon as your meditation is finished, record what you experienced. If the experiences are very subtle, you may have to contemplate them for a while to find language to describe them. It is important to do this, no matter how imprecise you feel the language is.

Offer your meditation to God, to your Guru, and for the upliftment of all beings.

See how long you can keep the sense of connection to your inner spaciousness. You can do this by bringing your attention into the heart, by focusing on the breath, or by repeating the mantra with awareness of the pulsation in the syllables.

Continue to practice these exercises each morning and evening for the rest of Week One.

God is much closer to us than our own soul, for he is the ground in which our soul stands.

JULIAN OF NORWICH

Week Two

Suggested Focus: Meditation on Consciousness

Meditation Instructions 1:

BECOME THE KNOWER

The following meditation is based on one of the classical Self-knowledge practices of Vedanta, often called the practice of *neti neti,* or "not this, not this." In this profoundly liberating process, we detach ourselves from identifying with the body, mind, and ego so that pure Awareness can reveal itself.

Begin with the preliminary practices 1–4 (pages 259–61).

Sitting comfortably, become aware of your experience of being where you are at this moment. Notice the sounds around you, the sensation of the air against your face, the clothes against your skin. Notice the sensations that go with sitting—your thighs meeting the floor or chair, the way your muscles grip to hold you in position. Be aware of the back muscles—how they contract to hold up the spine or relax against the back of the chair.

Now become aware of the internal sensations in your body. How is your stomach feeling? Are your cheeks and forehead relaxed or tight? Does some part of your body feel warm or cool?

Say to yourself, "I observe this body. If I can know my body, it must be outside me." Tell yourself, "I am aware of my body, but I am not my body."

Become aware of the breath, noticing how it flows in and out of your nostrils, how it moves downward to expand your lungs. As you follow the

Suggested Focus: Meditation on Consciousness

breath, tell yourself, "I am observing my breath. Since I can observe the breath, it must be outside me. I am not my breath."

Become aware now of the experience of your own energy. How is your energy? Do you feel alert? Dull or sleepy? Fresh? Wired?

As you observe your energy, tell yourself, "I witness the state of my energy. Since I can observe my energy, it must be outside me. It must be other than me. I am not my energy."

Become aware of the flow of thoughts and images in your mind, the running commentary, the mental static. Be aware, too, of any emotions that arise, of the underlying mood that prevails. Observe the flow of thoughts and feelings. Observe your mood.

Now tell yourself, "I know my thoughts. I am aware of my feelings. I witness my moods. Therefore, they are external to me. I am not my thoughts and feelings. I am not my moods."

Become aware of your feeling of "I-ness," your ego. Notice how there's a part of you that feels like a particular "me," that identifies itself as someone. Say to yourself, "I am the knower of this feeling of "I-ness." Since I am observing it, it must be outside me. I am not my ego."

Now ask yourself, "Who is the knower, the witness, of the body, the mind, the ego? Who is the knower?"

Just ask the question, "Who is the knower?" and wait to see what arises. If you are moved to do so, keep asking the question, waiting in silence, then asking again. You are not looking for an answer in words or for a particular experience. You are inviting the Self, the witnessing Consciousness, to reveal itself.

Finally rest in the knower. Meditate *as* the knower.

(As you experiment with this practice, you may find that you prefer to ask a different question such as "Who is the witness?" or "Who am I?")

Meditation Instructions 2:

MEDITATE ON YOUR OWN AWARENESS

Begin with the four preliminary practices (pages 259–61).

Focus your attention on the breath, following each breath as it comes in and goes out. With each exhalation, have the feeling that you are letting go of any tension in your body, any fear, any feeling of limitation. As thoughts arise, breathe them out. If emotions arise, breathe them out as well. Notice the inner space that remains each time you breathe out thoughts or emotions or limitations. Continue breathing out your thoughts, tension, fear, and limitation until your mind begins to become quiet.

Allow yourself to notice the Awareness through which you know your body, your breath, and your thoughts. Keep your attention on Awareness. As thoughts come up, as your attention moves to different objects, let the thoughts and objects go with the breath and focus on Awareness.

AFTER MEDITATION

Follow the instructions given in Week One.

Indeed, it is the Infinite, beginningless and endless, which exists as the pure experiencing Consciousness.

YOGA VASISHTHA

Week Three

Suggested Focus: Devotional Meditation

Follow the four preliminary practices (pages 259–61), then practice one of the techniques below.

Meditation Instructions 1:

BREATHING IN LOVE

Focus your awareness on the breath as it flows in and out. Feel that you are breathing in love and breathing out love.

Meditation Instructions 2:

DEVOTIONAL MANTRA REPETITION

Repeat your mantra with one of the following *bhavanas:*

1. Have the feeling that you are offering the mantra to the Beloved inside your heart or dropping it into the heart of God.

2. Imagine each repetition of the mantra as a flower being offered to the Beloved in your heart.

3. As you repeat the mantra, feel that it is God, your own divine Self, who is repeating it.

Meditation Instructions 3:

RESTING IN THE DIVINE HEART

Focusing your attention on the breath, allow each inbreath to bring you to the awareness of the inner space of the heart. It is not the physical heart you are touching here, but the subtle center in the chest region, at the place where the inhalation naturally comes to rest.

Say very gently to yourself, as if you were saying a mantra, "My heart is God's heart" or "My heart is the heart of the universe." Each time you repeat the words, pause and rest in the space created inside you by the thought that your heart is God's heart, the heart of the universe. Feel that you rest in the divine heart. If thoughts arise, let them dissolve into the space of the divine heart.

CHAPTER 14

The Process of Ripening

Much of the work of meditation takes place underground, and much of it is imperceptible. That is one reason why we measure our progress in meditation not so much by what happens during a particular session of meditation, as by the subtle ways in which a regular meditation practice changes our feelings about ourselves and the world. Otherwise our day-to-day experience in meditation often seems to follow no discernible progression. More often it is rather like moving through different weather patterns.

If you look at a weather map, you will see that it is marked with colors and swirls. In the blue zone, there is rain; in the red zone, sunshine. The green zone is having tropical storms, and the yellow

Do you remember how your life yearned out of childhood toward the "great thing"? I see that it is now yearning forth beyond the great thing toward the greater one. That is why it does not cease to be difficult, but that is also why it will not cease to grow.

RAINER MARIA RILKE

zone shows an unseasonable snowfall. It often feels like that in meditation. Different weathers seem to succeed each other. A period of profound, quiet meditation might be followed by a stormy period of agitation when the mind just won't get quiet, and then by a sort of gray period when meditation feels rather shallow or by a period when you feel resistance to meditating.

You might go through a day or a week of great lightness and bliss. Then on the next day, you are stuck in some heavy emotion. Your heart feels dry; your mind, thick and opaque. One day you have a full experience of the witness, and the next, your mind refuses to let go of thinking. On Tuesday you come out of meditation feeling brilliant, attuned to your world. You think, "Meditation is so great—it makes my mind sharp as a tack." On Wednesday you walk around feeling so dull or spacy that you can't help wondering, "Maybe meditation is making me lose my memory."

Why is it like this? It isn't because meditation changes. It is simply because, as we have seen, our journey inward is always taking us through different layers or terrains of our inner Consciousness. Swami Muktananda used to astonish us sometimes by his insistence on seeing whatever you brought him in a positive light. As everyone who knew him could attest, his favorite expression in Hindi was *"Bahut'accha—Very good."*

"I feel bliss," you would tell him. *"Bahut'accha,"* he would say. "You're experiencing the bliss of the Self." "I feel depressed!" you would tell him. *"Bahut'accha! You're experiencing purification."* "I feel nothing," you would say. *"Bahut'accha,"* he'd say. "You're experiencing the void." "Baba," you would say, "fifteen demons came out of the mantra and chewed me up and then set me on fire!" *"Bahut'accha,"* he would say. "You are being purified. Meditate on the place where you dissolved." Impatient for analysis or distrustful of the process, we would sometimes wonder if he understood how boring that void space was or how depressing the sadness.

As the years passed, we came to see that he understood very well and that, with the utter conviction of a man who has passed through every nook and cranny of the inner universe, he knew that it was all fine. Baba Muktananda's unshakable view was that human consciousness is divine and that whatever arises within it is dyed irrevocably with the hue of divinity. Besides, he knew that every bubble of feeling, thought, or image that comes up, whether we accept it wholeheartedly or reject it utterly, will ultimately dissolve back into the underlying fabric of Awareness, whose essence is love. Where else can thoughts and images or feelings and emotions go if not back into the Consciousness of which they are made?

Therefore, his chief concern was to keep us meditating, because he knew that eventually the very process of meditation itself would take us through whatever we needed to go through and out the other side. One of Baba Muktananda's principles was "Keep moving." He knew, I think, that our belief structures and fears—the ones that are always hanging about in the recesses of the personal mind—can start to jam us if we spend too much time thinking and worrying about our experiences. Contemplation is necessary. But trying to figure out the whys and wherefores of what we are experiencing, or letting ourselves be frightened or discouraged by a strange sensation or mood (or alternatively letting ourselves get overexcited by a "high" experience), can lock us right into one of our limiting concepts. The only solution is to keep on going. Consciousness itself will correct any imbalances that you feel. Meditation itself will show you what you need to know. Therefore, as Gurumayi once said, "You don't have to wonder whether you are at the beginning or the middle or close to your destination. Wherever you are, that is the perfect place for you to be."

When a pilot flies from New York to Paris, he is never exactly on course. He is always adjusting, always correcting slight deviations. So his flight pattern can be described as a process of error-correction, error-correction—until he finally arrives at his destination. Our inner process is much like this: a constant process of balance. Spiritual progress is not, as we sometimes imagine, a straight line. It is more like a zigzag, two steps forward and one step back. Yet if we keep at it with a strong intention, we do arrive at the destination.

RIPENING

Of course, it is all very well to say this or hear it. It is quite another to be stuck in the middle of the process, pushing against some inner wall and wondering if it will ever come down. Sometimes we want to storm the inner world, like Ramakrishna's first disciples who would wake up and say, "Another day gone, and still no vision of God!" Filled with aspiration and longing, we can't understand why the inner universe won't open up to us immediately.

At other times, we wonder if we will ever learn how to hold the mind still for longer than five minutes. We become discouraged because "bad" feelings that we think we should be rid of by now are still with us. We forget how much the process of meditation is about self-confrontation, self-recognition, and the humbling daily encounter with the gap between who we want to be and who we actually are.

In this practice, no effort is ever lost. Even a little of this practice protects one from great fear.

BHAGAVAD GITA

When you plant a peach tree, it has its season of sprouting. It grows through several seasons, bearing leaves, and then flowering. When it reaches a certain point of maturity, it bears fruit. How long this takes depends on many things—the soil, the weather, the type of tree, the quality of the water—but eventually the tree will bear fruit, and once it does, it goes on fruiting year after year. Spiritual growth is exactly like that. It is for most people a slow and gradual process, a matter of ripening. It happens in its own time. We don't know when fruition will happen. All we can know is that it will.

Let me give you one more personal example. I wrote in chapter 1 about one of the milestone experiences in what I would call the opening of my heart. In fact, this was a stage in a process that took years. After the intense sweetness of my early, post-*shaktipat* experiences, I entered a phase where whenever I sat for meditation, I would feel a hard and almost painful energy around my heart. Occasionally the shell over my heart would seem to dissolve, and I would find myself in an inner field of sweetness. Mostly, though, I spent my hours of meditation face to face with the wall around my heart. I came to take it for granted, to accept this prickly sensation of intense energy pushing up against the heart region. I would repeat the mantra, focus on the breath, and often go quite deep into a state of wide, expansive quiet. But the shell around my heart remained firmly in place.

During this time, I used to pray intensely to feel more love and for my heart to open fully. But it never happened for more than a few hours or, at most, days. It was terribly frustrating.

Then after nearly ten years of steady practice, I realized one day that, without my having noticed what had happened, my heart had become softer. The energy was no longer hard and painful. Gradually during the next few years, the feeling of softening and opening in the heart kept growing. Nowadays my normal daily experience is of a silky and tender sweetness around the heart that deepens during meditation into what I can only describe as a sensation of golden love.

In hindsight, of course, I understand why it took so long. Opening the knot of the heart is not a simple matter, not for anyone. I had many, many layers of armor around my heart, layers that had to be removed one by one—layers that are still being removed since we often tend to replace one form of armor with another. So much goes into these deep inner transformations, including a tremendous configuration of grace, personal effort, and the sheer work of time. That particular transformation involved years of inner practice, steady daily meditation, and chanting. It also included work performed as service, much prayer, and the process of life itself—the inner work of relationships, of the demands of living in a community, of doing work I liked and didn't like, of getting what I wanted and failing to get it. Running through all of this, powering it, and making it possible was the great imponderable, unquantifiable, undercover work of grace. Working through my practice and the situations that rubbed against my heart, grace gradually cleansed and made subtle my inner energy field. Layers came off so that I could feel the sweetness of what lay behind them. The subtle will got strengthened so that my body could hold more energy. More than that, during this time that loving inner energy, the energy of grace, soothed and healed many of my emotional wounds, the raw places that we all hold in our hearts so that finally I could let go of the carapace that I had built up to guard the wounded place inside. Then the love that was there could be felt and expressed.

The whole process becomes even more mysterious when I realize that even though I say "I" let go, the truth is that I didn't let go. I *couldn't* let go. Letting go simply happened. It happened in its own time, and it took as long as it took.

The process of ripening is like this. Our practice creates the arena that allows it to happen. But the shifts, the inner changes, and the openings—how do they happen? So naturally, so subtly, that when the process is done, we often feel that our efforts had nothing to do with the change. Yet it is the interaction of our efforts with grace that makes change possible.

Perhaps that is why it is a good idea to ask yourself periodically, "How have I been transformed since I started meditating?" You might look at the shifts in the way you feel about yourself, the changes in your character and in the way you relate to other people, the difference in the way you work. Look, too, at the more subtle shifts in your inner atmosphere, in the clarity of your mind, and in the flow of your energy. Write down what you discover, and also take some time to honor your own process and the power that plays through your meditation.

However firmly embedded the awareness of one's individuality may be, it ultimately merges into Consciousness. For this reason, one is always a pilgrim journeying toward Consciousness.

SWAMI MUKTANANDA

A LAST WORD

The purpose of this book and of the whole experience of meditation is to help you enter into a deeper relationship with yourself. The principles and disciplines in these pages—the commitment to daily meditation, to keeping a journal, and to entering meditation with conscious intention and respect—are offered not as rites you must follow but as clues to speed your own process. They are designed to create a structure within which you can soar. All the instructions should be taken as launching platforms for your inner exploration, vehicles through which

Kundalini can direct your meditation. The more you invest them—and any practice—with your own feeling, intention, and inspiration, the more the energy that unfolds will leap up and dance through your being and the more she will inspire you. So when inspiration arises, when new ways of meditating suggest themselves, think of them as gifts of the *shakti*. If you feel drawn to sit for meditation in a different place than usual or at an odd time, give in to the impulse and contemplate its effect. Let the thread of meditation weave its way through your life, and see how it makes you feel.

These practices can set a pattern for the rest of your life as a meditator, especially if you remember that what you seek in meditation is your own Beloved, your own inner intelligence, your own Awareness, your own Truth. The one who lives inside you reveals herself in so many ways. She dances as the subtle energy that gathers in your body when you close your eyes. She pulses in the breath and surges forth as the understanding that your breath is being moved by a greater force. She is there as the feeling of love or softness that sneaks in when you relax your tense muscles, as the pressure in your forehead, and as the awareness of Awareness. She comes as the peaceful feeling of inner quiet, as the insight into your own magnificence, as the highest thought you are capable of holding about yourself, and as the ease you feel when you breathe out tension. Even when your energy feels tense, ragged, opaque, or painful, even when thoughts and emotions whirl like dust devils through your inner space or when dullness lies like sludge in your heart, she is there at the bottom of your agitations and behind the feelings, memories, and sensations. She is in every moment of your meditation; she is your inner friend, your lover, and yourself. Keep looking for her, for him, for That—for the one whom Gurumayi calls the inner companion.

*I salute the Self!
Salutations to myself—the
undivided Consciousness,
the jewel of all the seen
and the unseen worlds!*

YOGA VASISHTHA

280

When you sense that presence, let yourself be with it. Let yourself be it. Meditate on your own Self, the one who is always there for you, the one who contains you in its stillness, the one who is always meditating on you.

May your practice of meditation unfold joyfully in all its seasons and bring you again and again to your own heart, the Heart of the universe, the great Self.

APPENDIX 1

Kundalini

This book is an expression of the Siddha Yoga tradition, based on the teachings and practices taught by Gurumayi Chidvilasananda and her predecessor, Swami Muktananda. At the core of this path is the awakening of *kundalini* through the grace of the spiritual master. In the following discussion, we will look at *kundalini* as this power is understood in the Indian tradition and in Siddha Yoga.

"Your life alone, great Mother, is the breath of every creature," wrote the nineteenth-century Bengali poet Ramprasad. His lines touch the mystery of *kundalini shakti,* the inner power that many yogic texts describe as the force behind spiritual growth. *Kundalini* is a mystery, a source of both fascination and confusion, and the subject of one of the most esoteric branches of spiritual literature. Mentioned in Indian yogic texts dating at least as far back as the sixth century C.E., *kundalini* is also described in the Taoist yoga manual *The Secret of the Golden Flower* and in many key texts of Tibetan yoga. In our time, traditional texts on *kundalini yoga* like the *Shiva Samhita* and the *Hatha Yoga Pradipika* are available in spiritual bookstores, along with shelves full of scholarly and popular books on the subject. Many longtime meditators, especially those who have been initiated by teachers of certain Indian and Tibetan Guru lineages, have experienced *kundalini* in the course of their practice. Even so, *kundalini* is often discussed—even, on the face of it— in many classical yogic texts, as if it were an almost mechanical energy, an energy that can be manipulated, an energy that one can learn to control or that can go awry.

In fact, *kundalini* is much more than that, and here is the heart of both its fascination and its mystery. As French scholar Jean Varenne says in *Yoga and the Hindu Tradition,* "The *kundalini* is *shakti,* the divine power incarnated in the body and inextricably involved in its destiny." The sages who compiled the Hindu Tantras, yogic texts in which *kundalini* is invoked and celebrated, regarded it as the living deity, Kundalini or Shakti, the Goddess, whose special gift to us is spiritual awareness. As a verse in the *Niruttara Tantra* states, "Without knowledge of *shakti,* liberation is unattainable."

In the Tantric tradition the name "Kundalini"—which means "coiled"—is actually a name for the cosmic creative energy, the *shakti* or power aspect of God, and to understand how she works within the human body, we need to understand this basic fact about her nature. This tradition, which includes the texts of Kashmir Shaivism, describes the ultimate reality as an inseparable dyad known as Shiva/Shakti. Often personified in mythology as a divine couple, Shiva and Shakti represent the two complementary poles of a single unbroken divine reality. Shiva is the still ground, the pure witnessing Consciousness that contains all that is. Shakti is the dynamic creative power inherent in reality, the power that, according to the tradition, manifests universes in blissful freedom. As the *Pratyabhijna Hridayam* puts it, "Supremely independent Chiti [a name for Shakti] is the cause of the manifestation, maintenance, and reabsorption of the universe. She manifests it upon her own screen." In a commentary on this verse, Gurumayi Chidvilasananda writes:

> Kundalini Shakti is so deft in Her own creation. Not only does She create but She creates everything upon Her own being. A potter makes pots using clay, but She creates everything out of Her own being, within Her own being, and upon Her own being. Therefore, She is called both transcendent and immanent. She is in the universe, She is also beyond the universe. She is within everything, yet She transcends everything also. She is both the womb and the child....

She is day, and She is night. She is the sun, and She is the moon. She is high tide, and She is low tide. She is loss, and She is gain. She is the power in all that exists and all that does not exist. She is a moment, and She is infinite aeons. She makes the eyes blink and the lips move. She bestows fortune and misfortune. If you know Her, you can smile at Her play. If you don't know Her, you live in misery. She must be known. Let's put it this way: She wants to be known. She is the Holy Spirit. She is sacred. She touches all, but remains untouched. She sees all, but remains unseen. She belongs to everyone, but no one owns Her. Without Her there is no universe.

Shakti, the Kashmiri Shaivite texts tell us, becomes the universe by a process of contraction—vast, formless, infinitely subtle energy becoming solidified into matter, rather as vapor condenses to form water and then ice. As the cosmic energy contracts, she veils her real nature, concealing herself behind the screen of forms. When Shakti is contracted, a human being—who is in essence pure, free Consciousness—remains blind to the truth about himself. This is an essential point of the Tantric worldview: The very power that has manifested the forms of this world works inside us to turn our senses outward and create the illusion that we are a particular individual, separate from all else. Therefore, there can be no experience of oneness unless the power consents, as it were, to turn the mind within and reveal the essence behind forms.

When we are in this state of contraction and limitation, *kundalini* is said to be "asleep." What is called the awakening of *kundalini* is actually the reversal of the energy's contracting or outward-flowing tendency, so that instead of concealing our real nature of pure energy, light, and bliss, the awakened *kundalini* begins to reveal it. But first the human body has to be prepared to experience itself as pure Consciousness. So the energy that has been turning the mind and senses outward and giving us the experience of separation and difference now begins to move through the subtle system, purifying it and giving it the power to turn inward. Most yogic traditions describe this as the movement of *kundalini* upward through a subtle channel called the *sushumna nadi*, which runs from the base of the spine to the crown of the head within our subtle, or energetic, system. *Kundalini* moves through the chakras, or spiritual centers, lying along the *sushumna nadi*;

285

it opens them, thus opening the doors to the mystical dimensions of experience. Eventually, as *kundalini* becomes stable in the topmost chakra in the crown of the head, the practitioner experiences union, oneness with all things. Over time, this experience begins to permeate the activity of the outgoing senses, allowing the experience of uninterrupted unity consciousness.

Since *kundalini* is a universal power, its effects have been felt — and recorded — by mystics of every tradition and also by many who would not call themselves mystics. The visions, raptures, insights, and mystical realizations described by Christian mystics like Teresa of Avila or Hildegard of Bingen, by Jewish mystics like Israel Baal Shem Tov, and by Sufi, Taoist, and Buddhist practitioners correspond to experiences of awakened *kundalini* described in Indian yogic texts. Vajrayana Buddhist writings, as well as some of the writings in Western hermetic and Kabalistic traditions, closely resemble descriptions of *kundalini* found in the Hindu Tantras. Elaine Pagels, in *The Gnostic Gospels,* quotes an early text of Gnostic Christianity that says: "In every human being dwells an infinite power, the root of the universe. That infinite power exists in two modes: one actual, the other potential. This infinite power exists in a latent condition in everyone."

Christian writers speak of this spiritual energy as the Holy Spirit. In Chinese yoga it is called inner *chi,* in Japanese, inner *ki,* to distinguish it from the external physical energy. The !K'ung bushmen of Africa speak of a powerful subtle energy called *n'um,* while the Hopi of the American Southwest describe the human spinal column as an axis containing vibratory centers. These centers correspond to the chakra system of *kundalini yoga.* In the Indian yogic texts, Kundalini is often depicted as a serpent (Sir John Woodroffe, the first Western scholar to write extensively about the Indian tradition of *kundalini yoga,* referred to *kundalini* as the serpent power); revered texts from Egypt and the Celtic traditions associate the image of the serpent with the ancient goddess religions. Contemporary writers in the Kabalistic tradition have pointed out that the serpent in the Garden of Eden might be best associated with *kundalini* and the initiation into higher knowledge. Carlos Suares, in *The Cipher of Genesis,* describes how Kabala refers to the serpent that appeared to Adam and Esha (Eve) in the Garden of Eden as the resurrection of Aleph, the principle of all that is and all that is not, from its entombment in earth. According to the Kabalistic tradition, when the serpent appears, Adam and Esha are just emerging from a state of deep oblivion. The task of the serpent is to awaken them and begin their journey of evolution. One Kabalistic text states that when the voice of God questions Esha about this event, what she actually says is not "The serpent beguiled me." Instead, she explains that the serpent has blended his earthly fire with her lost heavenly fire, which has come to life again.

How then is *kundalini* awakened? The Eastern texts tell us that it can happen in one of three ways: through certain *hatha yoga* postures and breathing exercises*; through concentrated meditation, worship, and prayer; or through the transmission of energy from a teacher. Kundalini has also been known to come awake spontaneously. Traditional texts say that the most natural and safe means of awakening *kundalini* is through the transmission of energy from a Guru whose own *kundalini* is fully unfolded. This process, called *shaktipat* in the Shaiva yoga tradition of India, is rare but extremely effective. When the teacher activates the energy, a connection is formed between teacher and student through which the energy is automatically regulated and guided. This transmission from the teacher is the basis of Siddha Yoga meditation.

The Siddha Yoga Gurus have followed the tradition of Kashmir Shaivism and the other Tantric texts in pointing out how important it is for a practitioner to understand the divine nature of *kundalini*. Swami Muktananda used to assure his students that since Kundalini is actually the divine power that creates and sustains the universe, she is all-knowing and benevolent and functions according to the individual's needs. Therefore when she has been awakened properly, her actions are always beneficial, although fear and lack of understanding can create problems for a practitioner who lacks proper guidance. Both Swami Muktananda and Gurumayi Chidvilasananda have stressed the importance of *understanding* the nature of Kundalini, nourishing the energy through regular practice and

---

*Swami Muktananda often warned students that when *hatha yoga* postures are practiced to activate *kundalini*, it can create a sudden or partial awakening that can be harmful to the practitioner.

287

discipline, and respecting her. "When you are meditating, if something happens that you don't understand, look upon it as the work of a living deity. Look at it with love and reverence, and then Shakti will help you," Swami Muktananda once told a student.

When *kundalini* awakens, it performs two main tasks within the body. Moving through the *nadis* (subtle channels that carry the vital force to the organs), it begins to purify the body, dissolving blockages, removing toxins, and even taking away latent illnesses. It also purifies the subtle system, the mind, intellect, and emotions, especially during meditation. While this is going on, a practitioner can experience a wide range of phenomena, many of which are discussed in chapter 9 of this book. In his spiritual autobiography, *Play of Consciousness,* Swami Muktananda describes the yogic movements, visions, and realizations that he experienced after receiving *shaktipat* initiation from Bhagawan Nityananda. Though he had practiced meditation for nearly twenty-five years before his initiation, the awakened *kundalini* opened him inwardly in ways he had never known, and this experience expanded over nine years of intense inner practice. At one point, he saw in a series of visions how this luminous energy traveled through his *nadis.* He saw how the energy was purifying him on all levels and inspiring a series of extraordinary mystical visions and realizations. Muktananda's journey culminated when he entered a permanent state of unity-awareness, experiencing total identity with the universe and its creative source. The ultimate effect of practice with an awakened Kundalini is this experience of union: the union of the human consciousness with the vast Consciousness of which it is a part, or as the yogic texts put it, the union between the individual soul and the supreme soul. In this state Kundalini recognizes herself, and we realize our own true identity as limitless Consciousness.

Gurumayi Chidvilasananda describes this experience of reunion that is the ultimate goal of Kundalini awakening and of the spiritual journey: "When Self-recognition takes place, reunion within also takes place. It is this reunion that gives rise to incredible ecstasy, incredible love. Then your old pettiness just falls away, and you become a shelter of supreme compassion. Every object you touch vibrates with your compassion. Every person you see is affected by your compassion. Your dwelling place grows lush with compassion."

APPENDIX 2

The Siddha Yoga Lineage

Siddha Yoga is a path to enlightenment guided by a living spiritual master, Gurumayi Chidvilasananda. It is based on the ancient spiritual traditions of India, brought to modern expression by Swami Muktananda.

The masters of this path are known as Siddhas. The word "siddha" means "accomplished," or "Self-realized," and it refers to a very rare and significant yogic attainment. A practitioner becomes siddha when he attains the full goal of spiritual practice, becoming firmly unified with the supreme Consciousness that is the source of the universe. In India and Tibet, there have been lineages of Siddhas, masters known not only for their depth of yogic attainment but also for their ability to pass on their own state to others. Siddha Yoga meditation has been handed down through such a lineage.

The founder of the contemporary Siddha Yoga lineage was Bhagawan Nityananda, one of the most revered saints of modern India. Nityananda was a mysterious, often silent yogi with a radically nondualistic attitude. ("Where are you looking for God?" he used to say. "God is your mother. God is your father. God is everywhere. God is in

Swami Chidvilasananda

you.") Nityananda had extraordinary and often visible spiritual power, which he employed for the benefit of his devotees and also to quicken the spiritual lives of his disciples. Nityananda offered the rare initiation of *shaktipat* (descent of universal energy), the transmission of awakening energy from a Guru to a disciple, that activates *kundalini*.

Swami Muktananda had been practicing yoga and meditation for twenty-five years when he received initiation from Nityananda, and he practiced for a further nine years before experiencing Self-realization. When Nityananda left his physical body in 1961, he passed on the power of the lineage to Muktananda, whom he had already established in an ashram near his own seat in the western Indian village of Ganeshpuri. Swami Muktananda, a dynamic and charismatic teacher, created the path that has become Siddha Yoga. He laid out a practice/curriculum of chanting of sacred names and texts, service, and study of the scriptures. He also established ashrams—centers of practice and study where students could focus intensively on spiritual development—and taught widely in India and the West. Swami Muktananda not only systematized his Guru's fundamental teaching of oneness (his aphoristic formulations became the core Siddha Yoga teachings "God dwells within you as you" and "See God in each other"), he also created a vehicle for offering *shaktipat* on a wide scale. Called the Siddha Yoga Meditation Intensive, this weekend course allows thousands of seekers to receive this rare initiation in a powerful and protected environment.

During his years of travel and teaching, Swami Muktananda also prepared his closest disciple, Swami Chidvilasananda, known as Gurumayi, to take the mantle of the lineage. He supervised her spiritual education, teaching her the arts of yoga and revealing higher knowledge to her. She was anointed as spiritual head of the Siddha Yoga lineage in 1982. She has expanded the Siddha Yoga teaching mission through her work with her students as well as through her own books, tapes, and teaching events, establishing Siddha Yoga as a cohesive global movement. Gurumayi travels and teaches widely, transmitting the spiritual energy of the lineage not only through traditional discourses but also through interactions, story, drama, music, and many other means. She has written a number of books, including *My Lord Loves a Pure Heart*, a guide to living a spiritual life in the world, *The Yoga of Discipline, Enthusiasm*, and *Courage and Contentment*. She also places special focus on the spiritual development of children and young people and on spiritual expression through music,

Swami Muktananda

art, and drama. While emphasizing the importance of taking time for spiritual retreat and practice, Gurumayi encourages her students to live their spirituality, to act from an inner platform of love, courage, and strength, so that their lives are of benefit to the world around them. Among the practical spiritual expressions that have grown under her hand are the PRASAD Project, which assists the needy in several countries with aid, community development, and medical and dental care, and the Muktabodha Indological

Bhagawan Nityananda

Research Institute, dedicated to preserving the sacred texts and religious practices of India.

Siddha Yoga meditation is taught around the world by trained teachers, both monks and lay people, who have studied and practiced this form of meditation for many years. There are about 250 centers of Siddha Yoga meditation around the world, as well as residential retreat centers in Ganeshpuri and in South Fallsburg, New York. Students are encouraged to spend regular time on retreat, and several types of retreats are offered at the main Siddha Yoga centers.

NOTES

PAGE 4   "Joy is within…" Swami Muktananda, *Mukteshwari* (South Fallsburg, N.Y.: SYDA Foundation, 1995) verse 428.

PAGE 6   *Bhagavad Gita* 13.25

PAGE 7   "The spirit is so near…" Robert Bly, *When Grapes Turn to Wine: Versions of Rumi* (Cambridge, Mass.: Yellow Moon Press, 1986).

PAGE 10   "In meditation…" Gurumayi Chidvilasananda, *My Lord Loves a Pure Heart* (South Fallsburg, N.Y.: SYDA Foundation, 1994) p. 136.

"I did not meditate…" Swami Muktananda, *Play of Consciousness: A Spiritual Autobiography* (South Fallsburg, N.Y.: SYDA Foundation, 2000) p. 145.

PAGE 12   "The true practice…" Shunryu Suzuki, *Zen Mind, Beginner's Mind* (New York: Weatherhill, 1970).

PAGE 14   "Set fire to the Self…" *Shvetashvatara Upanishad.*

PAGE 16   "The Infinite Goodness…" Dante Alighieri, from *12,000 Religious Quotations,* Frank Mead, ed. (Grand Rapids, MI: Baker, 1989).

PAGE 19   "There is a secret…" Robert Bly, *The Kabir Book* (Boston: Beacon Press, 1977).

PAGE 21   "Use your own light…" Stephen Mitchell, *Tao te Ching* (New York: HarperCollins, 1988) verse 52.

PAGE 24   "The one you are looking for…" Attributed to Francis of Assisi.

PAGE 25   "Knowing the Self…" David Godman, *Be As You Are: The Teachings of Sri Ramana Maharshi* (London: Arkana, Penguin Books, 1985).

PAGE 26   "The eye through which…" Stephen Mitchell, *The Enlightened Mind: An Anthology of Sacred Prose* (New York: HarperCollins, 1991).

"Be as you are…" David Godman, *Be As You Are: The Teachings of Sri Ramana Maharshi* (London: Arkana, Penguin Books, 1985) p. 69.

PAGE 27   "The naked, stark, elemental Awareness…" William Johnston, ed., *The Cloud of Unknowing and The Book of Privy Counseling* (New York: Bantam, Doubleday, Dell Publishing Group, 1973).

PAGE 28   *Kena Upanishad* 1.6

PAGE 29   "No words are necessary…" Coleman Barks, *Feeling the Shoulder of the Lion* (Putney, Vt.: Threshold Books, 1991).

PAGE 30   "The Supreme Self…" Gurumayi Chidvilasananda, *Resonate with Stillness* (South Fallsburg, N.Y.: SYDA Foundation, 1995) January 19.

PAGE 32   "No, my soul is…" Robert Bly, *The Soul Is Here for Its Own Joy* (Hopewell, N.J.: The Ecco Press, 1995).

PAGE 33   "The whole purpose of yoga…" Gurumayi Chidvilasananda, *Inner Treasures* (South Fallsburg, N.Y.: SYDA Foundation, 1995) p. 73-74.

PAGE 34   "Who is it…" Swami Muktananda, *The Self Is Already Attained* (South Fallsburg, N.Y.: SYDA Foundation, 1993).

PAGE 36   *Kena Upanishad* 1.5-6

PAGE 38   "Who could live…" Swami Prabhavananda, adapted from *The Upanishads: Breath of the Eternal* (Hollywood, Calif.: Vedanta Press, 1975) *Taittiriya Upanishad* 2.7.1.

"All things are born…" Swami Prabhavananda, adapted from *The Upanishads: Breath of the Eternal* (Hollywood, Calif.: Vedanta Press, 1975) *Taittiriya Upanishad* 3.6.1.

PAGE 39   "You feel love for God…" Gurumayi Chidvilasananda, *The Magic of the Heart* (South Fallsburg, N.Y.: SYDA Foundation, 1996) p. 94.

PAGE 40   "It is my nature…" Fiona Bowie, *Beguine Spirituality* (New York: Crossroad Publishing Co., 1990).

    Vijnana Bhairava 119-20.

PAGE 42   "He who goes…" Mencius, from *I Am With You Always*, Douglas Bloch, ed. (NY: Bantam, 1992).

PAGE 46   "There is an unseen presence…" Coleman Barks, trans., *The Essential Rumi* (New York: HarperCollins, 1995).

    "The Self reveals itself…" *Katha Upanishad* 1.2.23.

PAGE 47   "The Friend has such…" Daniel Ladinsky, *The Subject Tonight Is Love: Sixty Wild and Sweet Poems of Hafiz* (North Myrtle Beach, S.C.: Pumpkin House Press, 1996).

PAGE 48   "Gurumayi once remarked…" Gurumayi Chidvilasananda, *Enthusiasm* (South Fallsburg, N.Y.: SYDA Foundation, 1997) p. 135.

PAGE 50   "Place your faith…" adapted from Swami Muktananda, *Play of Consciousness: A Spiritual Autobiography* (South Fallsburg, N.Y.: SYDA Foundation, 2000) p. 282.

    "The established method…" adapted from Swami Kripananda, *Jnaneshwar's Gita* (South Fallsburg, N.Y.: SYDA Foundation, 1999) verse 18.1219.

    "If one could see…" Jnaneshwar Maharaj, *The Nectar of Self-Awareness* (South Fallsburg, N.Y.: SYDA Foundation, 1979) verse 2.68.

    "Unless taught by a teacher…" *Katha Upanishad* 1.2.8-9.

PAGE 51   "Think this over…" as quoted in Swami Muktananda, *The Perfect Relationship: The Guru and the Disciple* (South Fallsburg, N.Y.: SYDA Foundation, 1999) p. 71.

PAGE 53   "The Guru is not different…" *Nectar of Chanting* (South Fallsburg, N.Y.: SYDA Foundation, 1983) *Guru Gita* 9.

    "Affix to the bow…" Swami Prabhavananda, adapted from *The Upanishads: Breath of the Eternal* (Hollywood, Calif.: Vedanta Press, 1975).

PAGE 55   "I am the same Self…" *Bhagavad Gita* 9.29.

"I saw my Guru…" Swami Muktananda, *Bhagawan Nityananda of Ganeshpuri* (South Fallsburg, N.Y.: SYDA Foundation, 1996) p. 115.

PAGE 56   "From the blossoming…" Sogyal Rinpoche, *The Tibetan Book of Living and Dying* (New York: HarperCollins, 1992).

PAGE 57   "Give up to grace…" Coleman Barks, trans., *The Essential Rumi* (New York: HarperCollins, 1995).

PAGE 60   "This alone is obligatory…" *Malini Vijaya Tantra.*

PAGE 61   "Concentrate wherever…" *Yoga Sutras* 1.39.

PAGE 62   "This alone…" adapted from Mark S. G. Dyczkowski, *The Doctrine of Vibration: An Analysis of the Doctrines and Practices of Kashmir Shaivism* (Albany, N.Y.: The State University of New York Press, 1987).

"A yogi…" *Shiva Sutras* 3.16.

PAGE 65   "To know the Self…" Swami Muktananda, *The Self Is Already Attained* (South Fallsburg, N.Y.: SYDA Foundation, 1993).

PAGE 66   "When a man meditates…" Attributed to Ba'al Shem Tov.

"Kabir says this…" Robert Bly, *The Kabir Book: Forty-Four of the Ecstatic Poems of Kabir* (Boston: Beacon Press, 1977).

PAGE 67   "God is in your *bhava*…" Attributed to Tukaram Maharaj.

PAGE 68   "The Word…" T. S. Eliot, "Ash Wednesday," *The Waste Land* (New York: Harcourt Brace, 1958).

page 69   "The one truth…" M. P. Pandit, *Kularnava Tantra* (Pondicherry: All India Press, 1973).

PAGE 70   *Shiva Sutras* 2.3.

Parasurama Kalpa Sutra adapted from Swami Muktananda *Meditate: Happiness Lies Within You* (South Fallsburg, N.Y.: SYDA Foundation, 1999) p. 24.

PAGE 71   "During worship…" Swami Muktananda, *Lalleshwari* (Ganeshpuri, India: SYDA Foundation, 1981) verse 117.

PAGE 73   "If you want the truth…" Robert Bly, *The Kabir Book: Forty-Four of the Ecstatic Poems of Kabir* (Boston: Beacon Press, 1977).

"Mantra is our real nature…" David Godman, *Be As You Are: The Teachings of Sri Ramana Maharshi* (London: Arkana, Penguin Books, 1985).

PAGE 75   "Don't look for God…." adapted from Swami Muktananda, *Lalleshwari* (Ganeshpuri, India: SYDA Foundation, 1981) verse 22.

PAGE 76   *Pratyabhijna Hridayam* 17.

PAGE 77   "God is the midpoint…" Julian of Norwich, *Revelations of Divine Love.*

"At the still point…" T. S. Eliot, "Burnt Norton," *Four Quartets* (New York: Harcourt Brace, 1971).

Tripura Rahasya 17.2-3.

PAGE 79   "It is very…" Gurumayi Chidvilasananda, *Resonate with Stillness* (South Fallsburg, N.Y.: SYDA Foundation, 1995) October 20.

PAGE 82   "When you find…" Jane Hirshfield, *Women in Praise of the Sacred* (New York: HarperCollins, 1994).

"The Props assist…" Thomas H. Johnson, ed., *Final Harvest: Emily Dickinson's Poems* (Boston: Little, Brown and Company, 1961).

PAGE 84   "Thinking of the magnitude…" Garma C. C. Chang, *The Hundred Thousand Songs of Milarepa, Vol.* 1 (Boston: Shambhala Publications, 1962).

"The throbbing movement…" Swami Muktananda, *Nothing Exists That Is Not Shiva* (South Fallsburg, N.Y.: SYDA Foundation, 1997).

Vijnana Bhairava 46-47.

PAGE 88   "And let me tell…" Swami Muktananda, *Play of Consciousness: A Spiritual Autobiography* (South Fallsburg, N.Y.: SYDA Foundation, 2000) p.40.

PAGE 89   "The knowledge…" adapted from Swami Jagadananda, *Upadeshasahasri: A Thousand Teachings* (Mylapore, Madras: Sri Ramakrishna Math, 1949) verse 2.4.5.

PAGE 90   "Take a pitcher…" Robert Bly, *The Kabir Book: Forty-Four of the Ecstatic Poems of Kabir* (Boston: Beacon Press, 1977).

PAGE 92   "You who want knowledge…" Fiona Bowie, *Beguine Spirituality* (New York: Crossroad Publishing Co., 1990).

PAGE 93   "The entire world…" *Spanda Karikas* 2.5 as quoted in Swami Muktananda, *Secret of the Siddhas* (South Fallsburg, N.Y.: SYDA Foundation, 1994) p. 199.

PAGE 95   "Whether through immense joy…" Constantina Rhodes Bailly, *Meditations on Shiva: The Shivastotravali of Utpaladeva* (Albany, N.Y.: The State University of New York Press, 1995) stotra 5.

PAGE 97   "When, with a…" *Vijnana Bhairava* 63 as quoted in Swami Muktananda, *Secret of the Siddhas* (South Fallsburg, N.Y.: SYDA Foundation, 1994) p. 198.

PAGE 102   "The Mind…" Daniel Ladinsky, *The Gift: Poems by Hafiz* (New York: Penguin Putnam, 1999).

            "In the beginning…" Swami Muktananda, *Where Are You Going?: A Guide to the Spiritual Journey* (South Fallsburg, N.Y.: SYDA Foundation, 1994) p. 113.

PAGE 104   "Love your mind…" Swami Muktananda, *Resonate with Stillness* (South Fallsburg, N.Y.: SYDA Foundation, 1995), March 1.

            "You must stop…" Swami Muktananda, *The Perfect Relationship: The Guru and the Disciple* (South Fallsburg, N.Y.: SYDA Foundation, 1999) p. 137.

PAGE 108   *Yoga Sutras* 1.12

PAGE 109   "When we have…" Gurumayi Chidvilasananda, *Kindle My Heart* (South Fallsburg, N.Y.: SYDA Foundation, 1996) p. 86.

PAGE 111   "Our desires…" H. P. Shastri, *World Within the Mind (Yoga Vasishtha)* (London: Shanti Sadan, 1975).

PAGE 113   "In this nakedness…" Kieran Kavanaugh, *John of the Cross: Selected Writings* (Mahwah, N.J.: Paulist Press, 1987).

PAGE 114   "Pure Consciousness…" Ramana Maharshi. David Goodman, *Be As You Are: The Teachings of Sri Ramana Maharshi* (London: Arkana, Penguin Books, 1985).

PAGE 116   "You lose sight…" Trevor P. Legget, trans., *A First Zen Reader* (Boston: Charles E. Tuttle Co., 1991).

"A yogi should ponder…" Swami Muktananda, *Nothing Exists That Is Not Shiva* (South Fallsburg, N.Y.: SYDA Foundation, 1997) p. 53.

Pratyabhijna Hridayam 5.

PAGE 117   "The Essence of Mind…" Garma C. C. Chang, *The Hundred Thousand Songs of Milarepa, Vol.1* (Boston: Shambhala Publications, 1962).

PAGE 118   "The horse…" Swami Muktananda *Meditate: Happiness Lies Within You* (South Fallsburg, N.Y.: SYDA Foundation, 1999) p. 21.

PAGE 119   "O wavering mind…" Lex Hixon, *Mother of the Universe: Visions of the Goddess and Tantric Hymns of Enlightenment* (Wheaton, Ill.: Quest Books, 1994).

PAGE 123   "One deluded thought…" Timothy Freke, *Zen Wisdom: Daily Teachings from the Zen Masters* (New York: Sterling Publishing, 1997).

PAGE 125   "Wherever the mind goes…" *Vijnana Bhairava* 116.

PAGE 127   "When you are…" *Spanda Karikas* 1.22.

PAGE 130   "Your own mind…" Stephen Mitchell, *The Enlightened Mind: An Anthology of Sacred Prose* (New York: HarperCollins, 1991).

PAGE 134   "Although kundalini…" adapted from Arthur Avalon (Sir John Woodroffe), *The Serpent Power* (New York: Dover Publications, 1974).

PAGE 135   "If you learn how…" Gurumayi Chidvilasananda, *Resonate with Stillness* (South Fallsburg, N.Y.: SYDA Foundation, 1995) April 21.

PAGE 137   "I have realized…" Ramprasad, from *Mother of the Universe* by Lex Hixon (Wheaton, Ill.: Quest Books, 1994).

PAGE 138   "In one of the more lyrical…" Swami Muktananda, *Play of Consciousness: A Spiritual Autobiography* (South Fallsburg, N.Y.: SYDA Foundation, 2000) pp. 11-13.

"The *sadhaka*…" Swami Muktananda, *Play of Consciousness: A Spiritual Autobiography* (South Fallsburg, N.Y.: SYDA Foundation, 2000) p. 198.

PAGE 139   "When you feel…" Coleman Barks, *Unseen Rain: Quatrains of Rumi* (Putney, Vt.: Threshold Books, 1986).

"As she gently moves…" Gurumayi Chidvilasananda, *Resonate with Stillness* (South Fallsburg, N.Y.: SYDA Foundation, 1995) April 15.

PAGE 142   "The most exalted…" Lex Hixon, *Mother of the Universe: Visions of the Goddess and Tantric Hymns of Enlightenment* (Wheaton, Ill.: Quest Books, 1994).

"It is not just…" Gurumayi Chidvilasananda, *Inner Treasures* (South Fallsburg, N.Y.: SYDA Foundation, 1995).

PAGE 145   "Often when I step…" Plotinus. Grace Turnbull, *The Essence of Plotinus* (New York: Oxford University Press, 1934).

PAGE 146   "Please show me…" Attributed to Ramakrishna Paramahamsa.

PAGE 147   "You are no longer…" Lex Hixon, *Mother of the Universe: Visions of the Goddess and Tantric Hymns of Enlightenment* (Wheaton, Ill.: Quest Books, 1994).

PAGE 149   "Holy Spirit…" Stephen Mitchell, *The Enlightened Heart: An Anthology of Sacred Poetry* (New York: HarperCollins, 1989).

PAGE 151   "Trust the divine…" Aurobindo Ghose, *The Mother* (Wisc.: Lotus Press, 1998).

PAGE 152   "Emerging into…" Lex Hixon, *Mother of the Universe: Visions of the Goddess and Tantric Hymns of Enlightenment* (Wheaton, Ill.: Quest Books, 1994).

PAGE 156   "Be strong…" Robert Bly, *The Kabir Book: Forty-Four of the Ecstatic Poems of Kabir* (Boston: Beacon Press, 1977).

"Success in yoga" *Shvetashvatara Upanishad* 2.13.

PAGE 159   "In this body…" *Shiva Samhita*.

PAGE 161   "The unpracticed one…" *Yoga Sikha Upanishad* 1.26-30.

PAGE 165   "It is Her nature…" Gurumayi Chidvilasananda, *Resonate with Stillness* (South Fallsburg, N.Y.: SYDA Foundation, 1995) April 15.

PAGE 167   *Brihadaranyaka Upanishad* 4.4.3-6.

PAGE 169   "Student, tell me…" Robert Bly, *The Kabir Book* (Boston: Beacon Press. 1977).

PAGE 172   "During the period…" *Shvetashvatara Upanishad* 2.11.

PAGE 174   "Our Lord opened…" Grace Warrack, ed., *Revelations of Divine Love* (London: Methuen, 1952).

"Sometimes a very pure…" and "It is the state of omniscience…" Swami Muktananda, *Play of Consciousness: A Spiritual Autobiography* (South Fallsburg, N.Y.: SYDA Foundation, 2000) pp. 99-100.

PAGE 175   "Last night…" Robert Bly, *The Soul Is Here for Its Own Joy* (Hopewell, N.J.: The Ecco Press, 1995).

PAGE 176   "In that moment…" Attributed to Tevekkul-Beg.

PAGE 178   "The soul is not…" Grace H. Turnbull, *The Essence of Plotinus* (New York: Oxford University Press, 1934).

PAGE 182   "Darkness within darkness.…" Stephen Mitchell, *Tao te Ching* (New York: HarperCollins, 1988) verse 1.

PAGE 184   "Everything depends…" Evelyn Underhill, ed., *The Adornment of the Spiritual Marriage* (London: John M. Watkins, 1951).

PAGE 185   "The eye of your eye…" quoted in Swami Muktananda, *Play of Consciousness: A Spiritual Autobiography* (South Fallsburg, N.Y.: SYDA Foundation, 2000) p. 170.

PAGE 186   "Gaze intently…" Lex Hixon, *Mother of the Universe: Visions of the Goddess and Tantric Hymns of Enlightenment* (Wheaton, Ill.: Quest Books, 1994).

"The Lord of the universe…" Swami Muktananda, *Play of Consciousness: A Spiritual Autobiography* (South Fallsburg, N.Y.: SYDA Foundation, 2000) pp. 157, 158.

PAGE 188   "*Nirvikalpa is chit…*" David Godman, *Be As You Are: The Teachings of Sri Ramana Maharshi* (London: Arkana, Penguin Books, 1985).

PAGE 189   "Eye cannot see it…" Stephen Mitchell, *The Enlightened Heart: An Anthology of Sacred Poetry* (New York: HarperCollins, 1989).

"As my mind…" Swami Muktananda, *Play of Consciousness: A Spiritual Autobiography* (South Fallsburg, N.Y.: SYDA Foundation, 2000) p. 183.

PAGE 190   "The *turiya* state…" Gurumayi Chidvilasananda, quoted in *Darshan* magazine (South Fallsburg, N.Y.: SYDA Foundation, 1999) vol. 143, p. 42.

"The divine flashes forth." *Shiva Sutras* 1.5.

"My mind melted…" *Viveka Chudamani* 482.

PAGE 191   "Again the light…" Attributed to Symeon the New Theologian.

"Drinking this love…" Gurumayi Chidvilasananda, *Pulsation of Love* (South Fallsburg, N.Y.: SYDA Foundation, 2001) p. 15.

"The light…" E. Allison Peers, trans., *The Life of Teresa of Jesus: The Autobiography of Teresa of Avila* (New York: Image Books, Doubleday, 1991).

PAGE 193   "God alone reveals…" Attributed to Meister Eckhart.

"My I is God…" Catherine of Genoa, *Life and Doctrine of Saint Catherine of Genoa.*

PAGE 194   "As I went…" Gurumayi Chidvilasananda, *Pulsation of Love* (South Fallsburg, N.Y.: SYDA Foundation, 2001) p. 6-7.

PAGE 195   "I do not know…"Catherine of Genoa, *Life and Doctrine of Saint Catherine of Genoa.*

"When camphor…" Swami Muktananda, *Secret of the Siddhas* (South Fallsburg, N.Y.: SYDA Foundation, 1994) p. 57.

"For a while…" Jnaneshwar Maharaj, *The Nectar of Self-Awareness* (South Fallsburg, N.Y.: SYDA Foundation, 1979) verse 7.174-75.

PAGE 197   "He who without hesitation…" Constantina Rhodes Bailly, *Meditations on Shiva: The Shivastotravali of Utpaladeva* (Albany, N.Y.: The State University of New York Press, 1995) stotra 13.

"Ever immersed…" Rabindranath Tagore, *Songs of Kabir* (York Beach, Maine: Samuel Weiser, Inc., 1991).

"Even now…" Swami Muktananda, *Play of Consciousness: A Spiritual Autobiography* (South Fallsburg, N.Y.: SYDA Foundation, 2000) p. 210.

PAGE 198   "It is told…" Attributed to Martin Buber.

PAGE 200 "A person looks..." Jane Hirshfield, *Women in Praise of the Sacred* (New York: HarperCollins, 1994).

PAGE 202 "A great yogin..." commentary on *Pratyabhijna Hridayam* 19.

PAGE 204 "Let the Truth..." Gurumayi Chidvilasananda, *Resonate with Stillness* (South Fallsburg, N.Y.: SYDA Foundation, 1995) July 26.

PAGE 207 "Learn to listen..." Stephen Mitchell, *The Enlightened Mind: An Anthology of Sacred Prose* (New York: HarperCollins, 1991).

PAGE 210 "While you live..." Trevor P. Legget, trans., *A First Zen Reader* (Boston: Charles E. Tuttle Co., 1991).

PAGE 212 "The true man of God..." Stephen Mitchell, *The Enlightened Mind: An Anthology of Sacred Prose* (New York: HarperCollins, 1991).

"The essence of *sadhana*..." Swami Muktananda, *I Have Become Alive: Secrets of the Inner Journey* (South Fallsburg, N.Y.: SYDA Foundation, 1992) p. 54.

PAGE 215 "To attend..." Rabbi Rami M. Shapiro, *Wisdom of the Jewish Sages: A Modern Reading of Pirke Avot* (New York: Crown Publishers, 1993).

"When someone directs..." Gurumayi Chidvilasananda, *Smile, Smile, Smile!* (South Fallsburg, N.Y.: SYDA Foundation, 1999) p. 31.

PAGE 218 "The more awareness..." Coleman Barks, *Rumi: One-Handed Basket Weaving* (Athens, Ga.: Maypop Books, 1991).

PAGE 220 "A heart resolved..." Gurumayi Chidvilasananda, *Smile, Smile, Smile!* (South Fallsburg, N.Y.: SYDA Foundation, 1999) p. 34.

PAGE 222 "If you don't realize..." Stephen Mitchell, *Tao te Ching* (New York: HarperCollins, 1988) verse 16.

"Practicing the Opposite" *Yoga Sutras* 2.33.

"You have a right..." *Bhagavad Gita* 2.47.

PAGE 224 "The mountain..." Trevor P. Legget, trans., *A First Zen Reader* (Boston: Charles E. Tuttle Co., 1991).

PAGE 227   "Whenever the unsteady mind..." *Bhagavad Gita* 6.26.

PAGE 230   "Yoga is not..." *Bhagavad Gita* 6.16.

PAGE 232   "One thing I always did..." Swami Muktananda, *Play of Consciousness: A Spiritual Autobiography* (South Fallsburg, N.Y.: SYDA Foundation, 2000) p. 132.

PAGE 233   "Can you coax..." Stephen Mitchell, *Tao te Ching* (New York: HarperCollins, 1988) verse 10.

PAGE 235   "How could we forget..." Rainer Maria Rilke, Stephen Mitchell, trans., *Letters to a Young Poet* (New York: Vintage Books, 1986).

PAGE 237   "All the rough edges..." Gurumayi Chidvilasananda, *Courage and Contentment: A Collection of Talks on Spiritual Life* (South Fallsburg, N.Y.: SYDA Foundation, 1999) p. 66.

"When one is in the state..." *Spanda Karikas* 22.

PAGE 239   "Fighting and peacefulness..." Coleman Barks, trans., *The Essential Rumi* (New York: HarperCollins, 1995).

PAGE 241   "I have a feeling..." Robert Bly, *The Soul Is Here for Its Own Joy* (Hopewell, N.J.: The Ecco Press, 1995).

PAGE 242   *Pratyabhijna Hridayam* 8.

PAGE 243   "Think of the empty space..." William Mahony, *The Artful Universe: An Introduction to the Vedic Religious Imagination* (Albany, N.Y.: The State University of New York Press, 1998) *Brahmabindu Upanishad* 13–14.

PAGE 248   "Greatness exists..." *Courage and Contentment: A Collection of Talks on Spiritual Life* (South Fallsburg, N.Y.: SYDA Foundation, 1999) p. 140.

PAGE 249   "The pearl..." Hari Prasad Shastri, trans., *Indian Mystic Verse* (London: Shanti Sadan, 1984).

PAGE 251   "We must, then..." Kieran Kavanaugh, trans., *The Collected Works of St. Teresa of Avila, Vol.* 2 (Washington, D.C.: ICS Publications, 1980).

PAGE 254   "For one who is moderate..." *Bhagavad Gita* 6.17.

PAGE 256   "All this talk..." Stephen Mitchell, *The Enlightened Mind: An Anthology of Sacred Prose* (New York: HarperCollins, 1991).

PAGE 260   "God *must* act..." Stephen Mitchell, *The Enlightened Mind: An Anthology of Sacred Prose* (New York: HarperCollins, 1991).

PAGE 264   "When you let yourself..." *Courage and Contentment: A Collection of Talks on Spiritual Life* (South Fallsburg, N.Y.: SYDA Foundation, 1999) p. 117.

PAGE 267   The practice of becoming aware of the Self by disentangling yourself from identification with the body, thoughts, etcetera, has a long and honorable history. It appears in various forms throughout Vedantic literature: in texts like *Vivekachudamani* and *Yoga Vasishtha*, in Shankaracharya's famous hymn *Nirvanashtakam (Six Stanzas on Salvation)*, among others. Various modern versions of the practice also exist, the best-known being those taught by Ramana Maharshi and his followers. A particularly clear and helpful contemporary version appears in Ken Wilber's *One Taste* (Shambhala Publications, 2000).

PAGE 269   "Indeed, it is the Infinite..." adapted from Swami Venkatesananda, *Vasishtha's Yoga* (Albany, N.Y.: The State University of New York Press, 1993).

PAGE 274   "Do you remember..." Rainer Maria Rilke, Stephen Mitchell, trans., *Letters to a Young Poet* (New York: Vintage Books, 1986).

PAGE 276   "In this practice..." *Bhagavad Gita* 2.40.

PAGE 279   "However firmly embedded..." Swami Muktananda, *Secret of the Siddhas* (South Fallsburg, N.Y.: SYDA Foundation, 1994) p. 50.

PAGE 280   "I salute the Self!..." Swami Venkatesananda, *Concise Yoga Vasishtha* (Albany, N.Y.: The State University of New York Press, 1984).

PAGE 283   "Your life alone..." Ramprasad, from *Mother of the Universe* by Lex Hixon (Wheaton, Ill.: Quest Books, 1994).

PAGE 284   "The *kundalini* is *shakti*..." Jean Varenne, Derek Coltman, trans., *Yoga and the Hindu Tradition* (Chicago: University of Chicago Press, 1976).

           "Hindu Tantras" Tantra (literally, book) is a yogic tradition that was first written down in the tenth century CE; it is notable for dealing extensively with *shakti* and *kundalini*. Though in the west, tantricism has been associated with sex, it is in fact a broad-based and highly diverse tradition of practical yoga, which deals with the internal transmutation of energy and includes some of the loftiest philosophical texts in the Hindu tradition, including Kashmir Shaivism.

"Without knowledge…" quoted in Sir John Woodruffe, *Principles of Tantra* (Madras: Ganesh and Company).

"Supremely independent Chiti…" adapted from Jaideva Singh, trans., *Pratyabhijna Hridayam* (Delhi: Motilal Banarsidass, 1977) sutras 1-2.

"Kundalini Shakti is so deft…" Gurumayi Chidvilasananda, *Resonate with Stillness* (South Fallsburg, N.Y.: SYDA Foundation, 1995) April 16-17.

PAGE 286   "In every human being…" Elaine Pagels, *The Gnostic Gospels* (New York: Random House, 1979).

"The !K'ung bushmen…" John Marshall, *N/um Tchai: The Ceremonial Dance of the !Kung Bushmen* (Somerville, Mass.: Documentary Educational Resources, Inc., 1957).

"The Hopi…" Frank Waters, *The Book of the Hopi* (New York: Penguin Books, 1977).

Carlos Suares, *The Cipher of Genesis: The Original Code of Quabala as Applied to the Scriptures* (Boston: Shambhala Publications, 1981).

PAGE 287   "When you are meditating…" Swami Muktananda, *From the Finite to the Infinite* (South Fallsburg, N.Y.: SYDA Foundation, 1994) p. 82.

PAGE 288   "When Self-recognition takes place…" Gurumayi Chidvilasananda, *Resonate with Stillness* (South Fallsburg, N.Y.: SYDA Foundation, 1995) January 14.

GUIDE TO SANSKRIT PRONUNCIATION

For the reader's convenience, the Sanskrit and Hindi terms most frequently used in Siddha Yoga literature and courses appear throughout the text in simple transliteration. *Śaktipāta*, for instance, is *shaktipat*. The standard international transliteration for each Sanskrit term is given in brackets for Glossary entries.

For readers not familiar with Sanskrit, the following is a guide for pronunciation.

Vowels

Sanskrit vowels are categorized as either long or short. In English transliteration, the long vowels are marked with a bar above the letter and are pronounced twice as long as the short vowels. *E, ai, au,* and *o* are always pronounced as long vowels.

Short:
a as in c*u*p
i as in g*i*ve
u as in f*u*ll

Long:
ā as in c*a*lm
e as in s*a*ve
ī as in s*ee*n
o as in kn*o*w

ai as in *ai*sle
au as in c*ow*
ū as in sch*oo*l

Consonants

The main differences between Sanskrit and English pronunciation of consonants are in the aspirated and retroflexive letters.

The aspirated letters have a definite *h* sound. The Sanskrit letter *kh* is pronounced as in inkhorn; the *th* as in boathouse; the *ph* as in loophole.

The retroflexes are pronounced with the tip of the tongue touching the hard palate; *ṭ*, for instance, is pronounced as in ant; *ḍ* as in end.

The sibilants are *ś, ṣ,* and *s*. The *ś* is pronounced as *sh* but with the tongue touching the soft palate; the *ṣ* as *sh* with the tongue touching the hard palate; the *s* as in history.

Other distinctive consonants are these:

c as in *c*hurch
ch as in pit*ch-h*ook
ñ as in ca*ny*on

ṃ is a strong nasal
ḥ is a strong aspiration

For a detailed pronunciation guide, see
The Nectar of Chanting, published by SYDA Foundation.

GLOSSARY

ABHINAVAGUPTA

(c. 975-1025) An enlightened master from Kashmir; the most distinguished exponent of both the Trika and Kaula systems of spiritual philosophy. A great polymath, Abhinavagupta is popularly known for his treatise on aesthetics, which outlines the doctrine of the nine *rasas* (flavors of emotion) that is the basis of much Indian dramatic theory. His major philosophical works include *Tantraloka*, considered by many scholars to be the authoritative text on the Shaiva and Shakta Tantras, *Tantrasara* (a digest of *Tantraloka*), *Paratrimsika Vivarana*, and *Paramarthasara*. *See also* KASHMIR SHAIVISM; TANTRA.

AJNA CHAKRA [*ājñā cakra*]

The spiritual center located between the eyebrows, sometimes known as the "third eye."

The awakened *kundalini* passes beyond this chakra only by the command (*ajna*) of the Guru, and for this reason it is also known as the Guru chakra. *See also* CHAKRA.

AMRIT ANUBHAVA [*amṛtānubhāva*]

(*lit.*, nectar of Self-awareness) A text of radical nondualism, written in verse by the great Indian sage Jnaneshwar Maharaj (1275-1296), describing the experience of the supreme Reality, known here as Shiva, and his power of creation, Shakti. *See also* JNANESHWAR MAHARAJ.

ARJUNA [*arjuna*]

One of the heroes of the Indian epic *Mahabharata*, considered to be the greatest archer of his time. He was the friend and devotee of Lord Krishna, who revealed the teachings of the *Bhagavad Gita* to him on the battlefield. *See also* BHAGAVAD GITA; KRISHNA.

ASANA [*āsana*]

A *hatha yoga* posture practiced to strengthen and purify the body and develop one-point-edness of mind. *See also* HATHA YOGA.

ASHRAM [*āśrama*]

The dwelling place of a Guru or saint; a monastic retreat site where seekers engage in spiritual practices and study sacred texts and teachings.

ATMAN [*ātman*]

The core of Consciousness within the individual; the supreme Self; the soul.

AVADHUTA GITA [*avadhūtagītā*]

A Sanskrit text expounding the ultimate knowledge of nonduality; it speaks of ultimate reality as absolute freedom.

BHAGAVAD GITA [*bhagavadgītā*]

(*lit.*, song of God) One of the world's spiritual treasures and an essential scripture of India; the portion of the epic *Mahabharata* in which Lord Krishna instructs his disciple Arjuna on yoga, the nature of the universe, God, and the supreme Self. *See also* ARJUNA; KRISHNA.

BHAVA [*bhāva*]

(*lit.*, becoming; being) Attitude; emotional state; conviction; a feeling of absorption or identification.

BINDU [*bindu*]

(*lit.*, a dot, point) *See* BLUE PEARL.

BLUE PEARL

(Sanskrit, *nīlabindu*) Also referred to as Neeleshvari (the Blue Goddess); a brilliant blue light that is a compact mass of *shakti* gathered into a point of condensed power, containing the universe in an unmanifest state. Known in the esoteric literature of the Maharashtrian Siddha tradition as the light of pure Consciousness, the subtle abode of the inner Self.

BRAHMIN [*brahmin*]

A caste of Hindu society whose members are by tradition priests and scholars.

BRIHADARANYAKA UPANISHAD
[*bṛhadāraṇyakopaniṣad*]

One of the most important of the Upanishads. It teaches the identity of the individual and universal Self, describes the process of dying and the after-death experience, gives instructions on worship and meditation, and describes the steps of *sadhana* according to the philosophy of Vedanta. *See also* UPANISHADS; VEDANTA.

CHAKRA [*cakra*]

(*lit.*, wheel) A center of energy located in the subtle system of a human being, so called because it is a place where *nadis* (subtle nerve channels) converge like the spokes of a wheel. Six major chakras lie within the *sushumna nadi*, or central channel. They are: *muladhara* at the base of the spine; *svadhishthana* at the root of the reproductive organs; *manipura* at the navel; *anahata*, the "lotus of the heart"; *vishuddha* at the throat; and *ajna* between the eyebrows. When awakened, *kundalini shakti* flows upward from the *muladhara* to the seventh chakra, the *sahasrara*, at the crown of the head. *See also* AJNA CHAKRA; KUNDALINI; NADI; SHAKTIPAT; SUSHUMNA NADI.

CHIT; CHITI [*cit, citi*]

(*lit.*, supreme Awareness) The untrammeled, all-knowing creative power of universal Consciousness.

CHITTA [*citta*]

1) The mind-stuff, or energy out of which thoughts manifest. 2) The inner consciousness of a human being, including the capacities for volition, cognition, sensation, and emotion.

CLOUD OF UNKNOWING, THE

A Christian text on the unfolding of mystical experience, written by an anonymous contemplative living in fourteenth-century England.

CONSCIOUSNESS

The intelligent, free, bliss-filled Awareness/ energy that, according to the sages of Kashmir Shaivism and Vedanta, is the source and support of the universe. It is experienced in meditation as our own unmodified Awareness. *See also* CHIT; SHAKTI.

DHARANA [*dhāraṇā*]

1) Yogic concentration. 2) A centering technique, or meditation exercise. Many examples may be found in the *Vijnana Bhairava*, a key text of Kashmir Shaivism. *See also* VIJNANA BHAIRAVA.

ECKHART, MEISTER (JOHANNES OR JOHN)

(c.1260-1327) A Dominican friar, known as the father of German mysticism.

EGO

In yoga, the limited sense of "I" that is identified with the body, mind, and senses.

EKNATH MAHARAJ

(1528-1609) A householder poet-saint of Maharashtra, India, and the author of several hundred *abhangas*, or devotional songs, in the Marathi language.

GURU [*guru*]

(*lit.*, teacher) A spiritual master who lives in the constant experience of the divine inner Self and who is able both to initiate seekers and to guide them on the spiritual path to liberation. A true Guru is required to be learned in the scriptures and must belong to a lineage of masters. *See also* SHAKTIPAT; SIDDHA.

GURU GITA [*gurugītā*]

(*lit.*, song of the Guru) A sacred Sanskrit text consisting of mantras that describe the nature of the Guru, the Guru-disciple relationship, and techniques of meditation on the Guru. In Siddha Yoga ashrams, the *Guru Gita* is chanted every morning.

GURUMAYI

A term of respect and endearment often used in addressing Swami Chidvilasananda.

HATHA YOGA [haṭhayoga]

Yogic practices, both physical and mental, performed for the purpose of purifying and strengthening the physical and subtle bodies. *See also* ASANA; YOGA.

HILDEGARD OF BINGEN

(1098-1179) Benedictine abbess and mystic of medieval Germany, known for her extensive spiritual writings, her musical compositions, and for a series of paintings based on her mystical visions. She founded several monasteries along the Rhine River, and preached reform of the Church of her day.

INTENSIVE

An important Siddha Yoga meditation program, which was designed by Swami Muktananda both to give spiritual initiation (*shaktipat*, in Sanskrit) by awakening the *kundalini* energy and to aid in its continued unfoldment. *See also* KUNDALINI; MUKTANANDA, SWAMI; SHAKTIPAT.

JNANESHWAR MAHARAJ

(1275-1296) The Guru of many of the saints of Maharashtra, India, and a child yogi of extraordinary powers. He wrote the *Jnaneshvari*, an eloquent and powerful verse commentary in the Marathi language on the *Bhagavad Gita;* his commentary is acknowledged as one of the world's most important spiritual works. He also composed a shorter work, the *Amrit Anubhava,* and over one hundred *abhangas,* or devotional songs, in which he describes various spiritual experiences following the awakening of *kundalini. See also* AMRIT ANUBHAVA; BHAGAVAD GITA.

KABIR

(1440-1518) A great poet-saint and mystic who lived as a weaver in the city of Varanasi in North India. His poems describe his mystical experiences, offering a radically nondual approach to spiritual knowledge and worship.

KASHMIR SHAIVISM

A nondual philosophy, propounded by Kashmiri sages, that recognizes the entire universe as a manifestation of *shakti,* the divine conscious energy. Also known as the Trika System, it explains how the formless, unmanifest, supreme principle manifests as the universe, and how a human being is liberated by recognizing his own identity with that supreme principle. Kashmir Shaivism contains authoritative explanations of *shaktipat* and the role of grace in spiritual progress. Together with Vedanta, Kashmir Shaivism provides the basic scriptural context for Siddha Yoga meditation.

KRISHNA [kṛṣṇa]

The eighth incarnation of Lord Vishnu, the sustaining power of the universe according to Hindu theology. Krishna's stories are told in several of the Puranas, including *Shrimad Bhagavatam,* and his spiritual teachings are contained in the *Bhagavad Gita. See also* BHAGAVAD GITA.

KRIYA [*kriyā*]

(*lit.*, activity) A physical or subtle movement initiated by the awakened *kundalini*. *Kriyas* purify the body and nervous system, thus allowing a seeker to experience higher states of consciousness. *See also* KUNDALINI.

KSHEMARAJA

(10th century) A disciple of Abhinavagupta and author of many commentaries on Kashmir Shaivite scriptures, including the *Pratyabhijñā Hṛdayam. See also* ABHINAVAGUPTA; KASHMIR SHAIVISM; PRATYABHIJNA HRIDAYAM.

KUMBHAKA [*kumbhaka*]

Yogic breath retention. This practice stabilizes the mind, permitting the meditator to experience the Self, which lies beyond the mind.

KUNDALINI [*kuṇḍalinī*]

(*lit.*, coiled one) The primordial *shakti*, or cosmic energy, often personified in Indian spiritual literature as a goddess or as the "serpent power" that lies dormant, coiled like a sleeping serpent at the base of the spine. Once awakened, this extremely subtle force begins to purify the body and mind, and gives rise to inner spiritual experiences. As *kundalini* travels upward through the *sushumna nadi,* a subtle nerve channel that runs along the spinal column, the energy pierces the various chakras, or spiritual centers, finally reaching the highest chakra at the crown of the head. When *kundalini* stabilizes in this center, the individual experiences his or her identity with the supreme Self and attains the state called Self-realization. *See also* CHAKRA; SHAKTIPAT.

KUNDALINI YOGA [*kuṇḍalinīyoga*]

The process of attaining union of the individual self with the supreme Self through the spontaneous unfolding of awakened *kundalini* energy. *See also* KUNDALINI; YOGA.

MAHARASHTRA

(*lit.*, the great country) A state on the west coast of central India, famous as the home of an indigenous devotional movement dating from the middle ages. Maharashtrian saints include Namdev, Jnaneshwar, Eknath, Tukaram, and others. Gurudev Siddha Peeth, the mother ashram of Siddha Yoga meditation, and the *samadhi* shrines of Bhagawan Nityananda and Swami Muktananda are located there.

MALINI VIJAYA TANTRA [*mālinīvijayatantra*]

A foundational text of the North Indian tradition of *agama,* considered to be authoritative in its treatment of *shaktipat,* the role of the Guru, and mantra.

MANSUR AL-HALLAJ; MANSUR MASTANA

(852-922) An ecstatic Sufi poet-saint who lived most of his life in Baghdad. He was hanged as a heretic for his pronouncement *ana'l-haq,* "I am God," which orthodox Muslims of those days would not tolerate.

MANTRA [*mantra*]

(*lit.*, sacred invocation) Names of God;

sacred words or divine sounds invested with the power to protect, purify, and transform the individual who repeats them. A mantra received from an enlightened master is said to be filled with the power of the master's attainment, which is then transmitted to the recipient. *See also* OM NAMAH SHIVAYA.

MAYA [*māyā*]

The power that veils the true nature of the Self and projects the experiences of multiplicity and separation from the whole, creating the illusion that the real is unreal, the unreal is real, and the temporary is everlasting.

MEISTER ECKHART

See ECKHART, MEISTER.

MUDRA [*mudrā*]

(*lit.*, seal) 1) A symbolic gesture or movement of the hand expressive of an inner state, such as joy, fearlessness, or liberation. Deities and saints are often pictured performing these gestures to bestow their blessings. 2) Hatha yoga techniques practiced to hold the *prana* (life force) within the body. *Mudras* may occur spontaneously after one receives *shaktipat*.

MUKTANANDA, SWAMI

(1908-1982) A Siddha of the modern age, a disciple of Bhagawan Nityananda and Guru of Gurumayi Chidvilasananda, often referred to as Baba. Muktananda systemized the disciplines and practices known as Siddha Yoga, and brought the initiation known as *shaktipat*

to popular consciousness in India and the West. *See also* NITYANANDA, BHAGAWAN; SHAKTIPAT; SIDDHA.

NADA [*nāda*]

(*lit.*, sound) Spontaneous inner sounds that may be heard during advanced stages of meditation; *nada* may take the form of sounds such as bells, the blowing of a conch, and thunder.

NADI [*nāḍī*]

(*lit.*, duct, nerve) A channel in the subtle body through which the vital force flows. A network of seventy-two million *nadis* spreads throughout the human body. The hubs or junctions of the *nadis* are known as chakras. *See also* CHAKRA; KUNDALINI; SUSHUMNA NADI.

NANAK, GURU

(1469-1538) The founder and first Guru of the Sikh tradition. He lectured widely, spreading liberal religious and social doctrines including opposition to both the caste system and the division between Hindus and Muslims.

NITYANANDA, BHAGAWAN

(d. 1961) A great Siddha master, Swami Muktananda's Guru, also known as Bade Baba ("elder" Baba). He was said to be a born Siddha, living his entire life in the highest state of consciousness. His *samadhi* shrine is located in the village of Ganeshpuri, near Gurudev Siddha Peeth, the mother ashram of Siddha Yoga meditation.

OM [*om*]

The primordial sound from which the universe emanates; the inner essence of all mantras.

OM NAMAH SHIVAYA [*oṃ namaḥ śivāya*]

(*lit., Om*, salutations to Shiva) The Sanskrit mantra of the Siddha Yoga lineage; also one of the traditional Shaivite mantras. It is known as "the great redeeming mantra" and, when given as an initiation mantra, is said to grant both worldly fulfillment and spiritual realization. *Om* is the primordial sound; *Namah* means to honor or bow to; *Shivaya* denotes divine Consciousness, the Lord who dwells in every heart.

PATANJALI

A third-century sage and the author of the *Yoga Sutras*, a Sanskrit text which sets forth one of the six orthodox philosophies of India and is the authoritative text of the path of *raja yoga*, the "kingly path," the path of meditation. *See also* YOGA SUTRAS.

PRANA [*prāṇa*]

The vital life-sustaining force of both the human body and the universe.

PRATYABHIJNA HRIDAYAM

[*pratyabhijñāhṛdayam*]

(*lit.*, the heart of the doctrine of recognition) An eleventh-century treatise by Kshemaraja that summarizes the *pratyabhijna* branch of Kashmir Shaivism. It describes how supreme Consciousness manifests the universe through

a process of self-contraction, and how the individual can ultimately recognize (*pratyabhijna*) his or her essential identity with that Consciousness. *See also* KASHMIR SHAIVISM; KSHEMARAJA.

RAMAKRISHNA PARAMAHAMSA

(1836-1886) A great saint of Bengal; the Guru of Swami Vivekananda and the founder of the Ramakrishna order of monks.

RAMANA MAHARSHI

(1870-1950) A widely revered saint and Guru who spent most of his life near Arunachala, a sacred hill in South India. After his spiritual awakening at age sixteen, he meditated intensely for many years and later taught disciples to practice self-inquiry by asking the question "Who am I?" In modern times, he is perhaps the best-known exponent of the path of pure Advaita (nondual) Vedanta.

RUMI, JALAL AL-DIN

(1207-1273) A great Sufi Guru and founder of the Mevlani order of dervishes. He settled in Turkey, where he mastered all the recognized Islamic sciences at an early age and was a respected doctor of law. After meeting Shams-i-Tabriz, an ecstatic wandering saint, he was transformed from a sober scholar into an intoxicated singer of divine love. His poetry is among the treasures of world literature.

SADHAKA [*sādhaka*]

A seeker on the spiritual path.

SADHANA [*sādhana*]

1) A spiritual discipline or path. 2) Practices, both physical and mental, on the spiritual path.

SAHAJA SAMADHI [*sahajasamādhi*]

(*lit.,* natural union) The ultimate state of meditative union with the Absolute, attained by rare practitioners at the culmination of their spiritual journey. It is described as "natural" because it is experienced without any special effort, remaining continuous throughout the waking, dream, and deep-sleep states.

SAMADHI [*samādhi*]

1) The state of inner absorption. 2) Meditative union with the Absolute. 3) The state of final absorption in the Self.

SAMSKARA [*saṃskāra*]

An impression of past actions and thoughts that remains in the subtle body. They are brought to the surface of one's awareness and then eliminated by the action of the awakened *kundalini* energy.

SELF

The *atman,* or divine Consciousness residing in the individual, described as the witness of the mind or the pure I-awareness.

SHAIVISM

See KASHMIR SHAIVISM.

SHAKTI [*śakti*]

1) The divine Mother, the dynamic aspect of the absolute Reality, and the creative force of the universe. 2) All-pervasive, divine spiritual energy.

SHAKTIPAT [*śaktipāta*]

(*lit.,* descent of grace) Yogic initiation in which the Siddha Guru transmits spiritual energy into the aspirant, thereby awakening the aspirant's dormant *kundalini shakti. See also* GURU; KUNDALINI.

SHANKARACHARYA; SHANKARA

(788-820) One of the most celebrated of India's philosophers and sages, he expounded the philosophy of nondual Vedanta. Among his many works is *Viveka Chudamani (The Crest Jewel of Discrimination).* In addition to teaching and writing, he established ashrams in the four corners of India. The Saraswati order of monks, to which Swami Muktananda, Swami Chidvilasananda, and the other Siddha Yoga monks belong, was created by Shankaracharya.

SHIVA [*śiva*]

1) A name for the one, all-pervasive supreme Reality. As the deity and highest principle of the Shaivite tradition, he performs the five cosmic functions of creation, dissolution, maintenance, concealment, and grace-bestowal. 2) One of the Hindu trinity of gods, representing God as the destroyer, often understood by yogis as the destroyer of barriers to one's identification with the supreme Self.

SHIVA SUTRAS [*śivasūtra*]

A Sanskrit text said to have been revealed by Lord Shiva to the ninth-century sage Vasuguptacharya. It consists of seventy-seven *sutras*, or aphorisms, that, according to tradition, were found inscribed on a rock in Kashmir. The *Shiva Sutras*, which describe the path to full union with supreme Consciousness, are the primary scriptural authority for the philosophical school known as Kashmir Shaivism. *See also* KASHMIR SHAIVISM.

SHREE MUKTANANDA ASHRAM

The Siddha Yoga meditation ashram in South Fallsburg, New York, established in 1979 as a spiritual retreat site and as the international headquarters of SYDA Foundation, . the nonprofit organization that administers Siddha Yoga publications and courses. *See also* ASHRAM.

SIDDHA [*siddha*]

(*lit.,* accomplished) An enlightened yogi or fully Self-realized master; one who lives in the state of unity-consciousness; one whose experience of the supreme Self is uninterrupted and whose identification with the ego has been dissolved.

SIDDHA YOGA [*siddhayoga*]

(*lit.,* the yoga of fulfillment) A path to union of the individual and the divine that begins with *shaktipat*, the inner awakening by the grace of a Siddha Guru. Siddha Yoga is the name Swami Muktananda gave to this path, which he first brought to the West in 1970; Gurumayi Chidvilasananda is the living master of this lineage. *See also* GURU; SHAKTIPAT; SIDDHA.

SPANDA [*spanda*]

The vibration of divine Consciousness that pervades all life; it is perceived by the yogi in higher states of meditation.

SPANDA KARIKA [*spandakārikā*]

A ninth-century collection of fifty-three verses composed by the Kashmiri sage Vasuguptacharya. An important work of Kashmir Shaivism, it describes the universe as the play of *spanda*, divine vibration, and sets forth the practices for attaining Self-realization by awareness of *spanda*. *See also* KASHMIR SHAIVISM; SHIVA SUTRAS.

SUSHUMNA NADI [*suṣumṇānāḍī*]

The central energy channel; the most important of all the *nadis*. Extending from the base of the spine to the crown of the head, it is the pathway of the awakened *kundalini*. *See also* NADI.

SUTRA [*sūtra*]

Aphorism; a condensed and often cryptic statement that contains the essence of a spiritual teaching. In India, the major points of an entire philosophical system may be expressed in a series of *sutras*, such as the *Shiva Sutras* or the *Yoga Sutras*.

TANTRA [*tantra*]

1) An esoteric discipline in which one makes

use of one's own life-energy (*prana*) to become united with the divine. The goal of Tantra is Self-realization, achieved when one unites Shiva and Shakti within oneself through the awakened *kundalini*. As an approach to practice, it is notable for its practicality and its recognition that the ordinary experiences of life can be pathways to spiritual enlightenment. 2) Divinely inspired scriptures of this tradition that reveal the secrets of attaining Self-realization through *kundalini* awakening and through uniting the two principles, Shiva and Shakti. *See also* SHAKTI; SHIVA.

TUKARAM MAHARAJ

(1608-1650) A revered and popular householder saint who was a grocer in the village of Dehu in Maharashtra, India. Tukaram wrote thousands of *abhangas*, devotional songs, describing his spiritual experiences, the realization of God, and the glory of the divine Name.

TURIYA [*turīya*]

(*lit.*, the fourth) The transcendental state, beyond the waking, dream, and deep sleep states, in which the true nature of Reality is directly perceived; the state of *samadhi*, or deep meditation, in which one is in direct contact with the experiencing consciousness. *See also* SAMADHI.

UPANISHADS [*upaniṣad*]

(*lit.*, sitting close to; secret teachings) The inspired teachings, visions, and mystical experiences of the forest-dwelling sages of ancient India; the concluding portion of the Vedas and the basis for Vedantic philosophy. With immense variety of form and style, all of these scriptures (exceeding one hundred texts) give the same essential teaching: that the individual soul and God are one. *See also* VEDANTA; VEDAS.

VAIRAGYA [*vairāgya*]

Dispassion; renunciation.

VEDANTA [*vedānta*]

(*lit.*, end of the Vedas) One of the six orthodox schools of Indian philosophy, usually identified as Advaita ("nondual") Vedanta, describing how the one supreme principle that is the foundation of the universe resides as the inmost self of a human being. Vedanta arose from the meditative experience of ancient sages. It teaches that the universe is nothing but absolute Consciousness, within which the world—as we know it—is merely an appearance or a reflection. *See also* UPANISHAD; VEDA.

VEDAS [*veda*]

(*lit.*, knowledge) Among the most ancient of the world's scriptures, the four Vedas are regarded as divinely revealed, eternal wisdom. They are the *Rig Veda, Atharva Veda, Sama Veda,* and *Yajur Veda.*

VIJNANA BHAIRAVA [*vijñānabhairava*]

A seventh-century text on yoga, one of the *agamas*, or revealed scriptures of Kashmir Shaivism; a compilation of 112 *dharanas*, or centering techniques, designed to open inner doorways and give rise to an immediate experience of union with God.

WITNESS, THE

The transcendental Consciousness that lies at the root of the mind and from which the mind can be observed. *See also* CONSCIOUSNESS; SELF.

WITNESS-CONSCIOUSNESS

The pure impersonal Awareness that remains apart from the activities of the mind and body and witnesses them.

YOGA [*yoga*]

(*lit.,* union) The spiritual practices and disciplines that lead seekers, according to the classical definitions of the *Bhagavad Gita,* to evenness of mind, to the severing of their union with pain, and to skill in action through detachment. Ultimately, the path of yoga leads to the constant experience of the Self.

YOGA SUTRAS [*yogasūtra*]

A collection of aphorisms by the third-century sage Patanjali; it expounds different methods for the attainment of the state of yoga, or union, in which the movement of the mind ceases and the witness of the mind rests in itself.

YOGA VASISHTHA [*yogavāsiṣṭha*]

An important text of Advaita ("nondual") Vedanta, probably written in the twelfth century, that records dialogues in which the sage Vasishtha describes to his disciple Lord Rama the path to liberation by understanding the true nature of mind.

YOGI [*yogi*]

1) One who practices yoga. 2) One who has attained perfection through yogic practices. *See also* YOGA.

INDEX

Abhinavagupta, 38, 91. *See also* Kashmir
  Shaivism
Action, *kundalini's* power of, 141
Addiction, to information, 256
Aids to meditation. *See* Meditation, aids to
Ajna chakra, 145, 158, 165
Al'Bistami, Abu Yazid, quoted, 256
Alighieri, Dante, quoted, 16
Ananda. See Bliss; Joy
Ananda shakti (power of bliss), 141-42
Anger. *See* Emotions; Feelings; Negativities
Antidote(s), to fear, 235-38; to negativities,
  88, 94-95, 107-08
Anxiety. *See* Emotions; Feelings;
  Negativities
Armoring, 277-78
Arthur, King, in story, 120-22
Atman. See Self
Atma vichara, 216. *See also* Self-inquiry
Attentiveness, to awakened *kundalini*,

134-35; development of, 227; in eating,
253-54; seen as love, 54; to Self, in daily
life, 211-24; in self-inquiry, 216-18. *See
also* Awareness
Auditory meditators. *See* Sound(s)
Aurobindo, quoted, 151
Awakening, of *kundalini*, 4
Awareness, 27-30; as crucible for emotions,
126-29; in daily life, 209-24; for dissolving resistance, 238-40; as doorway to Self,
27-29; exercises on, 27-28, 97; holding
mantra in, 69; *kundalini's* power of, 141-
42; maintenance of, 200-03; in mantra,
74-76; meditations on, 81-85, 269; in
negative states, 94; as open-eyed practice,
213; as pulsation, 82-84; in transcendental state, 159, 189-94; transformative
power of, 215-16; of uncentered state, 212,
214; in waking state, 200-03; witnessing
of, 82-85. *See also* Attentiveness;

SUGGESTED READING

By Swami Muktananda

Play of Consciousness: A Spiritual Autobiography

This book has been called one of the great spiritual autobiographies of modern times; in it Swami Muktananda describes the "secret" experiences of the higher states of meditation. It is also an amazing meditation manual, as well as an unparalleled description of the process of the awakened *kundalini*.

Meditate: Happiness Lies Within You

Swami Muktananda's practical and philosophical teachings on meditation. *Meditate* is like a short course in meditation; for many years it has been the basis of my own practice.

Kundalini: The Secret of Life

Swami Muktananda was one of those rare teachers who knew how to awaken and guide the *kundalini* energy in his students. This book explains *kundalini* both practically and from the point of view of an enlightened meditator.

I Am That: The Science of Hamsa from the Vijnana Bhairava

A short meditation text that explains the practice of the natural breath mantra, *Hamsa*.

The Mystery of the Mind

Another essential text for meditators, in which Swami Muktananda offers the fundamental teachings from the yogic and Shaivite traditions on how to work with your own mind.

From the Finite to the Infinite

A real treasure: hands-on answers to common and uncommon questions about every aspect of the spiritual path.

Nothing Exists That Is Not Śiva: Commentaries on the Śiva Sutra, Vijnanabhairava, Gurugita, and Other Sacred Texts

My personal favorite text, this is a mind-expanding series of commentaries on Kashmir Shaivite texts written from the viewpoint of someone who actually experiences the universe as a play of one energy.

By Swami Chidvilasananda (Gurumayi)

Inner Treasures

Joy, peace, and love are the names we give to states we all long for and don't always know how to touch. Gurumayi's explanations of how to enter these states are not just uplifting, they also show you how to do it.

My Lord Loves a Pure Heart: The Yoga of Divine Virtues

Gurumayi's specialty is making spiritual life practical. This book explores the qualities that allow us to live an awakened life.

The Yoga of Discipline

An advanced text on essential yogic disciplines, filled with specific guidance and practical examples.

Remembrance

Imaginative, poetic, and devotional essays, which offer surprising and powerful ways to expand awareness and open to the inner heart.

Enthusiasm
Gurumayi explores the awakened state as a state of unbounded enthusiasm, describing the obstacles to experiencing natural ecstasy, and how to overcome them.

On The Siddha Yoga Tradition

Meditation Revolution: The History and Theology of the Siddha Yoga Lineage
by Douglas R. Brooks, Swami Durgananda, Paul Muller-Ortega,
William Mahony, Constantina Rhodes-Bailly, S. N. Sabarathinam
Essays on different aspects of the Siddha Yoga tradition, exploring the theological and historical significance of a traditional yogic path that has taken strong root in the West

On Kundalini

The Sacred Power
by Swami Kripananda
A concise, highly informative text on the theory and practice of working with an awakened *kundalini*, written by a senior teacher in the Siddha Yoga tradition.

Devatma Shakti: Divine Power
by Swami Vishnu Tirtha
The style is somewhat thick and old-fashioned, but this text is indispensable for someone wanting to understand the process that goes on after *kundalini* is awakened.

The Serpent Power: The Secrets of Tantric and Shaktic Yoga
by Arthur Avalon (Sir John Woodroffe)
Another traditional text, this one compiled by an English Indologist from the teachings of the Sanskrit Tantric texts that are the source of our knowledge of *kundalini*.

On Yogic Practice

*Yoga Philosophy of Patanjali: Containing His
Yoga Aphorisms with Vyasa's Commentary in Sanskrit
and a Translation with Annotations Including
Many Suggestions for the Practice of Yoga*
BY SAMKHYA-YOGACHARYA SWAMI HARIHARANANDA ARANYA
The basic text of meditation in the Indian tradition, and the source of the tradition
of yoga, including ashtanga yoga.

*How to Know God:
The Yoga Aphorisms of Patanjali*
TRANSLATED BY SWAMI PRABHAVANANDA AND CHRISTOPHER ISHERWOOD
This translation and commentary on Patanjali's *Yoga Sutras* expands and paraphrases
the sutras for the benefit of readers and devotees of any religion or spiritual path.

The Bhagavadgita
TRANSLATED BY S. RADHAKRISHNAN
Not only the source of teachings on how to live a yogic lifestyle but also one of the
definitive statements about the nature of human life, meditation, the Self, God,
karma, and the secrets of Self-realization.

Jnaneshwar's Gita: A Rendering of the Jnaneshwari
BY SWAMI KRIPANANDA
A sublime, subtle commentary on the *Bhagavad Gita* by an enlightened master of the
13th Century, Jnaneshwar Maharaj. In this version, Swami Kripananda has rendered
the translation into lucid and poetic English.

The Upanishads: Breath of the Eternal
TRANSLATED BY SWAMI PRABHAVANANDA AND FREDERICK MANCHESTER
A clear, poetic, and authoritative translation of some of the most ancient and essential texts on the nature of the inner Self and the practice of meditation. See particularly the *Svetashwatara, Mundaka, Kena* and *Katha Upanishads.*

What's On My Mind?: Becoming Inspired with New Perception
BY SWAMI ANANTANANDA
Working with one's own obstructive tendencies through practical techniques, many
of which are based on the principles of Kashmir Shaivism.

On the Principles of Kashmir Shaivism

The Doctrine of Recognition: A Translation of Pratyabhijnahridayam
BY KSHEMARAJA, TRANSLATED BY JAIDEVA SINGH
A digest of essential Shaiva teachings, describing how Consciousness manifests
the universe, limits itself, and then liberates itself once again through grace and
yogic sadhana.

Shiva Sutras: The Yoga of Supreme Identity
WITH COMMENTARY BY KSHEMARAJA, TRANSLATED BY JAIDEVA SINGH
Considered the fundamental text of the Shaiva system, the *Shiva Sutras* describe the
practice and experience of yogis on the path to enlightenment.

The Aphorisms of Shiva:
The ShivaSutra with Bhaskara's Commentary, the Varttika
TRANSLATED BY MARK S. G. DYCZKOWSKI
This work illumines the *Shiva Sutras* with additional commentary, bringing forth further
nuances and layers of meaning from the scripture.

The Yoga of Vibration and Divine Pulsation: A Translation of the Spanda
Karikas with Kshemaraja's Commentary, the Spanda Nirnaya
TRANSLATED BY JAIDEVA SINGH
A companion piece to the *Shiva Sutras*, describing how the creative energy of
the universe works through both ordinary and exalted states of mind, forming the
experience of limitation and suffering as well as that of expansion, joy, and freedom.

The Doctrine of Vibration:
An analysis of the Doctrines and Practices of Kashmir Shaivism
BY MARK S. G. DYCZKOWSKI

An inspired survey of the principles of Kashmir Shaivism.

The Triadic Heart of Shiva:
Kaula Tantricism of Abhinavagupta in the Non-Dual Shaivism of Kashmir
BY PAUL EDUARDO MULLER-ORTEGA

Explores the essential Shaivite teaching of the Heart as the symbol for absolute Consciousness.

Vijnanabhairava or Divine Consciousness
TRANSLATED BY JAIDEVA SINGH

A Kashmir Shaiva text of practice rather than theory, this concise and ancient treatise offers 112 methods of mystical union with the divine.

Aspects of Kashmir Shaivism
BY B. N. PANDIT

A modest and informative series of essays expressing the principles of Kashmir Shaivism, including the Shaiva conception of liberation, creation, realism, and yoga.

The Philosophy of Sadhana
BY D. B. SEN SHARMA

A useful survey of the Shaivite teachings on yogic practice, initiation through shakti-pat, the role of the Guru, and the stages of inner development.

On Hatha Yoga

Light on Yoga
BY B. K. S. IYENGAR

A definitive guide to the philosophy and practice of hatha yoga.

Yoga: The Iyengar Way
BY SILVA MEHTA, MIRA MEHTA, AND SHYAM MEHTA
A comprehensive, practical guide to the hatha yoga method developed by B. K. S. Iyengar, containing detailed instruction and photographs.

CDs and Tapes

Meditation Instructions Volume I
BY GURUMAYI CHIDVILASANANDA
This recording includes two sets of instructions, leading gently into meditation with guidance in posture, breath, and mantra.

Tamboura
The hum of this ancient Indian stringed instrument creates a powerful atmosphere for meditation, shutting out ambient noise and stilling the mind.

The Power of the Mantra
Gurumayi Chidvilasananda chants *Om Namah Shivaya*, the initiation mantra of Siddha Yoga meditation, which is charged with the power of the entire Siddha Yoga lineage.

Om Namah Shivaya (Bhupali Raga)
The dignified *bhupali raga* inspires feelings of contentment, harmony, and detachment. This recording features group chanting with Gurumayi Chidvilasananda.

Anusara Yoga 101
WITH JOHN FRIEND
A powerful, clear and inspiring hatha yoga class in the form of a two-CD set. John Friend is a master of alignment and the founder of Anusara ("flowing with grace") yoga. This CD can be used as the basis for daily practice.

PERMISSIONS ACKNOWLEDGMENTS

PIRKE AVOT: From *Wisdom of the Jewish Sages* by Rabbi Rami M. Shapiro. Copyright © 1993 by Rami M. Shapiro. Used by permission of Bell Tower, a division of Random House, Inc.

EMILY DICKINSON: "The Props Assist the House." Reprinted by permission of the publishers and trustees of Amherst College from *The Poems of Emily Dickinson*, Thomas H. Johnson, ed., Cambridge Mass.: The Belknap Press of Harvard University Press. Copyright © 1951, 1955, 1979 by the President and Fellows of Harvard College.

T. S. ELIOT: "The Word…" from "Ash Wednesday" in Collected Poems 1909-1962 (London: Faber & Faber, 1963). Reprinted by Permission. From "Burnt Norton" in *Four Quartets*. Copyright © 1936 by Harcourt Inc. and renewed by T.S. Eliot. Reprinted by permission of the publisher and by permission of Faber & Faber for the estate of T.S. Eliot.

HADEWIJCH: "You who want…" from *Beguine Spirituality* (London: SPCK Publications 1991). Fiona Bowie translator and editor. Reprinted by permission of SPCK and Fiona Bowie.

Hafiz: Selections from *The Subject Tonight is Love*. Daniel Ladinsky, trans. Copyright © 1996 Daniel Ladinsky (North Myrtle Beach, SC: Pumpkin House Press, 1996). Reprinted by permission of the translator.

Hakuin: "While you live..." from *A First Zen Reader*, Trevor P. Leggett, trans. (Boston: Charles E. Tuttle Co. 1991). Reprinted by permission.

Hildegard de Bingen: "Holy Spirit" from *The Enlightened Heart: An Anthology of Sacred Poetry*, edited by Stephen Mitchell. Copyright © 1989 by Stephen Mitchell. Reprinted by permission of HarperCollins Publishers, Inc.

Hui-Neng: "One deluded..." from *Zen Wisdom: Daily Teachings from the Zen Masters*, Timothy Freke trans. Copyright © 1997 Godsfield Press, Ltd. Reprinted by permission.

Jiminez: "I have a feeling..." from *The Soul is Here for its Own Joy* by Robert Bly. (Hopewell, NJ: The Ecco Press, 1995) Copyright © 1995 Robert Bly. Reprinted by permission of the author.

Kabir: Selections from *The Kabir Book* by Robert Bly. Copyright © 1971, 1977 by Robert Bly. Copyright © 1977 by The Seventies Press. Reprinted by permission of Robert Bly and by permission of Beacon Press, Boston. "The Pearl..." from *Indian Mystic Verse* by Hari Prasad Shastri. Copyright © 1984. (London: Santi Sadan, 1984). Reprinted by permission.

Kumagai: "The Mountain..." from *A First Zen Reader*, Trevor P. Leggett, trans. (Boston: Charles E. Tuttle Co. 1991). Reprinted by permission.

Lao Tzu: Excerpts from the *Tao te Ching by Lao Tzu*, A New English Version, With Foreword and Notes by Stephen Mitchell. Translation copyright © 1988 by Stephen Mitchell. Reprinted by permission of HarperCollins Publishers Inc. USA and Macmillan London, UK.

Jikme Lingpa: "From the Blossoming Lotus..." in *The Tibetan Book of Living and Dying* by Sogyal Rinpoche and edited by Patrick Gaffney and Andrew Harvey. Copyright ©

Library of Congress Cataloging-in-Publication Data.
    Kempton, Sally
        The heart of meditation : pathways to a deeper experience/
    Swami Durgananda.
            p.   cm.
        Includes bibliographical references and index.
        ISBN 0-911307-97-4 (pbk.)
        1. Siddha Yoga (Service Mark)   2. SYDA Foundation.   I. Title.
    BL1283.755 .D87   2002
    294.5'435 — dc21
                                                    2001001092

You can learn more about the teachings and practices
of Siddha Yoga meditation by contacting

SYDA FOUNDATION
PO BOX 600, 371 BRICKMAN RD
SOUTH FALLSBURG, NY 12779-0600, USA

TEL: 845-434-2000

or

GURUDEV SIDDHA PEETH
PO GANESHPURI, PIN 401 206
DISTRICT THANA, MAHARASHTRA, INDIA

Please visit our website at
www.siddhayoga.org

For further information on books in print by Swami Muktananda
and Gurumayi Chidvilasananda, editions in translation, and
audio and video recordings, please contact

SIDDHA YOGA BOOKSTORE
PO BOX 600, 371 BRICKMAN RD
SOUTH FALLSBURG, NY 12779-0600, USA

TEL: 845-434-2000 EXT. 1700

Call toll-free from the United States and Canada: 888-422-3334
FAX toll-free from the United States and Canada: 888-422-3339

ABOUT THE AUTHOR

Swami Durgananda

With her thirty years of meditation experience, Swami Durgananda is one of today's most knowledgeable and effective teachers of meditation. She has studied and taught under the guidance of the meditation master Gurumayi Chidvilasananda for the last two decades, offering courses and workshops in Siddha Yoga meditation and yoga philosophy all over the world.

Formerly a journalist who wrote on the culture of the 1960s and 1970s for major publications, the author became a full-time student of meditation under the late master Swami Muktananda, and edited many of his books. She currently lives in California.